ADVANCE PRAISE FOR *IN THE NAME*

'As fond as O'Rawe is of Gerry Conlon, this is not a [hagiography?]. [Conlon is] shown in all his imperfect splendor, his contradictions and complexities, as both a victim of the conflict in Northern Ireland and ultimately a survivor whose inherent humanity and decency rise above ancient animosities and modern human failings. Written by someone who emerged from the same cauldron that swallowed so many of their generation, O'Rawe's unsparingly honest account does many things, none more so than make us fervently wish that Gerry Conlon lived much longer, because he had so much more to teach us.'

–Kevin Cullen, columnist and former
Ireland correspondent for *The Boston Globe*

'A vivid, bracing, often funny account of the wild and tragic but ultimately inspiring life of Gerry Conlon. With great affection and compassion for his subject, Ricky O'Rawe has written a biography that captures Conlon's self-destructive demons, but also his infectious lust for life.'

–Patrick Keefe, *The New Yorker*

'Rick O'Rawe has written a searingly honest, deeply moving and all encompassing account of the life of Gerry Conlon. Gerry's lust for life was only matched by his unquenchable thirst for justice not just for the Guildford 4 but for all those who have fallen foul of an often corrupt and politically loaded judicial system. The author deserves praise for refusing to allow his lifelong, deep friendship with Conlon to whitewash many of Gerry's own personal failings. Yet in the end O'Rawe still does justice himself to the memory of a remarkable, courageous and lovable character.'

–Henry McDonald, *The Guardian*

'Gerry Conlon's remarkable life deserves the honest integrity O'Rawe brings to his task. It is a labour of love but without being a hagiography of his friend … [and] contributes to the ongoing quest for truth – how the State got it so wrong and why no one has been brought to justice for the Guildford Pub Bombings … These are questions Gerry Conlon fought to have answered and which O'Rawe lays out with forensic detail.'

—Kevin R. Winters, international human rights lawyer

Richard O'Rawe and Gerry Conlon grew up together in Belfast's Lower Falls area – they were life-long best friends and confidantes. O'Rawe is a former Irish republican prisoner and was a leading figure in the 1981 Hunger Strike in the H Blocks of the Maze prison. He is the author of the best-selling book *Blanketmen: An Untold Story of the H-Block Hunger Strike* (2005) and *Afterlives: The Hunger Strike and the Secret Offer that Changed Irish History* (2010).

In the name of the son

In the name of the son
THE GERRY CONLON STORY

RICHARD O'RAWE

MERRION PRESS

First published in 2017 by
Merrion Press
10 George's Street
Newbridge
Co. Kildare
Ireland
www.merrionpress.ie

© Richard O'Rawe, 2017

9781785371387 (Paper)
9781785371394 (Kindle)
9781785371400 (Epub)
9781785371417 (PDF)

British Library Cataloguing in Publication Data
An entry can be found on request

Library of Congress Cataloging in Publication Data
An entry can be found on request

All rights reserved. Without limiting the rights under copyright reserved alone, no part of this publication may be reproduced, stored in or introduced into a retrieval system, or transmitted, in any form or by any means (electronic, mechanical, photocopying, recording or otherwise) without the prior written permission of both the copyright owner and the above publisher of this book.

Interior design by www.jminfotechindia.com
Typeset in 11.5/14.5 Adobe Caslon Pro

Cover design by www.phoenix-graphicdesign.com
Cover front: Gerry Conlon in New York, 1990. Photo courtesy of the Conlon family.
Cover back: Courtesy of Hugh Russell/*The Irish News*

Contents

Foreword by Johnny Depp   ix
Acknowledgements   xvii
Prologue   xix

One   1
Two   20
Three   34
Four   48
Five   63
Six   77
Seven   90
Eight   103
Nine   111
Ten   119
Eleven   130
Twelve   138
Thirteen   147
Fourteen   157
Fifteen   170
Sixteen   185
Seventeen   202

Endnotes   211
Bibliography   223
Index   224

Upon Thinking of My Long-Lost Brother, Gerry ...
20.8.17

    I first met Gerry Conlon, by absolute chance, in the hallway of a talent agency in Los Angeles, somewhere around 1990, I believe. It was a rare occurrence for me to visit the place, which made the moment with Gerry all the more charmed.

    I had pressed the button and was en route to my destination floor. Upon arriving, the doors opened. As I exited, I spooked a couple of guys to my left, who looked, as did I, sorely out of place. The guts of this heinous, monolithic terrarium of steel, glass and dubious "art", sparsely shaming those ghastly "modern" walls, was not a typical setting for folk such as myself, or gents of this breed, who, in my personal and moderately professional estimation, were satisfactorily saturated and teetering along the same invisible ledge, as though they'd been out on the prowl, for an especially impressive stretch. Indeed, they looked just like the depraved, miscreant, unhinged maniacs I always tended to hang out with. One of them possessed the squinty scrutinising eyes of the streets, and was as skinny as a dried lizard. He also seemed to have been divined with a prevailing lack of residents in the tooth department. The questionable few choppers that had not been evicted, were lonely, jagged and rotting. His stringy, straight hair - greasy to his shoulders. This was Joey Cashman. A hilariously clever and quick-witted Irishman, from just outside Dublin. He was the manager of one of my favourite humans of all time, the infamously tattered genius of lyric and song, Shane MacGowan, from the Pogues. Joey was a lovely man, who held strong to those he loved. Devoted and solid. I would later survive many adventures with this man, and to this very day, I have been informed of Joey's tragic and "sudden" demise, and miraculous resurrection, at least fourteen times. The other fella was from heavier stock. He laid a big, beautiful, slightly crazed Cheshire Cat smile on me, which showed that this man had at least met a dentist once in his life. But it was his eyes that got me. Eyes that simultaneously exuded wisdom and a childlike purity; a desire to live and love. There was no question that these powerful eyes had seen and experienced much. This was Gerry Conlon. He approached me and introduced himself and his mate Joey, with the exuberance of a man who held nothing back. He gave of himself freely. His eyes sparkled like ten thousand stars had just given birth to ten thousand more ...

Gerry Conlon had first gotten my attention when he stomped out of the Old Bailey in London in October 1989, fists raised high and declared to the world that he was an innocent man who had spent fifteen years in jail. The authorities had tried to shove him out the back door, in order to avoid the inevitable media frenzy, but he had refused, instead imparting something along the lines of "Fuck you, I'm a free man, youse fuckin brought me in the back door, I'm going out the front!" My curiosity had then been further fired when I'd learnt that he'd witnessed his father, Giuseppe, another innocent man, die in a British prison. And now here he was, Gerry himself, stood right before me, in this, the most incongruous of places possible. Fortunately, to prevent matters from being overtly one-sided, he recognized me from something or other and lunch was duly arranged.

Gerry was altogether an articulate, personable, funny, self-deprecating and fierce humanitarian. He was an absolute gentleman, who possessed all the knowledge of law in the streets of Belfast. Chivalrous, loyal and highly sensitive to any injustice, no matter how large, or minute. If he loved you, you were blessed to be invited into his circle, where there existed no edits with him. Gerry said what he felt and meant what he said. He had no difficulty in getting his point across. Ever. He had grown so used to having his prison clique around him that those of us who spent significant amounts of time with him became a newfangled version of just that. He was a 100% trusted friend and brother, to the very end.

During lunch, he broached the subject of my playing him in the film that was to be produced about his life during his unfathomably unjust arrest and incarceration. More than touched at this profoundly personal invitation from this man, I was already on the deck wiping away tears (as was he), when he gave me the first details of his abduction and torture by the British authorities. During this, our first proper encounter, he spoke more of his experiences in prison. Despite the hardship that had been visited on him, I came away with the impression that here was a character whose passion for life had been in no way diminished. He was starving for it. As much as he could get ahold of.

Later, during the summer of 1991, I found myself fortunate enough to be invited on holiday with Gerry and his family. Despite being more of a grape man, the only flavours I recall from that trip are Black Bush, Jameson's, Irish Coffee and of course, the Guinness. The Conlons were lovely people, one and all, but I had a special place in my heart for Gerry's mother, Sarah, and his sister, Ann. These were sweet, strong and kind folk whose lives had been torn asunder and putting them back together wasn't going to be easy. But, if my experiences with these wonderful people told me anything, it was that their humour remained perfectly intact. In fact, I specifically remember some sloppy conversation with both Gerry and I employing words and sentences that our mouths were shamefully unfit to speak, as our eyes began to see double. At some point Gerry decided that we must go to Dingle to see Fungie, the dolphin. Very important. Gerry had no need to convince me, of course I was going to say yes. Who wouldn't want to go to a place called Dingle to see a dolphin named Fungie? Gerry proceeded to inform me that his cousin, David, would be coming down that night to Dublin from Belfast, and would drive us to Dingle in the morning. And indeed, as promised, later that evening, David appeared in the door of the bar, screaming, "Gerry, ya fucken cunt!" I turned to see a big, thick and angry-looking brute, with ginger hair and pincers for arms. We were introduced. I shook one of his metallic claws and looked him squarely in the eye. "It's a pleasure to meet you," I said. He replied with what may have been an eleven-syllable fuck-off. I still don't know. The man was utterly pickled. If worry was going to come into the picture it would have done so at exactly that moment. We sat down to have a drink. And drink we did. What seemed like an instant later, it was brought to our attention that we were fast approaching 8.30 a.m. It was time to go. Worry never seemed to enter the picture. We had merely forgotten to sleep. But, whilst not feeling all that bright-eyed and bushy-tailed, we remained determined to make our rendezvous with this mysterious dolphin called Fungie. Fungus. I felt like fungus. Gerry looked like fungus, and David was immune to fungus. Of course, I was chosen to ride in the front seat with David. His co-pilot, as it were. It is potentially the only time I have put a seatbelt on without hesitation. Or actually thought about one for that matter. But David, it turns out, was a fantastic driver. His claws were quite handy for storing pints of Guinness, but it didn't matter, because his feet were steering. So, as I also clutched two pints of Guinness, similar to Gerry in the back seat, I thought that if we were to die, it would be the most interesting trio of obituaries. Anyways, we soldiered onward towards Dingle, but at some point there came the inevitable need to replenish our glasses. The next road sign informed us that Limerick, also known as Stab City, lay just ahead. We would find a pub, have a bite, and get back on our way with enough Guinness to carry us through to Dingle. Wrong. Our brief pitstop in Limerick proved to be one of the most chaotic nights that I can ever remember, and/or, kind of not remember. Suffice to say, we conquered Stab City. The three of us took over a pub, all in the name of Gerry Conlon. He was a hero to these people and it was a joy to bear witness. Courtesy of his devilish charm, he owned the place. It was a riotous celebration. The following morning, I awoke in an unfamiliar room, in what appeared to be an old hotel. Complete with red-eyes and full-on throbbing gristle somewhere within whatever had been spared of my brain, I somehow managed to contact Gerry in the adjoining room. "Where is the Lord Mayor of Limerick?" I asked, referring to David, who had been bestowed the honor the night previous. "He's taking a shower" Gerry said, in a pained drawl. Apparently he woke up with some chick. He didn't know where he was, let alone who she was. Gerry went on to tell me that David had said good morning and asked the girl very simply, "Did we fuck?" "I'm not sure," came the reply from the sweet lady to the armless thalidomide, whose pincer claws had been hurled across the room. David thought for a moment, before calmly stating, "Well, we had better make sure ..."

After picking myself up off the floor, we again made for Dingle, where we finally met Fungie. The three of us were in no state to do anything whatsoever, let alone get in a fucking boat with a bunch of tourists. I can recall us being looked down upon by our fellow shipmates, especially the children, for some reason. I felt dirty. But Gerry was as excited as an eight-year-old, as we clipped through the water watching out for the dolphin to occasionally rear a head and deign us with its glory on this most joyous of grey days that I can ever recall. Gerry always possessed the magical ability to ensure such miracles.

The pain of losing his father never left Gerry. He blamed himself for Giuseppe's death and nothing I, or anyone else, could say to him would shift that blame. In quieter moments, he would tell me of his pain, of how troubled he was at having confessed to the Guildford pub bombing. In his mind, if he hadn't confessed, his father might still be alive and the Maguire family, who were also wrongfully convicted of the pub bombings, would never have been sent to prison. He might have been dealt the torturous methods employed by the authorities to haul out the counterfeit admissions, but in his rush to self-condemnation, he set that aside. He could not forgive himself.

Gerry Conlon was a leader who became the central figure in the struggle to have the Birmingham Six released from prison, even addressing a Congressional Committee on the matter. Gerry was also an international human rights activist and he highlighted the harsh treatment meted out to the Australian aborigines and Native Americans. His activism didn't stop there: he protested capital punishment wherever it reared its ugly head. For prisoners around the world, many of whom had been wrongfully convicted, Gerry Conlon was their only hope.

Yet, by his own admission, this man was a flawed character, as so many of us are. He often told reporters that he took drugs to ward off his demons. In 1998 he took the decision to go clean, but what followed was a six-year struggle, during which he repeatedly goaded himself to commit suicide. But he beat the monster; he got off his knees and he beat the monster.

This book is a tour de force, a warts-and-all depiction of the life of Gerry Conlon from the minute he walked out of the Old Bailey. Knowing him as I did, he wouldn't have wanted it any other way. On every page, the colourful characters that inhabited Gerry's life reach their hands out to the reader and invite them into a world rich in pathos, humour and irony. This is not a sad story. No, far from it. This is a chronicle of the triumph of the human spirit over extreme adversity. It is a story of hope. It is the story of a man I loved and would have taken a bullet for, as I know he would have done for me and all his loved ones. It was an honor to have known Gerry Conlon and to call him my friend.

Once we'd just left a bookstore in Dublin. Me with a handful of Brendan Behan's books, and Gerry with a present - a beautifully handworked leather wallet, with one word etched onto it ... "Saoirse", meaning Freedom. It's in my pocket as I write these words.

Johnny Depp
Vancouver
August 2017

Acknowledgements

About a year before he died on 21 June 2017, Gerry Conlon and I were having breakfast in a Belfast city centre café. Afterwards, as we casually strolled along Royal Avenue, he asked me to write his biography from the time he was released from the Old Bailey in October 1989: 'I've a great story in me, O'Rawe.' I believed him; Gerry was one of life's adventurers. But there was no great hurry, we'd get around to it ... little did we know that the clock was ticking.

When Gerry was in hospital he sent for me. It was a week before he tragically passed. He reminded me of our agreement and I reaffirmed my commitment to write his story.

The first person I approached about fulfilling my promise to Gerry was his sister, Ann McKernan. She never hesitated. She gave me interview after interview and handed me four large grip bags containing prison and medical records, as well as personal notes from Gerry. In this book, I called this invaluable source of information, 'The Gerry Conlon Papers'. To my friend Ann I express my warmest thanks.

Special thanks go to Johnny Depp who, when asked if he would write the foreword, never hesitated, replying that it would be 'an honour'. Huge thanks also to Stephen Deuters.

Others who helped and who were very generous with their time were Joey Cashman, Gearóid Ó Clei, Finola Geraghty, 'Minty', Marion McKeone, Siobhan MacGowan, Fiona Looney, Shane MacGowan, Victoria Mary Clarke, Paddy-Joe Hill, Bridie Brennan, Martin Loughran, Mary-Kate McKernan, David Pallister, Darragh McIntyre, Sandy Boyer (deceased), John McDonagh, Mark Durkan, Margaret Walsh, Barry Walle, John McManus, Peter Ong, Seamus Doherty, Kevin Winters, Brendan Byrne, Henry McDonald, 'Angie', Frank Murray (deceased), Noel Doran, Hugh Russell, and the staff in *The Irish News*, Niall Stannage, 'Celtic Pat' McDonnell, Malachi O'Doherty.

I am especially indebted to Conor Graham of Merrion Press and his staff: Fiona Dunne, Myles McCionnaith and Maria McGuinness.

I am much obliged to Peter O'Connell Media for the great job they did in publicising this book.

To my literary agent and teacher, Jonathan Williams, I express my deepest appreciation.

My special thanks go to my daughter Berni, who accompanied me around the UK and Ireland.

As ever, my wife Bernadette gave unconditional support, as did my daughter Steph and son Conchúr.

Now that I wrecked my brain trying to remember everyone who helped me with this book, it strikes me that there is someone out there whom I have forgotten. If that someone is you, please forgive me – and let me know. If you can prove that I missed you, I'll buy you a pint!

Prologue

On the night of 21 March 1994, two limousines pulled up at Hollywood's Chateau Marmont hotel for the contingent of *In the Name of the Father*. The film's producer, Jim Sheridan, screenwriter Terry George, Gerry Conlon and his friend Joey Cashman all climbed into the back of the same limousine. Knowing they would never again be back at an Oscars ceremony, Conlon and Cashman were determined to make the best of it. As soon as the vehicle had taken off, Cashman asked if the driver would stop at a drinks store so he could buy Tequila. It would be surprising if warning bells did not ring in Jim Sheridan's head at Cashman's request. Giving these two boys access to bottles of hard liquor on the way to the biggest awards ceremony in the film-producing world was questionable at best. Prudently, Sheridan said he did not think that was a good idea. Predictably, Gerry sided with Joey: 'If Joey wants to stop at an offie [an off-licence], we stop at the fucking offie.'

The limousine stopped at a drinks store and several bottles of Tequila were bought. Not long after that the fun began. Conlon and Cashman stuck their heads out of the top of the limousine, started shouting and waving to pedestrians in the streets and guzzled down their bottles of Tequila as if tomorrow was for saints and suckers. There was a huge queue of limousines waiting to pull up outside the Dorothy Chandler Pavilion.

Cashman said: 'We were off our heads before we even got there, and Jim was really embarrassed by it all. Just before we hit the red carpet, Jim managed to get Gerry down, and then he almost had to sit on him to keep him from going back up again!'

Mustering all the decorum at their disposal, Conlon and Cashman got out of the limousine. While Sheridan was being interviewed by the press, no one was paying Conlon any attention, so he went up to the podium where only the top stars are interviewed and introduced himself to a television producer. Soon after, with his Tequila-guzzling buddy standing alongside him, Conlon gave a very coherent interview, during which he endorsed the film.

The Oscars ceremony lasts for approximately four hours. Conlon and Cashman found the whole thing excruciatingly boring, so, after two hours, they retreated to the toilets for the remainder of the ceremony, where they wiled away the time smoking crack cocaine. Then, realising they were hungry, they left the building and searched the neighbourhood for a restaurant. The two made sure they were back in the Chandler Pavilion before the ceremony ended – just in time to join the first of the night's parties: the Governors Ball. Cashman had fond memories of the event:

> Afterwards, you just walk out the door and there was a party in the building, or connected to it. It was really big, and the public had no access. And there was loads of booze and champagne and all that. There was plenty of good stuff to eat there, you know, caviar, smoked salmon, grilled shrimps. I like that sorta stuff. So me and Gerry dug into that. Then we gatecrashed the different parties for the rest of the night, and we ended up back in our hotel and all these women stripped off and jumped into the pool. I stripped off and jumped in, and Gerry jumped in after me. We'd great craic. I'll tell ya – it certainly beat going down to the local. Like, I can look back and if someone asks me, 'Where were you at the weekend?' I can say about that weekend: 'I was at the Oscars.' Know what I mean?

One

At 3.30 p.m. on 19 October 1989, in the homeland of Magna Carta and the cradle of parliamentary democracy, the underbelly of a Trojan horse opened and justice saw the light of day.

Confronted with indisputable evidence of police deception and perjury at the original trial in October–November 1975, appeal court judge Lord Lane had little option but to quash the convictions of the Guildford Four. These were individuals who had been found guilty of no-warning bombing attacks in Guildford, Surrey, and Woolwich, London, on 5 October and 7 November 1974, in which seven people died. It was a seminal and ugly moment in the history of British jurisprudence, but how did that Trojan horse ever get inside the hitherto impenetrable walls of the British judicial system in the first place? To answer that question, we must revert to the people who really *did* put the bombs in Guildford and Woolwich, and to Flat 7, Waldemar Avenue, Fulham.

By 1974, it was dawning on the seven-man IRA Army Council that the armed campaign to force the British government to withdraw from Northern Ireland was stuttering. In fact, the British, far from being thrown back into the Irish sea, had weathered the best that the IRA could throw at them. Not only were the British still on the field of battle, they were planning new strategies to wipe out the IRA. Against a growing realisation that the war could not be won if it was limited to the borders of Northern Ireland, the Army Council sanctioned a no-warning bombing campaign against British army targets in London, Birmingham and other major cities in England.

The prospect of civilians being blown up, as well as British soldiers, was raised by the prominent Irish journalist Mary Holland when she interviewed Army Council member Dáithí Ó Conaill a week after The

Kings Arms pub in Woolwich was attacked. Holland asked Ó Conaill about civilians being killed in the bombing campaign, and he chillingly replied: 'They [the IRA] warned civilians not to frequent places where military personnel are known to have established haunts.'[1] The upshot of that answer was that, if civilians got blown to smithereens, then so be it; it was their own fault, not the IRA's. Ó Conaill then went on to say: 'As regards military targets, there are no warnings. There will be no warnings.' He then promised that the bombing campaign in England would be intensified.

Bombing England was hardly a novel tactic: in the middle of the nineteenth century and during World War II, republican activists had waged bombing campaigns in London and other British cities, but to little or no effect. On 8 March 1973, the very court in which the sentences against the Guildford Four had been delivered and eventually quashed – the Old Bailey – had been car-bombed by the IRA, and one innocent person, Frederick Milton, was killed. Undeterred by the lack of success, the Army Council unleashed an IRA Active Service Unit (ASU) in August 1974 in Fulham.

The officer commanding the ASU was a County Kerry man, Brendan Dowd, and the engineering officer was Joe O'Connell from County Clare. Another member of the IRA unit was Liam Quinn from San Francisco. At 5.30 p.m. on 21 September 1974, Dowd hired a Ford Escort car from Swan National car hire and signed a contract under the false name 'Martin Moffitt'. That night, Dowd, O'Connell and an unidentified third man reconnoitred various pubs in Guildford for possible targets. Dowd and the third man did a second reconnoitre a week later, which confirmed in Dowd's mind that the two pubs to be bombed should be The Horse and Groom and The Seven Stars.

At 2.30 p.m. on 4 October, Dowd again used the false name 'Martin Moffitt' to hire a white Hillman Avenger from Swan National. The next morning, he and O'Connell made the two six-pound bombs in the Fulham flat. That evening Dowd drove the white Avenger containing O'Connell, the third man and two young IRA women to Guildford, where Dowd parked on the top floor of a multistorey carpark. After priming the bombs in the car and placing them in each of the IRA women's handbags, he then accompanied one of the females into The

Horse and Groom, while O'Connell accompanied the other to The Seven Stars, along with the third man (who has never been charged with the bombings).

In The Horse and Groom, Dowd and his female compatriot pretended to be a courting couple, kissing and holding hands. The woman slipped the handbag containing the primed bomb under her seat. Meanwhile, O'Connell, the second female and the third man had found seats in the corner of the bar of The Seven Stars. The female left her handbag containing the bomb on the floor, and the third man gently pushed it under a bench with his feet. By 8.15 p.m., the five members of the bombing team were back in London and having a drink in The Durell Arms on Fulham Road.

The first bomb exploded in The Horse and Groom at 8.50 p.m. No warning was given. A reporter who was at the scene within a minute wrote: 'People were running, shouting and screaming. Many of them were young girls and many were clutching bleeding heads. There was blood everywhere. The entire front of The Horse and Groom was blown out – there was rubble everywhere, glass, bricks, timber. People were scrabbling amongst the debris, trying to pull people out of the mess. It was panic and chaos.'[2] Five people died in The Horse and Groom and some 200 were injured, many seriously. On hearing of the bomb attack on The Horse and Groom, Owen O'Brien, the manager of The Seven Stars, had the sharpness of mind to evacuate 200 customers from the pub, and when the bomb exploded, no one was killed.

On 10 October 1974, Harry Duggan from County Clare, Eddie Butler from County Limerick and Hugh Doherty from Donegal joined the ASU. In the month that followed the Guildford bombings, Dowd and his cell were unrelenting, carrying out four more bomb attacks, none of which had fatal consequences. Then, on 7 November 1974, in Sedding Street, close to London's King's Cross station, Joe O'Connell got into the passenger seat of a stolen white Corsair, with Dowd in the driving seat. Duggan and Butler sat in the back of the car. The men drove to the side of The Kings Arms pub in Woolwich, in south-east London, and, after making sure that it was packed with people, some of whom they presumed were British soldiers, Joe O'Connell threw a seven-pound gelignite bomb through the window, killing two people and injuring twenty-six others. A local man, Michael Hulse, described the scene as 'like a battlefield. I was watching television when it went off. The windows shook and rattled. It was like a 25-pounder cannon going off. I went outside and there were about a dozen bodies lying on the road.'[3]

The Assistant Chief Constable of Surrey, Christopher Rowe, had been put in charge of the Guildford bombings inquiry, but neither he nor those around him had a clue as to who had carried out the attacks, although they suspected it was the work of the IRA. As Gerry Conlon put it, 'They were killing people in huge numbers. The IRA caused absolute terror. And they [the British police] couldn't find them.'[4] Nevertheless, 'they' soon found him.

On 28 November 1974, 21-year-old Paul 'Benny' Hill was arrested by police in Southampton, and the next day he signed statements confessing to the Guildford and Woolwich bombings. During police interrogations, Hill named Gerry Conlon, Paddy Armstrong and Armstrong's 17-year-old English girlfriend, Carole Richardson, as his fellow bombers. Hill also told police that he and Gerry Conlon had stayed with Gerry's aunt, Annie Maguire, while they were in London. This, and a false confession from Gerry Conlon that was exacted by police under duress, were enough to have Mrs Maguire and six other members of her family arrested. Mrs Maguire's protestations of innocence accounted for nothing when police alleged they had found traces of the explosive, nitroglycerine, on her hands and on the person of the six other members of her extended family. Included in what became known as the 'Maguire Seven' was Giuseppe Conlon, Gerry's father, who hadn't even been in England when the bombings occurred, and who had travelled over to England from Belfast only on 1 December to help co-ordinate his son's legal defence. Prophetically, on the evening of 5 December, Giuseppe Conlon was in his police cell when Detective Chief Superintendent Wally Simmons of the Surrey bomb squad shouted in to him: 'You want to know about your son? Well, he's going to get thirty years. We'll see to it that you die in gaol. I'll see you later.'[5]

By 7 December, the Guildford Four had all confessed to the bombings and were subsequently charged with multiple murders. Gerry Conlon described his time in police custody:

In my cell I could suddenly see myself and what I was doing, maybe for the first time. I wanted to please the police just so I wouldn't be beaten any more, screamed at, abused with dirty names. I actually wanted to please these bastards. I was in a terrible state of confusion and fear. I was crying. I was breaking down and falling apart. And all I wanted to do was to please these policemen – to please them and get away from them.[6]

For the police, it was seemingly a job well done. For the real bombers, it was business as usual, and for the next year their campaign of violence continued unabated as they shot people dead and bombed targets all over London, almost at will. In the period up to the IRA ceasefire, which commenced on 9 February 1975, police records show twenty-nine incidents that were directly attributable to that particular IRA cell.

When the cell continued its campaign in August 1975, after a collapse of the IRA ceasefire, its members were no less industrious, and between November and December they carried out six bomb and bullet attacks, including the doorstep assassination of Ross McWhirter, the co-founder, along with his brother Norris, of *The Guinness Book of Records*. Ross had put up a reward of £50,000 for the convictions of those involved in the IRA onslaught and that, in the IRA's view, made him a target. It was not until the Balcombe Street siege in December 1975 – almost a year after the Guildford Four and the Maguire Seven had been charged – that most of the IRA cell were finally arrested.

During questioning, Eddie Butler and Joe O'Connell told police that they had bombed Woolwich. Moreover, they said they did not know any of the Guildford Four. Despite this confession, the police failed to inform the Guildford Four's defence counsel about the IRA men's admissions, but they did tell the Office of the Director of Public Prosecutions. Curiously, the DPP's office never acted on the senior policemen's report; they buried it. Accordingly, no further action or inquiries were initiated, no one went back to Butler or O'Connell to challenge their accounts, and neither man, nor any member of that IRA cell, was charged with the Guildford and Woolwich bombings. No one in the DPP thought it prudent, or desirable, to question whether or not the Guildford Four or the Maguire Seven might be innocent. Besides the IRA, it took a formidable effort by the police and the judiciary to put and keep the Guildford Four in prison.

On 16 September 1975, Mr Justice John Francis Donaldson, Master of the Rolls, opened the trial of the Guildford Four. Donaldson had been president of the National Industrial Relations Court and had antagonised trade unionists so much that they tried to impeach him 'for political bias'.[7] Michael Foot, the former Labour Party leader, accused him of having a 'trigger-happy judicial finger'.[8] His trigger-happy judicial finger pointed the jury in only one direction. In the matter of Paddy Armstrong's evidence, where Armstrong had said he had made a confession only because he was high on drugs, Justice Donaldson told the jury: 'He was high on drugs when he was arrested and when the effects of them wore off thereafter, he said, he was induced to sign them because he was very frightened of the Surrey police.' Justice Donaldson thereafter told the jury that, '*I* would not have made a false confession, but Armstrong may be different from me.' One could be forgiven for asking the obvious questions: how would his honour know if he would have made a statement or not? Had he ever been high on drugs?

Gerry Conlon, Paddy Armstrong and Carole Richardson pleaded not guilty, but Paul Hill, when asked to plead, said: 'I refuse to take part in this. I refuse to defend myself. Your justice stinks.' Hill may have been correct in his assessment, but to a London jury in 1975, a plea of non-recognition of the court – which was essentially what Hill had first entered – was akin to admitting to membership of the IRA, and wasn't it the IRA that had carried out these atrocities? After conferring with his client, Hill's counsel, Arthur Mildon QC, entered a plea of not guilty on Hill's behalf.

Sir Michael Havers, the Conservative Shadow Attorney General, led the prosecution team. The only evidence against the four was their jumbled confessions, but that was enough. During his summing up of the evidence against Paul Hill, which was applicable to all the defendants, Justice Donaldson said: 'Finally, as with all these confessions, you may wonder how it is possible to produce quite so detailed a confession if it is not true. You will wonder whether there is any other reason, because certainly none has been suggested, for making such a suggestion, other than it being true. There it is.'

There it was indeed.

Oblivious of the fate of Gerry Conlon and his three co-defendants, the IRA cell launched 'phase two' of its bombing campaign on 27 August 1975, when cell members Harry Duggan and Hugh Doherty placed a ten-pound bomb under a seat in The Caterham Arms, in Caterham, Surrey. Twenty-three civilians and ten soldiers were injured in the no-warning blast, with eight victims being critically injured. More attacks followed. It was as if nothing had changed. Nothing had for the real bombers.

Shortly after two o'clock on 22 October, the jury returned unanimous guilty verdicts on all counts against the four accused. Bemoaning the fact that he could not put the black cap on his learned head, Justice Donaldson, in his sentencing, expressed regret that the four individuals had not been charged with treason, which carried a mandatory death sentence. Nevertheless, he took some comfort in sentencing the four to life imprisonment. Justice Donaldson recommended that Paul Hill never be released from prison, and Gerry Conlon should serve a minimum of thirty years.

But Justice Donaldson was not finished with this matter. On 27 January 1976, he presided at the Maguire Seven trial. His final words to the jury on that occasion could not have been clearer: 'But if, members of the jury, having considered all these matters, you are sure, then it is your duty, *your duty* in accordance with the oath that you have taken, to bring in a verdict of guilty.' When the guilty verdicts were returned, Justice Donaldson gave Annie Maguire, who was surely the IRA's most unlikely bomb-maker, the maximum sentence of fourteen years' imprisonment. Her husband Paddy received the same sentence. Giuseppe Conlon was sentenced to twelve years. Seán Smyth and Pat O'Neill were sentenced to eleven years each. Sixteen-year-old Vincent Maguire was given five years, and his brother Patrick, a fourteen-year old, four years. Of Annie Maguire, her son Vincent later told Grant McKee and Ros Franey, authors of the book *Time Bomb*, that 'My mother couldn't even put a plug together. She was nearly blind. She had to wear real strong glasses to see what she was doing. I don't even think she could put a screw in a plug, let alone make bombs.'[9]

Absurdity was heaped on top of absurdity when, on 24 January 1977, the trial of Joe O'Connell's IRA ASU opened. Judge Sir Joseph

Donaldson Cantley OBE QC presided. In accordance with IRA protocols, none of the defendants entered a plea. However, O'Connell went further. 'I refuse to plead,' he said, 'because the indictment does not include two charges concerning the Guildford and Woolwich pub bombings. I took part in both, for which innocent people have been convicted.' Here was a claim from the real bombers that miscarriages of justice had occurred in the trials of the Guildford Four and the Maguire Seven.

The Crown prosecutor, John Mathew QC, moved quickly to dismiss O'Connell's explosive declaration by telling the jury: 'Guildford and Woolwich are not a matter for you.' Joe O'Connell and the IRA men had never been schooled in the niceties of judicial decorum and they begged to differ. So much so that they instructed their defence counsel not to prove that they were innocent of the Guildford and Woolwich pub bombings, but to prove that they *were* guilty. Conversely, this approach placed an onus on the Crown prosecutor to prove that the IRA cell did *not* carry out the pub bombings. It was a bizarre state of affairs.

One of the most important witnesses at the Balcombe Street trial was independent forensic scientist Douglas Higgs, who had also given evidence at the Guildford Four trial in September 1975. It emerged during the Balcombe Street trial that Higgs had prepared a statement for the Guildford Four court on 24 January 1975, which provided an analysis of the bomb-throwing attacks. In his statement, Higgs had said that five attacks, carried out between 22 October 1974 and 22 December 1974, were so similar in nature that they had obviously been perpetrated by the same individuals. Among the attacks to which Higgs referred in his statement was the Woolwich pub bombing. But the alleged Woolwich pub bombers, the Guildford Four and the Maguire Seven, had all been arrested by 3 December 1974. The logic of this was if, as Higgs confirmed, the same individuals had carried out all the bombings and some of those bombings had occurred *after* the arrests of the Guildford Four and Maguire Seven, then they could not possibly have bombed the Woolwich pub. An upshot of this is that the statements of admission made by the Guildford Four, in which they said they had bombed the Woolwich pub and Guildford, would have to have been deemed worthless – since they would be patently untrue – and the judge would have had to acquit them of all charges. Unfortunately for the Guildford Four and the Maguire Seven, the Crown did not forward Higgs's 24 January 1975 statement to the Guildford defence, but they did send them a further statement that Higgs had composed on 17 June 1975. This was similar to his previous statement, with the exception that any reference to the Woolwich bombing had been omitted.

After persistent questioning, Higgs said that it was the police who had asked him to leave out the reference to Woolwich in his second statement. Judge Cantley wondered aloud who, in particular, had asked him. The answer to that question emerged in court when, under cross-examination, Chief Superintendent Jim Nevill divulged that it had been the Director of Public Prosecutions, the late Sir Norman Skelhorn, who had sent a directive down the line to Douglas Higgs to remove the Woolwich reference from his 17 June statement.

Sir Norman Skelhorn was a man who neither shirked his responsibilities nor hid his prejudices. In October 1973, at the Harvard Law School Forum, he told the audience he accepted that torture had taken place in Northern Ireland, but, 'When dealing with "Irish terrorists", any methods are justified.'[10] This end-justifies-the-means approach from Sir Norman explains why he had no qualms about sending instructions to Douglas Higgs to doctor his statement. Only one conclusion emerges from this revelation: Sir Norman Skelhorn attempted to pervert the course of justice in order to make sure that the Guildford Four and the Maguire Seven should serve out their full sentences. While the prominent High Court Judge and Master of the Rolls Lord Denning did not accuse Sir Norman of perverting the course of justice, he nevertheless identified him as the single most culpable person in the false imprisonment of those convicted of the Guildford and Woolwich bombings. In 1990, a reporter for *The Spectator* asked Lord Denning to comment on the evidence that the Guildford Four were innocent and the judge replied: 'That troubles me a lot, because I knew Sir Norman Skelhorn, the Director of Public Prosecutions at the time, a first-rate man. He's dead now. He's unable to explain what happened, and it was his responsibility.'[11]

Detective Chief Superintendent Hucklesby of the Metropolitan Police was asked to retake the witness stand and was forced to concede that he had recommended to Sir Norman Skelhorn that Eddie Butler and Joe O'Connell *should* be tried for the Woolwich pub bombing. The police, to all intents and purposes, had a strong case in the form of damning forensic evidence and, by this stage, five admissions of guilt from the IRA cell, which, crucially, they were prepared to stand over in court: it does not get any better for prosecutors. Predictably, Sir Norman Skelhorn did not act on Hucklesby's recommendation, and thus once more left himself open to the charge that he was intent on perverting the course of justice and keeping innocent people in prison.

Questions remain to be answered: did Sir Norman Skelhorn act alone, or was he merely the cutting edge of an establishment conspiracy? Did he receive instructions from above – from the Home Secretary, Roy Jenkins, or even from Prime Minister James Callaghan? Gerry Conlon's view on this matter was unambiguous: 'And in our case, and that of the Birmingham Six, we are now, at this moment, actively pursuing the release of confidential documents that have been held from 1974 under the Official Secrets Act that are not to be released for seventy-five years. Now that only proves our innocence from day one, and it proves state collusion between the government, the judiciary, the police and the press.'[12]

As anticipated, the four members of the IRA cell were all sentenced to life imprisonment, but they had prevailed in the trial of contradictions: they had demonstrated that it was they, and not the Guildford Four or the Maguire Seven, who had carried out the Guildford and Woolwich pub bombings.

Category 'A' prisoner 462779, Gerry Conlon, now locked up in a cell on the third floor of 'A wing' in Wakefield Prison, Yorkshire, was closely following events in court. Writing to his mother, Sarah, on 31 January 1977, Conlon said:

> It's the first time I've shed a tear in prison. Mum, you'll never know how happy I was to read it [the IRA cell's assertion that they, and not the Guildford Four, had carried out the Guildford and Woolwich bombings] and see for the first time since I was arrested

that the truth is coming out. Now it's been publicly admitted in a court of law that we were not responsible for the charges on which we were convicted. I'm feeling confident about the outcome. Everyone must know now that I should be out, as the police fitted up the wrong people and it's now out in the open, Mum.[13]

Gerry's optimism was premature and was soon to be dashed. On 10 October that year, the Guildford Four appeal opened at the Old Bailey. Lord Roskill presided, accompanied by Mr Justice Boreham and Lord Justice Lawton. Once again, the indefatigable Sir Michael Havers led for the Crown.

The Guildford Four's appeal was based on affidavits taken by Conlon's and Hill's lawyer, Alastair Logan, from members of the IRA ASU while they were in prison, and from the evidence garnered at their trial. It included 135 discrepancies between the IRA men's accounts of the bombings and those of the Guildford Four. Such was the strength and quality of detail in their evidence that Havers, after grilling Eddie Butler, said he accepted Butler had been present at the bombing. Then he found Harry Duggan's evidence 'convincing'. Of Joe O'Connell's testimony that he had been at both the Guildford and Woolwich bombings, Havers said there was 'such a ring of truth' about it, the Crown accepted that 'a great deal of what he says is true'. On hearing these astounding admissions, Gerry Conlon and the other three defendants must surely have thought that their ordeal was over and that they would soon be walking out of the front door of the Old Bailey. How elated they must have been when they heard even Lord Roskill fall in behind Havers: 'We are content to assume that O'Connell's story of his presence [at Guildford] and preparation may indeed be true and that Dowd may also have taken part.' How sweet those words must have been to the ears of the Guildford Four, but they would have been wise to remember Banquo's words in *Macbeth*, 'What, can the devil speak true?'[14]

Havers, rather astutely, had anticipated it would be almost impossible to counter the deluge of intimate detail that the real culprits would bring to the court and instead offered a new proposition: far from having arrested and sentenced the people who had carried out the

Guildford and Woolwich pub bombings – which had been the Crown's position right up until the appeal – there were now another four culprits: the IRA ASU. It must have been a mouth-dropping moment for Gerry Conlon and his co-accused. Since the Guildford Four were innocent of all the charges, Havers could not offer the court a single piece of evidence to link them with the IRA ASU, despite the fact that when police searched the IRA men's safe houses, they had found documents, letters and eighteen sets of fingerprints, none of which matched any of the Guildford Four's.

In a case noted for its anomalies, observers were left wondering why, having accepted that the Balcombe Street IRA unit had bombed Guildford and Woolwich, no direction was given to police from the bench that they should be charged with the murders of the five people killed in the pub bombings. Despite the absence of evidence, the appeal court judges accepted Havers's proposition that the Guildford Four had been in league with the Balcombe Street IRA team and they upheld their convictions.

In many ways, the British judiciary was a prisoner of its own inflated ego. In the Guildford Four appeal, it appears that it mattered little what defence counsel said or proved, because Lord Roskill and his fellow judges were never persuadable. Rather, their judgement was always infected by self-interest and fear, and by that which they held most dear – the British judicial system. Given the manifold implications of allowing this appeal to succeed, their view was that they had no option but to send these four innocent people back to prison. Lord Denning succinctly summed up his fellow judges' mindset when it was put to him that, had the Guildford Four been hanged, they (the judiciary) would have hanged the wrong people: 'They'd probably have hanged the right men. Not proven against them, that's all.'[15] Lamenting the days when judges had the power to sentence three men to hanging before lunch and two afterwards, Denning went on to say: 'The Guildford Four should have been sentenced by twelve good men of Hampshire to be hanged. Then we should have forgotten all about them.'[16] Unfortunately for His Lordship, Gerry Conlon and his co-accused were not forgotten about, even if they had to spend another twelve years in prison before they obtained their freedom.

ONE

During those twelve years, Conlon crossed paths with some of Britain's most notorious psychopaths. At the turn of the New Year 1979, Sarah Conlon visited her husband Giuseppe in the hospital wing of Wormwood Scrubs prison in London. Accompanying the matriarch was her daughter Ann and her husband Joe McKernan, along with their one-year-old daughter, Sarah. Giuseppe, although gravely ill, was in reasonable spirits. Gerry was brought into the hospital wing, handcuffed to a prison officer, while another prison officer kept hold of a guard dog. The visit began and the usual pleasantries were exchanged. Suddenly Giuseppe's gaze shifted to something or someone beyond the visiting party. Ann McKernan recalled:

> I don't know where my daddy got the strength from, but he pushed aside the bedclothes and got out of bed. We were telling him to get back into bed, but he wasn't listening. Then he shuffled across the room to this man who was mopping the floor and grabbed him by his shirt. My daddy was right into the man's face, and he said to him, 'If I ever get you putting your eyes on my grandchildren again, I'll personally kill you.' We didn't know who the man was or what was happening. Then our Gerry shouted, 'It's that bastard, Ian Brady!' I didn't know who Ian Brady was. It wasn't until later that I found out that he was the Moors Murderer [Brady and his lover, Myra Hindley, murdered five children between 1963 and 1965 and buried their bodies on Saddleworth Moor]. Anyway, our Gerry jumped up and said, 'Get the fuck out of here, you fucking bastard!' Well, Brady dropped his mop and ran out of the wing, and we helped my daddy back to his bed. His breathing was shallow; the exertion had almost killed him. When he recovered his breathing, he sent for the doctor and told him, 'See in future, when I'm getting visits, keep that animal away from my family.' The doctor settled my daddy down.[17]

Despite being terminally ill with emphysema and lung cancer, Giuseppe Conlon's fighting spirit never wavered, nor did his love for his family. This was never more apparent than when, several weeks later, Gerry was taken out of his cell in Wormwood Scrubs and brought to Hammersmith Hospital. He was led, handcuffed, into a room that was crowded with priests, Home Office officials, prison wardens, police officers and doctors. Gerry was taken to the side of his father's bed. On seeing him, Giuseppe pulled away his oxygen mask and told Gerry: 'I'm going to die.'

'No, you're not. You're not going to die.'

'Yes I am. Don't be worrying. I want you to promise me something.'

'Yes, okay.'

'I mean it.'

'Yes, I promise you.'

'When I die, I don't want you attacking no screws. I want you to start clearing your name. My death's going to clear your name and when you get your name cleared, you clear mine.'[18]

Nine more years would pass before Gerry's name would be cleared, while Giuseppe's name would not be fully cleared until Tony Blair, as British prime minister, apologised to the Guildford Four and the Maguire Seven in February 2005.

It was towards the end of those nine years that Gerry Conlon first met Paddy Joe Hill, one of six men falsely accused of the Birmingham pub bombings in 1974, in which twenty-one people died. Conlon had an instant special affection for Paddy Hill, and Hill was similarly struck with Conlon:

> When me and Gerry were together, it was fucking mayhem. When we [the Birmingham Six] were brought to Long Lartin for our appeal, I went over to Gerry's wing, and I said to the screws, 'Is Conlon on the wing?' and one of them says, 'Aye, he's up the stairs' and I shouts up, 'Conlon, get your fucking arse down here, and bring your snout, and your money, and your fucking drugs.'[19]

In *Proved Innocent*, Conlon confirms that a dynamic presence had arrived on the prison wing that night:

> I was up in my cell when I thought I heard my name. It was yelled out amid an unholy commotion that had suddenly swept into the wing, a bellowing Irish voice that I'd never heard before.

'Conlon, you gobshite! Get your arse down here.'

I thought I must have misheard, so I didn't move. The third time I couldn't mistake my own name being roared out.

'CONLON! Get fucking down here, now.'

I saw this small, solid, and incredibly animated figure, leaning against the railing at the bottom of the stairs, giving out to all these people around him. His dentures had been damaged when he was beaten at Winson Green prison, so you hardly ever see the man with teeth. His mouth is like one of the puppets on *Rainbow* [a children's TV programme], the one with the zipper over his lips. But I'd like to see someone brave enough to try to zipper Paddy's mouth.

He looked up, recognized me at once and stuck his hand through the railing.

'What took you so long, you bollocks? Paddy Joe Hill, good to meet you, son.'[20]

With the Birmingham Six appeal imminent, and with an outside chance of being released, Hill pledged to Conlon: 'Well, if I get out at this appeal, you're coming out too. Because I'll be going everywhere, doing whatever I can for you. OK?'[21]

On 28 January 1988, the appeal of the Birmingham Six was turned down, and Hill was returned to prison to serve out his life sentence. In prison, character is the cement that holds a person together, and Paddy Hill had character to give away. If he was entertaining pangs of despair, Hill soon fought them off, convincing himself that he could see a 'light shining at the end of the tunnel more brightly than ever before'.[22] He was right inasmuch as there was a light at the end of the tunnel, but it would shine, first, on the Guildford Four, not on the Birmingham Six.

'It was on the 16 October 1989. I'll never forget it,' Paddy Hill said in Belfast in 2015. 'After Long Lartin, Gerry and me was moved to Gartree, and we'd been knocking about together for nearly two years. Now, we were sitting in the workshop and a screw says to Gerry that he has to go back to his cell immediately. I went with him, and when we got to the wing, the Principal Officer told him, "There's a van waiting to take you to London immediately."'[23] After helping Conlon to pack up his meagre belongings, Hill walked him over to the prison reception. 'He was nearly crying,' Hill recalled, 'but I said to him, "Never fucking mind that. Just do what you have to do." And fair play to him, when he got out, he did the business.'

While Gerry Conlon no doubt pondered his fate in the back of a prison van as it made its way to London's Brixton Prison, his family in Belfast was unaware that anything was afoot. The next day, however, a phone call from Gerry's solicitor in London, Gareth Peirce, would change everything.

Ann and Joe McKernan had been buying wallpaper in Belfast city centre and on their way home they stopped at a shop in Church Lane which sold religious items. For Ann it was a weekly chore: 'My mother had been buying her candles out of the holy shop every Tuesday for fifteen years, 'cause Tuesday was St Martha's day, and St Martha's was the patron saint of servants and cooks, and for my mammy coming out of work, we had to have her candles there.'[24]

It was 11.05 a.m. and the McKernans had just got into their family home at 52 Albert Street in the Lower Falls area when the phone rang. Joe answered it. He listened carefully, put down the phone and turned to Ann: 'That was Gareth Peirce. She says Gerry's getting out on Thursday.' At Ann's insistence, Joe rang Gareth back and she reiterated her message, saying to Joe, 'Go tell Mrs Conlon.'

The McKernans got a taxi up to the Royal Victoria Hospital, where Sarah Conlon had worked as a catering assistant for sixteen years. 'I cried all the way there,' Ann said. 'When I told her, she collapsed against the wall. She couldn't believe it. It was such a shock.' If Sarah Conlon's faith in the power of prayer had been challenged during those lonely, desolate years, she never showed it and now it seemed as if her prayers had been answered. But sometimes good news can be too good and, like a geyser, a degree of scepticism now burst forth, with Sarah casting doubt on the veracity of what Ann and Joe were telling her. Eventually Ann persuaded her mother that Gerry *was* about to be released, and Sarah left work to the cheers and applause of her workmates.

Money was tight and times were hard. Flying to London was an expensive business for a working-class Belfast family. Sarah was troubled, Ann remembers. 'She kept repeating, "How am I going to get over to London for our Gerry's appeal?'" Trying to come to terms with one miracle – the imminent release of her son – was hard enough, even for someone as immersed in the Catholic faith as Sarah Conlon, but what happened next must surely have convinced her that prayer had no master. The house-phone rang. Again Joe answered it. This time, instead of Gareth Peirce, it was a reporter from the British television news station ITN, who offered to fly the Conlon family over to London *in a private jet* for the appeal, in the expectation that the station's helpfulness to the family would see them rewarded with that exclusive first interview with Gerry Conlon upon his release. The offer was gratefully accepted.

That night, after flying to London, with almost empty purses, the Conlon family – Sarah, Gerry's two younger sisters, Bridie and Ann, and two relatives – put their heads down in a one-bedroom flat in Westbourne Terrace Road, Maida Vale. The flat was occupied by Sarah's brother, Hughie Maguire, and his wife, Kate. The Conlons slept on 'the floors, the settee and chairs'.

The next day, Sarah, Bridie and Ann visited Gerry in Brixton Prison. He was as baffled as they were about the speed of events, but he had enough of a grasp of the situation to put in an order for new jeans and a shirt – in case he had to stand in front of the television cameras. His mother protested, saying that she did not have the money to buy him new clothes. But, as mothers often do, she found it. Sarah's brother, Hughie, on hearing of Gerry's request, put his hand into his pocket and handed his sister enough money to buy the jeans and shirt.

On 19 October 1989, two black London taxis brought the extended Conlon family to the Old Bailey. At a side entrance, they were met by a court official who led them up a set of back stairs and into the upper gallery of Court Number Two, the court where the original verdicts had been pronounced fifteen years earlier. At the same time as Sarah and her family were entering the court, the Guildford Four walked up the stairs from the cells below and stood in the dock. Before long, they heard evidence that at their original trial in 1975, the police had deleted, and added to, parts of Paddy Armstrong's original interview notes. This could be viewed only as an attempt by police to enhance their case against him. The case was then declared unsafe and the verdicts quashed.

Finally, having emerged from the underbelly of the Trojan horse, Gerry Conlon, in a cyclone of righteous fury, stormed out of the Old Bailey and told the world's press: 'I've been in prison for fifteen years for something I didn't do. For something I didn't know anything about. A totally innocent man. I watched my father die in prison for something he didn't do. He is innocent. The Maguires are innocent. Let's hope the Birmingham Six are freed.'

It is not hard to imagine old men in long wigs and ermine groaning and gnashing their teeth as they watched Conlon on television. Never one to hold his tongue, Lord Denning said publicly what many of his fellow law lords would, no doubt, have been saying in private: 'British justice is in ruins.'

Later, in an interview with ITN, Conlon said of his Old Bailey pronouncement: 'That wasn't me speaking. That was my dad. That was my dad.'

Gerry's mother was not a lady who courted the limelight. While Gerry and his sisters Ann and Bridie were driven in a limousine to the Holiday Inn, near Swiss Cottage (where ITN had organised a champagne reception), Sarah and other family members took a taxi to the hotel. On the way across London, Gerry was full of verve. Ann McKernan recalled: 'He couldn't sit for a second. There was a sunroof in the limo, and he opened it and stuck his head out the top of the car, and he was waving the whole way to the hotel, and people were shouting at him as if they knew what had happened and who he was.'[25]

When Conlon was led into the reception room in the Holiday Inn, the first person he saw was his mother, whom he lifted off her feet, whirled around and kissed. For Sarah Conlon, it must have been a bittersweet moment; she had finally been reunited with her son, but her husband would never be coming home.

Also present was Diana St. James, Gerry's pretty American girlfriend. Diana, with whom he had been corresponding while in prison, would travel back to Belfast with him.

The mood was light for the rest of the evening, but Gerry felt uneasy about the pervasive attention. Strangers were coming up to him and shaking his hand, asking him to relate his experiences of prison. Later that night, as he was going up in the lift to his room, he noticed that two burly men had walked into the elevator with him. When he proceeded down the corridor to his room, they followed him. He turned and asked them what they were doing and they told him they had been hired as bodyguards by ITN to ensure his safety. As the bodyguards stood on either side of his bedroom door, Conlon felt that they represented a life experience he wanted to put behind him: 'To my mind the only difference between these two and a couple of screws were the clothes.'[26]

There was a party that night in Gerry's penthouse suite, with the mini-bar being continually emptied and restocked. Then, at around five o'clock in the morning, Gerry took a panic attack. He went to his mother's room and explained to her how miserable he was feeling. He wept. At this point, his Uncle Hughie brought him back to his flat in Westbourne Terrace Road.

At breakfast in the hotel the next morning, Ann McKernan asked Hughie what had happened to Gerry, and Hughie said: 'I gave him my leather jacket and we went for a walk in the rain.'

'And then what happened?'

'And then Gerry said to me, "Isn't this brilliant? I haven't walked in the rain for fifteen years."'

Hughie went on to tell Ann that Gerry later phoned his solicitor and friend Gareth Peirce to come and collect him. Gerry was discovering that there was a lot more to freedom than simply not being locked up: he had got out of jail, but jail had not got out of him.

On 31 December 1974, Gerry Conlon was flown from Belfast to England on a draughty RAF transport plane. Handcuffed to a hostile detective, he was bewildered at the enormity of the charges being levelled against him, and he was terrified. Perhaps his teeth were chattering; perhaps he was shivering. For sure, he had no idea of the hardships and tribulations that lay ahead. On 21 October 1989, he returned to Belfast with no hostile detective. He was not handcuffed, and he was not on board a chilly RAF transport plane. Instead, he was on a plush private jet with his sister Ann, Diana St James and friends, courtesy of ITN. During the flight, he helped himself to smoked salmon and champagne. Gerry Conlon probably thought he was free at last. He wasn't.

Two

'I hope your arse is well greased, Hill.'

'It's buttered-up like a big Belfast bap, Conlon.'

'It'd better be 'cause I've a wee parcel here to keep you entertained in them there dark nights.'[1]

As he casts his agile memory back to his visit with Gerry Conlon in Gartree Prison on 28 October 1989, Paddy Hill lifts a rolled-up cigarette from the glass dining table and lights up. He inhales deeply and exhales slowly. How did Gerry smuggle in the hash and the tobacco? 'Between his bum cheeks,' Hill answers matter-of-factly. And how did the transfer take place? 'Gerry looked around to see if any screws were watching and, when he saw there wasn't, he shoved his hand down the back of his trousers and when it came back up again, there was a cylindrical parcel wrapped in cling-paper in it.' Hill takes another draw on his cigarette. 'The next thing, he casually reached over the table to me, as if shaking my hand, and passed me the parcel. I bangled [secreted in rectum] it immediately. "There's two ounces of snout and two ounces of hash in there", he said. Believe me; that brought a smile to my face.'

It still brings a smile to his face. Hill casually relights his cigarette. It does not seem to have crossed his mind that, just over a week after Gerry had thundered out of the Old Bailey, declaring to the world that he had spent fifteen years in prison for something he did not do, and after being on the front page of practically every newspaper in the western hemisphere, Gerry Conlon had risked being returned to prison for smuggling two ounces of hash into prison.

'Nah, that wouldn't have happened. Y'see, we knew all the moves.'[2]

But in the jungle of everyday life, outside of prison, Gerry barely knew any moves, and in the years after his release, he would return to a recurring theme: 'There are days when I wish I was still in prison.'

It is not hard to see why there was a brotherly bond between Conlon and Hill: they were both intelligent, had the same lively nature and were fighters at heart. In an interview with *The Irish News* on 23 October 1989, Conlon said:

> You wouldn't believe how emotionally attached I am to Paddy Hill. He uses thirty quid a week on stamps to write to people to highlight his case – he doesn't stop working and every letter he wrote mentioned the Guildford Four and every letter I wrote mentioned the Birmingham Six. So I couldn't live with myself if I did nothing about the Birmingham Six, because I know if Paddy Hill were sitting here now talking to you, Paddy Hill's thoughts would be with me as my thoughts are with him.[3]

Other people's thoughts were with Gerry Conlon and some of them were not that friendly. Seán Smyth, who, as one of the Maguire Seven, had been sentenced to eleven years in prison, could never be accused of couching his criticism of Conlon in soft terms:

> The person I blame to the day I die for those lost years is Gerry Conlon. He had no call to do that. He should have kept his mouth shut. We all did. I got beatings, threats, psychological torture – the lot, but I never once admitted anything or implicated anyone. I remember watching Gerard Conlon on television when he got out of the Old Bailey. Okay, so he was innocent. He didn't deserve to be in prison but if it wasn't for him we would never have been in prison either. Any of us. He is running around like Jack-the-Lad. Imagine if we had implicated anyone and got them nine years in jail.[4]

Smyth's condemnation of Conlon was perfectly understandable given that, when he was arrested, Conlon identified the aunt with whom he had stayed when he first came to London, Anne Maguire, as the bomb-maker, which in turn led to the arrests of the other members of the Maguire Seven. However, to lay the blame entirely at Conlon's feet presupposes that the physical abuse and psychological cruelty that

Smyth and his co-accused suffered was on a par with that meted out to Conlon, when it was not so. Conlon's interrogations included being hooded, stripped naked, deprived of sleep and bedding, starved of food and water, and being beaten continuously; the Maguire Seven did not experience anything similar. That aside, the question arises: would it be right to blame Conlon for a confession that was extracted out of him under extreme duress? The heartbreaking irony in Smyth's criticism is that here was the innocent blaming the innocent for the brutality and inhumanity of the guilty. On a more practical note, Gerry Conlon's confession would not, on its own, have been enough to secure the convictions of the Maguire Seven: the jury accepted the fraudulent forensic evidence that all the accused had handled explosives. The tragedy in Smyth's bitter accusation was that it was clearly heartfelt and was shared by others of the Maguire Seven, but that does not make it any less irrational.

A new era had opened for Gerry Conlon, when, amid much handshaking, backslapping, autograph-signing and shouts of 'Welcome home, lads', Paul Hill and he climbed onto the stage at a Birmingham Six rally outside the GPO in Dublin's O'Connell Street on 5 November 1989. Plucked from the obscurity of their prison cells, both men now enjoyed celebrity status, especially Conlon, whose Old Bailey display had endeared him to Irish people everywhere. Conlon told the 2,000-strong crowd that he was 'very happy to be standing here amongst my own people'. He went on to say: 'I don't want any other Irish person to come out of a British prison like my father did – in a box.' Continuing in the same vein, he said: 'There is no British justice for Irish people.'[5]

Yet, once the initial euphoria of his release had worn off, Conlon admitted that he was finding it difficult to adjust and to come to terms with freedom. In an ITV documentary, *The Guildford Four: Free to Speak*, Conlon spoke frankly about how he was 'longing for Gartree and my friends'. With a sense of deep foreboding, he said: 'I feel like I am a more responsible person now. But I am deeply scarred and I am badly emotionally affected, and I don't know if I am ever going to be really happy again.'[6]

Like a jack-in-the-box, Sir Norman Skelhorn, the Director of Public Prosecutions at the time of the Guildford pub bombings, popped up again in the news, when the alibi statement of Charles Edward Burke was released by BBC's *Newsnight* on 14 November 1989. Unlike in the film *In the Name of the Father*, where he was portrayed as an elderly vagrant, the real Charlie Burke was a young man who had a steady job working in a greengrocer's shop. Burke and a Belfast man called Patrick Carey had shared a room in the Hope House Hostel on Quex Road, London, with Conlon and Hill. In his 1975 statement to police, Burke said that, at the time of the Guildford pub bombings, he had been with Conlon in the hostel and that Conlon had been drunk and had tried, unsuccessfully, to borrow a pound from him. It subsequently emerged that Crown Counsel had written to the Guildford Four defence counsel on 13 August 1975, and had given them a list of witnesses who had been interviewed by police but whom the Crown would not call on at the trial. Unsurprisingly, Charlie Burke's name was not on the list. Neither was that of Sister Michael Power, a nun who worked in the hostel and who had made a statement to police confirming that her records showed that Burke had been in the hostel on the day of the Guildford pub bombings (this strengthened Burke's alibi statement). It was not until 1989 that Conlon's then solicitor, Gareth Peirce, uncovered Burke's and Power's statements. Peirce and fellow Guildford Four solicitor, Michael Fisher, berated Sir Norman's department, accusing the DPP of a cover-up. Fisher said: 'Paul Hill's case has always been under considerable pressure. He invented and elaborated upon a cock-and-bull story knowing that it couldn't be corroborated, that he and the others named had alibis, and, therefore, believing that it wouldn't stand up in court. What then happened was that steps were taken to ensure that his cock-and-bull story did stand up in court.'[7]

Sarah Conlon, as ever, was worried for her big son. At his own expense, he was organising a lobbying campaign on behalf of the Birmingham Six, and he was preparing to go alone, if necessary, to the United States on 5 November. Sarah prevailed upon Gerry's cousin Martin Loughran to accompany him on the trip, saying that he would have been out of prison a mere seventeen days by the time he set forth for the US and he needed someone to guide him. Martin, who was six years older than Gerry, was working on building sites in London and his initial reaction was to refuse the request: 'I told my Aunt Sarah that I couldn't leave my work. But she pleaded with me. She said, "He really, really needs somebody – family." And I only went because his mother, as I say, had asked me. I did it for my aunt Sarah and my mother.'

While in Washington, Conlon and Loughran stayed with Kerry Bowen of the human rights organisation, American Protestants for Truth about Ireland. 'Just down from Kerry's apartment in Connecticut Avenue there was a bar called Murphy's, and the barman was called Paddy Joe Walsh,' Martin Loughran recalls, 'and he was a scream, a real ducker-and-diver. Paddy Joe was from the Falls area. He and Gerry got on like a house on fire, and he showed us around Washington.' After the sightseeing, Conlon was out of the traps, meeting with important US politicians from both the Democratic and Republican parties, including Congressmen Brian Donnelly, Ted and Joe Kennedy, and the Speaker of the House, Tom Foley. Martin Loughran has a vivid memory of Conlon's meeting with Joe Kennedy:

> We met Joe Kennedy in his office. He was a nice fella and was, by a long shot, the most interested politician we met. He asked questions and he listened intently. You could tell he was genuine. Anyway, after Gerry had said his piece and answered all Joe's questions, Joe sat back, put his hands behind his head and his feet up on his desk, and remarked that he was going to Ireland soon to do a bit of fishing. I have to give it to Gerry. He saw an opportunity and pounced on it. Gerry said to him, 'Why don't you go to England and visit the Birmingham Six when you're over? Visit Paddy Hill; he'd appreciate seeing you.' And Joe kinda looked away as if, you know, tossing it over in his head, and then he looked back and said, 'That's not a bad idea. Yeah, I'd like that.'[8]

On 20 November 1989, it was reported in *The Irish News* that, 'Two of America's most influential politicians are to visit the Birmingham Six after meeting Gerard Conlon of the Guildford Four.'[9]

The congressman was as good as his word. In 1990, Joe Kennedy went up the Falls Road in Belfast, and while there, dropped into the Conlon home in Albert Street. He later went to England to visit the

Birmingham Six. 'They wouldn't let him in to visit Paddy Hill at that time, although he eventually did get in to see Paddy around July 1990, I think,' Martin Loughran said. 'But it was all about the publicity and all that came about with Gerry asking Joe to visit the Birmingham Six.'

It wasn't long after their meeting that Kennedy and Conlon met Congressman Tom Lantos. Lantos, the only Holocaust survivor on Capitol Hill, was a highly respected and compassionate Hungarian-American politician. He was also the co-chair of the influential Congressional Human Rights Caucus, a bipartisan group representing 200 members of Congress. The traditional focus of the caucus had always been human rights abuses in totalitarian countries such as the Soviet Union, South Africa, China and Cuba, but occasionally its attention was drawn to human rights violations in democratic countries. United States politicians had rarely taken more than a cursory look at British human rights abuses, but that was all to change irrevocably, and it was Gerry Conlon who would be the catalyst for that change.

During his meetings with Kennedy and Conlon, and after listening to the Irishman's impassioned presentation, Lantos pledged that the case of the Birmingham Six would be the subject of the caucus's first hearing in the new year. If Conlon thought this breakthrough was a cause for celebration, he did not show it. There was still work to be done.

After Conlon's success in Washington, he and Loughran went to New York. The socialist human rights activist Sandy Boyer remembers getting a phone call in his Brooklyn apartment and a Belfast voice saying, 'This is Gerry Conlon. I'm in New York for the Birmingham Six, and my lawyer, Gareth Peirce, told me to get in touch with you.' Sandy later learned that this was high praise from Gerry. 'If Gareth recommended somebody, Gerry was sure he or she could be trusted. He had complete faith in her.'[10]

Gerry, Martin and Gerry's girlfriend, Diana St. James, met Sandy Boyer that afternoon in O'Reilly's pub (then Joyce's pub), at Sixth and 31st, and they discussed how to shape the Birmingham Six campaign in the United States. Forty-five-year-old Boyer was impressed with Conlon's political nous: 'We agreed immediately that it had to be as mainstream as possible, and that any connection with NORAID (the Republican Movement's fund-raising organisation) or republicanism would be fatal. I then began to suggest people whom Gerry should meet.'

With fifteen years of high-octane energy in the tank and the passion of someone who not only knew his own worth, but who saw himself as being on a sacred mission, Conlon hurled himself into the task of obtaining the release of the Birmingham Six. Boyer recalls: 'Gerry moved from one contact to the next and he quickly moved beyond the people I knew. He kept checking in with me, partly because he needed to talk to someone who knew the scene, and, maybe more, because he needed to talk to someone who had no agenda beyond the Birmingham Six.'

Conlon expressed his appreciation in a radio interview, hosted by Boyer, in 2013:

> As you know, Sandy, you were one of the first people I met in America when I got out and you helped open doors – for Ed Koch (the former mayor of New York); you got me to Cardinal O'Connor, and your help was invaluable in securing the release of the Birmingham Six because you facilitated me and you pointed me in the right direction. And I remember when I took the delegation of Paul Dwyer, Brian Donnelly, Joe Kennedy and met Charlie Rangel and people like that. And we met Jack O'Dell from the Rainbow Coalition and of course Tom Lantos, a great congressman from California, who gave us a congressional hearing on human rights' abuses on Irish people in British prisons.[11]

Conlon certainly had the Irish gift of the gab, but he baulked before the presence of Cardinal John O'Connor, a prelate who upheld the sanctity of life, whether that be in the womb or on death row. Boyer had arranged for Conlon to meet Cardinal O'Connor after Mass at Saint Patrick's Cathedral. 'By that time, Gerry was living on the edge of his nerves,' Boyer says. 'We were supposed to meet the cardinal at the left side of the altar after the Mass. When no one was there, Gerry turned and bolted out the door. In a few minutes someone found out that we were supposed to meet at the cardinal's residence. I had to take off and try to catch up with Gerry. Fortunately I guessed right and he was going down Fifth Avenue. Gerry seemed to get a lot of comfort from talking to the cardinal. Afterwards he told me the cardinal asked if the people with him were friends and warned him against hangers-on.'

In an interview with New York's *Irish Echo* on 2 December 1989, Conlon said that he had met Cardinal O'Connor on the previous two Sundays, and he found him to be 'very honest, sincere and aware'.

For the remainder of his life, Gerry Conlon straddled two continents. He had a great affection for the United States, and over the years would become a regular visitor to that country. But he liked coming home, whether that home was in Belfast or London. At the end of November 1989, he returned to Ireland just in time to appear on RTÉ's prime television talk show, *The Late, Late Show*, along with Paul Hill. Earlier, the Irish Taoiseach, Charles J. Haughey, had met both men and had given them his credit card on the understanding that they should use it to fit themselves out with new clothes. It was an offer neither man could refuse, and when they appeared alongside the show's host, Gay Byrne, they were suitably attired in designer suits. When Byrne asked Conlon what he would like to do now, he replied that he would like to go to the World Cup football finals in Italy the following summer. A travel agent, watching the interview, wrote to Conlon offering him and Hill a free trip to Italy. Conlon immediately took up the offer.

In that same month, Conlon was given a £50,000 interim compensation payment from the British government. It would be the first tranche of £546,000 that he would eventually receive. Conlon was unimpressed: 'They gave me £546,000 for taking me, torturing and framing me, taking my father, torturing him and having him in prison; then leaving me sinking in the quicksand of my own nightmares.' He went on to say that, 'Giving money to victims of miscarriages of justice is like giving them a bottle of whiskey and a revolver. You may as well say, "Here's the money, now go and kill yourself."'[12] Conlon did not go and kill himself, but he thought about committing suicide many times as he struggled to readjust to a normal life. It could be argued that, when he moved away from Belfast and his family home in 1974, Conlon lost all sight of what a normal life looked like. He had lived in squats and hostels, had been unable to hold down a job and had begun experimenting with drugs.

At four o'clock on the afternoon of 9 December 1989, Gerry Conlon, Paul Hill, Paddy Armstrong, and relatives of the Birmingham Six led the 'Parade of Innocence' through central Dublin to celebrate the release of the Guildford Four and to highlight the continued incarceration of the Birmingham Six. As dusk fell, 10,000 people lit candles and walked behind them. Around 200 costumed actors, some on floats, played the parts of prisoners, judges, policemen and torch-bearers. When the parade reached the River Liffey, a boat made of tabloid newspapers from the 1975 media campaign against the Guildford Four, Maguire Seven and the Birmingham Six was ceremoniously burned. Three hours after the parade had begun, the last of the marchers reached the Central Bank plaza where they were treated to passionate speeches from Gerry Conlon, Paul Hill and the former MP for Mid-Ulster, Bernadette McAliskey, amongst others.

At the end of the pageant, the manager of The Pogues, Frank Murray, introduced himself to the ex-prisoners and brought them around to Blooms Hotel in Temple Bar. After a few drinks, arrangements were made to meet up later. Several hours after that, Murray was in a bar and restaurant called 'Suesey Street' in Leeson Street.

> You could drink fairly easy there. You could definitely get wine and champagne after hours, and every so often the police would come in, but we knew they were coming in so the wine bottles and the drink would disappear off the tables for ten minutes until the police went away. Well, I heard this commotion outside the door, you see, so I went to have a look out and saw the security men and Gerry, and sharp enough, he recognised me immediately and shouted over, 'Frank! Frank, it's me.' Once I told the security men who they were, they were let in. So we went to the bar and we were having a drink for about five minutes and word got around and all of a sudden Gerry was swarming with women and they were saying hello to him, and Gerry, naturally enough, was in like Flynn.

That was Gerry; he had a glint in his eye, a beautiful mischievous glint that the women loved.[13]

On his release from prison, Conlon wanted to live in Belfast with his family, but Belfast is a relatively small city, made even smaller by the sectarian divide that dissects it. One of the consequences of this tribal divide at the time of Conlon's release in 1989 was the omnipresence of loyalist assassins, who opted to believe the hints emanating from certain British newspapers that Conlon had been guilty and had been released only by dint of a judicial faux pas. In light of this, loyalist paramilitaries would have viewed him as a particularly desirable target. Moreover, the Conlon household was situated in the strongly republican Lower Falls, a district where the IRA and the British army frequently fought each other in gun battles. Gerry never hid the fact that he had inherited his father's pacifist views, and his forthright rejection of war and political violence was interpreted by some within his own community as somehow being anti-IRA. He was anti-IRA, but he was also anti-British army and anti-loyalist paramilitaries. Given the myopia and cataclysmic social upheaval that had infected Belfast and its citizens for over two decades at that time, it was hardly surprising that Conlon opted to get away from it all and live in cosmopolitan London.

He liked London and found the English generally endearing: 'There is not a lot of bitterness in my heart. I feel bitter towards the judiciary, towards the police who framed me, who fabricated evidence, but I have nothing but time and respect for all the English people who helped, and there have been so, so many of them.'[14] Later he would say, 'English people are brilliant people.'[15] And so it was that Gerry moved into the detached Victorian house of Gareth Peirce and her husband, Bill, in London's Kentish Town in December 1989. This was one of his better decisions because Peirce provided a degree of stability and good judgement that he badly needed. She understood him and had a feel for the mountains that all the miscarriage of justice victims would have to climb if they were ever to readjust back into society: 'They [the Guildford Four] came out with no money and no counselling,' she said. 'They had no references. It's difficult to open a bank account; you can't get a mortgage. They have no GP. They don't belong.'[16]

Gerry Conlon never professed to be a saint nor, in numerous subsequent press interviews, did he hide his failings and transgressions. Speaking bluntly of the time before he was arrested for the Guildford bombings, he said: 'We [Paul Hill and he] were working on building sites. We were getting drunk; we were known to the community [a euphemism for being petty criminals]. We were fucking arseholes.'[17] But that was then. Now he wanted a new beginning. He wanted to travel and to savour humanity in all its majesty. He was still only thirty-five years old, and he wanted to catch up with a life that had zipped passed him fifteen years earlier. Perhaps he saw Gareth Peirce as a bridgehead of sensibility, a sobering influence who, to some extent, cramped his style, but by the start of 1990 he was looking for his own accommodation.

Jeremy Corbyn, the future British Labour Party leader and the MP for Islington North, had highlighted the case of the Guildford Four, and he secured Conlon a small one-bedroom council flat in the Holloway Road area of north London. After buying a sofa-bed, Martin Loughran moved in with Gerry. It was a claustrophobic existence, far removed from the home comforts of Gareth and Bill's house, but crucially, the name Conlon was on the rent book. Before long, further compensation began to filter through, and Gerry was able to buy a two-bedroom basement flat in Tufnell Park, north London. Now he was, for the first time in fifteen years, the architect and builder of his own world.

'When we moved into Tufnell Park, I went back to my work on the building sites,' Martin Loughran says. 'Gerry was a whirlwind. He was still very active on the Birmingham Six front – I remember he went to a big conference in Copenhagen – but he was also meeting people and partying. Y'see, Gerry made friends easily. And he was a party-animal. I didn't like parties; I preferred a quiet pint in my local pub.' Loughran has no recollection of Conlon taking any drugs other than marijuana:

> I would say his biggest vice in those days was his gambling. He had no appreciation of money. He just saw money as a means to get him where he wanted to go and then just rake it up. I saw me sitting in the flat in Tufnell Park and there was a bookies

way down the street, and he'd say to me, 'There's a grand. Away and put it on such and such a horse.' And maybe it was beat. Broke my heart, like. But, then again, I've seen me walk into the bookies and take thousands from them and bring it back to him. Y'see, Gerry was a lucky gambler. He'd sit in the house and smoke a bit of blow, and his head would've been buried in the paper, studying the form; he knew when a horse was right and when it wasn't. And he'd never have stood all day in a bookies like a lot of gamblers. And another thing, people have said he was an alcoholic. He wasn't. No way. Certainly not when I was with him.[18]

David Pallister also felt the rush of Conlon's personality. A reporter with *The Guardian* since 1974, Pallister had extensively covered the 'Troubles' in Northern Ireland. He had also been in both Guildford and Birmingham on the day after the explosions had occurred and had reported on both sets of appeals. Moreover, he had written copiously about miscarriages of justice. With these qualifications, it is little wonder that Gareth Peirce judged him to be the writer best suited to bring to life the Gerry Conlon story in a book.

At the solicitor's invitation, Pallister first met Gerry in Gareth's home in early 1990, where they collectively discussed the mechanics of the journalist ghostwriting Gerry's biography. The reporter liked Gerry: 'He was good company and we got on well. He remarked approvingly of my gait, "Just like you'd see on the Falls Road."'[19]

From the outset, it was agreed that in order to give Gerry and David the best possible chance to concentrate on the task in hand, they had to get away from the many distractions of London. David's suggestion of two weeks in sunny Tunisia went down exceedingly well with Gerry, but tying down the *bon vivant* to a strict work regime would prove problematic: 'Even though he was tremendously engaging, very articulate, thoughtful and funny at the same time, it was sometimes hard getting him to stick to the bigger picture we were after,' Pallister said. 'But after the damage of fifteen years in prison I was content to be indulgent about his indiscipline and self-indulgence. The poor guy had been through hell and he was understandably angry and bitter.'

Pallister's idea of going to Tunisia in the first place had been to find anonymity because Gerry had already attained a considerable media profile. While the idea was sound, it was only as foolproof as Gerry wanted it to be – and playing the role of the perennial bore did not come naturally to him. He was Gerry Conlon of the Guildford Four, after all, and where was the harm in telling his fellow tourists that he was the man who had ridden out of the Old Bailey on a chariot of righteous indignation?

Even though it was always going to be a difficult commission for Pallister, the two men did manage to get through a substantial amount of work as they sat on the balcony of the journalist's room every morning with a tape recorder. And every evening Pallister sent the tape of that day's work back to London to be transcribed. A significant portion of what had been recorded pertained to Gerry's survival exploits while in prison. Pallister said: 'He had some highly amusing and graphic tales, which he recounted with relish. He also had stories of financial scams. He smoked dope all day. He had brought it in, he explained, wrapped in film between his buttocks.'

When they got back to London, Pallister was confronted by Gareth Peirce, who had had access to the recordings made in Tunisia. She was less than enthusiastic. 'Gareth was unhappy about the stories of his exploits,' Pallister said. 'She wanted something more about the grief and the pain and his relationship with his father. There was pressure from the knowledge that Ronan [Bennett] was doing Paul Hill's book [*Stolen Years: Before and After Guildford*],' Pallister said. 'Before I could progress, I was summarily taken off the project and paid off. I had a final highly emotional meeting with Gerry in a café on Kentish Town Road, close to Gareth's house, where he laid out his true feelings.'

Robin Blake, another journalist, finished the book with Gerry. Tellingly, Pallister was not invited to the launch of Conlon's book, *Proved Innocent*, in the House of Commons on 11 June 1990. He professed that he was 'not bitter about all of this ... but I was annoyed that the book turned out to be so dishonest.'[20] No amount of coaxing would persuade Pallister to elaborate on what exactly had driven him to question the book's honesty, or to give an account of his final meeting with Gerry in Kentish Town. Perhaps he believed that some things were better left unsaid.

Leaving things unsaid was not the way of the next set of characters to enter Gerry Conlon's convoluted life. For Joey Cashman and Shane MacGowan, of the Irish punk rock band The Pogues, Gerry's devil-may-care attitude to life paralleled their own laissez-faire philosophy. For the more circumspect Hollywood superstar Johnny Depp, Gerry was the 'friend' with whom he got drunk and raked about, while the two men and the Conlon family toured Ireland.

The lad was on the rocky road to somewhere – he just didn't know where.

Three

Gerry Conlon was astute enough to know that American political influence casts a long shadow and that sometimes that shadow engulfed 10 Downing Street. He also knew that, as a miscarriage of justice victim, he was in a unique position to exhort American politicians to persuade the British government that it was not in their vested interest to continue to deny justice to the Birmingham Six. So, in early March 1990, along with his trusted cousin Martin Loughran, Conlon returned to Washington to attend the Congressional Human Rights Caucus hearing on the Birmingham Six case, which Congressman Tom Lantos had promised he would convene during the Irishmen's previous trip. The hearing was co-sponsored by Congressman Joe Kennedy of the Ad Hoc Congressional Committee on Irish Affairs.

There were high expectations of a successful outcome to the caucus hearing, not least because Conlon had a masterful grasp of his brief and had the ability to deliver a faultless presentation. More than any other facet, it was his personality that made him a reliable persuader: in temperament, he was a composite of nervous energy and cordiality; in conversation he had the gift of giving the speaker his undivided attention; in practice, he was blessed with a prodigious memory, which meant that he could remember dates, places and people's names, even if he had not seen those people for a while, sometimes for years. This meant that if he had been introduced to a politician in the past, or his wife, or his kids, he remembered their names and details. This was impressive data storage, which did not go unnoticed by almost everyone with whom he came into contact.

Once again Conlon availed of Sandy Boyer's services to help co-ordinate his activities. Even before Conlon had left for the United States, Boyer, an unsung hero of the Birmingham Six narrative, had been busy sorting out the Irishman's agenda: 'In the week or so before the hearing, I was speaking to Joe Kennedy's staffer regularly. We were going over the schedule for the hearing and I was able to answer questions about the case.'[1] The significance of Boyer's contribution cannot be underestimated because, as a result of his discussions with Kennedy's staffer, a briefing document for members of the caucus was produced, which said: 'Their [the Birmingham Six] convictions were based upon signed confessions and forensic tests which indicated that the defendants may have been severely beaten at the time the confessions were obtained. Furthermore, the forensic tests were shown to be incomplete and unreliable.'[2]

Boyer had meticulously prepared the ground, and now it was time for the Guildford Four man to deliver. Boyer recalls:

Gerry and I met in Washington two days before the hearing. We went to talk to the Kennedy staff member who was organising the hearing. She wanted us to meet Joe Kennedy the next day and started to tell us that they had a new office. When, rather than her telling me where the new office was, I told her, Gerry gave me a big wink. The point isn't that I had done anything especially brilliant, but that Gerry, without even thinking about it, was sending me a compliment, just between the two of us. Little things like that made it such a pleasure to work with him.[3]

Sandy Boyer recollects that when the caucus convened on 12 March 1990, Joe Kennedy's staffer was buoyed up because there were more members of the US Congress in attendance than there were staffers. As well as Conlon, the caucus was addressed by Gareth Peirce; the Catholic Primate of All-Ireland, Cardinal Tomás Ó Fiaich; human rights advocate and barrister Lord Tony Gifford QC and Seamus Mallon, the Social Democratic and Labour Party MP for Newry and Armagh. Mallon made it clear that it had been the IRA, not the Birmingham Six, who had carried out the bombings.

If knots were tightening in Conlon's stomach as he waited to address the congressmen, he did not show it. Neither did he show any concern about the fact that he had no prepared notes to refresh his memory – his memory did not need refreshing. Sandy Boyer recalled: 'Gerry was the star. In his testimony he said, "I know what happened to the Birmingham Six because the same thing happened to me. I was held for six days in four police stations without food or sleep. I was beaten, humiliated, degraded and stripped naked. At the end of six days I signed a confession. I was never allowed to see a solicitor."'[4]

As it turned out, many praised Conlon's presentation. Congressman Joe Kennedy said: 'It's one thing to hear all the very sound legal arguments put forward by Tony Gifford, but nothing compares to hearing Gerry Conlon. It certainly left an indelible imprint on my mind.'[5] Colman McCarthy, a member of the *Washington Post* Writers Pool, later wrote: 'Gerry Conlon, with unclipped coal-black hair, dark mournful eyes, and a wrinkled suit, had the look of a villager in one of Ireland's wild moors. He might well have been in one today – farming, raising a family – had the British government not imprisoned him for 15 years as one of the Guildford Four.'[6]

In his concluding remarks to the caucus, Congressman Chairman Tom Lantos said: 'It is clear in this instance that British justice has failed, and we will pursue this matter to its end.' Thanks to Gerry Conlon, Sandy Boyer, and others – Amnesty International in particular – the long shadow of American political influence once again engulfed 10 Downing Street, and it could not be ignored.

For Gerry Conlon it was time to take off that wrinkled suit and hit the bright lights of the Big Apple, where he stayed with friends in the Floral Park neighbourhood of Queens. At the Limelight nightclub in downtown New York, a young Irish girl called Ann McPhee introduced herself to Conlon and said that she was nanny to the Irish actor Gabriel Byrne's children. She told him that Gabriel was handing out Gerry's book to everyone who visited him, encouraging them to read it. It was through Shane Doyle, Gerry's friend and owner of Sin-é Café in Saint Mark's Place, that a meeting was arranged with Gabriel Byrne.

Gerry found Gabriel impressive: 'Gabriel Byrne called. He said he'd read the book and loved it and thought it had the potential to make a great film.'[7] After their discussion, Gerry decided that Gabriel was the man who could get his film produced. However, with no screenplay, no definitive outline, no money, and nothing more than a wildcat idea, the two men shook hands and concluded a gentleman's agreement for a nominal figure of one dollar, which gave Byrne the option to develop a film based on Conlon's life.

On 26 March 1990, RTÉ, the Irish broadcasting company, screened *Dear Sarah*, a £1 million television drama based on letters written by Giuseppe Conlon to his wife Sarah while he was in prison. The drama, written by Irish journalist Tom McGurk, told the story of how Sarah had visited Giuseppe for the first time, and of how they had to sit at opposite ends of a glass screen, unable to even touch hands. It also showed Sarah Conlon's immense courage and fortitude, as she fought, almost alone, to clear her husband's and son's names, and of how she coped with the strain of travelling between Belfast and Britain to visit her dying husband.

Giving a background analysis to *Irish News* reporter Pete Silverton, McGurk said: 'Sarah had an invalid husband and a son she spoiled stupid, and one day a steamroller hit her.' Silverton pointed an accusing finger at Gerry Conlon for the trouble that had befallen the Conlon and Maguire families:

> The steamroller made two passes over Sarah, of course. First her son was arrested – drinker, druggie, gambler, layabout, petty criminal. Like the rest of the Guildford Four, you couldn't have relied on him to burgle the local chippie, let alone organise a pub bombing. Then his 'confession' – naming the Maguires – led directly to his own father's arrest. Would it be any wonder if the Maguire family refused even to speak to Gerry again? Of all his relatives, they must have thought, why did he pick on us? What did we ever do to him?[8]

Had Conlon been in an uncharitable mood, he might well have returned the question to Silverton: 'What did I ever do to you?'

Speaking of *Dear Sarah*, Ann McKernan said: 'There were dramatic moments in the film ... my father being trailed up the stairs in the prison when he wasn't able to walk, my mother's letters being taken from him. These things they did to my father because they couldn't beat him as he was a sick man.'

Commenting on the drama, RTÉ executive producer Joe Mulholland said, 'It is a haunting and disturbing true story of a bewildered and ailing man caught up in an implacable system. But it is, moreover, a love story of two people whose faith in each other never wavered.'[9]

Proved Innocent was launched in Buswells Hotel in Dublin on 11 June 1990, and later that night in the Palace of Westminster. The book is an earthy story of the author's upbringing in a strictly Catholic home in Belfast's Lower Falls, where the rosary was recited every night and all family members had to attend. Conlon relates how he looked on this period of his life as a happy and carefree time, even though money and luxuries were scarce. He goes on to narrate how, after leaving school, he pursued a career as a petty criminal and shoplifter, and of how he got the boat to England to escape the violent conflict that was engulfing Northern Ireland. Fast-moving, sometimes hilarious, always fascinating, Conlon was like a gondolier on Venice's Grand Canal, as he navigated his readers through the crowded, choppy waters of his life. The book became an instant bestseller. When asked what he hoped to achieve by publishing *Proved Innocent*, Conlon said: 'There is no one person whom I would like to single out for retribution. That and revenge is something that I do not want. All I am hoping to achieve with my book is to point out that sometimes the British justice system does fail. The British don't have sole copyright on injustice.'[10]

At the Dublin book launch, Conlon called on the IRA to call off its armed campaign in order to get all the Irish prisoners in English prisons released. In Belfast, on 13 June, hundreds of people formed queues in the street outside Waterstones bookshop and a mighty cheer went up when Conlon appeared. Inside, he signed book after book, inscribing each with a personal message. In a newspaper interview, given on the same day, he once again committed himself to campaigning for the Birmingham Six, saying: 'I couldn't live with myself if I walked away. I would do anything or go anywhere to help them.'[11] He also revealed that he was 'living out of a suitcase; my time is not my own. I don't see enough of my family.'[12]

On his return to London, Conlon had barely time to unpack his bags before he was getting on another plane, this time to Copenhagen, with other Birmingham Six campaigners, to lobby representatives at a conference for Security and Co-operation in Europe. Twenty-three out of twenty-eight European and North American countries had sent delegations to the Danish capital. While Conlon could not, and did not, claim credit for convincing the delegates to pass a vote calling on the British government to re-examine the convictions of the Birmingham Six, his participation was nevertheless telling: 'Gerry's contribution was crucial,' wrote Paul May, who chaired the London-based campaign to free the Birmingham Six. 'Gerry described powerfully how it felt to be brutalised and imprisoned as an innocent man.'[13]

In between campaigning for the Birmingham Six at home and abroad, Conlon was contractually bound to promote his book in different cities around the United Kingdom and Ireland, while also trying to get a film of his book produced. At the same time, he was struggling to rebuild relationships with his family. The sad reality was that the Conlon family, particularly Gerry, had had to insulate themselves from the world in order to survive their ordeal: they had *all* been prisoners and each of them was deeply affected by the traumatic events that had been visited upon them. If that was not enough, Gerry had to somehow find a way to temper the guilt that haunted him over the death of his father in prison. Siobhan MacGowan, the sister of The Pogues vocalist Shane MacGowan, met Conlon soon after his release and became a close friend and confidante for the rest of his life. She shared her experience:

> Gerry was really deep. We would've talked about all sorts of things – his family when he came out and how he couldn't look them in the eyes because he felt so guilty. He was really soft. That's why he kept away from Belfast for so long; he couldn't get past it. He wanted to go home but he couldn't. And especially his mother – when he looked her in the eye. He was emotionally wounded.[14]

The extent of this emotional wounding was made apparent in a report compiled by Barry Walle, a counsellor and psychotherapist, to whom Conlon had been referred by senior house officer Dr Joanna Bromley and consultant psychiatrist Dr Geoff Tomlinson in 2000:

> Gerry can be described as split: three parts adapted to prison, one part outside. His internal world is almost entirely taken up by vivid and detailed 'memories' of his arrest, interrogation/torture, conviction, and prison, so vivid that he is, in effect, reliving it. It is his reality for most of the time without the benefit of the support and companionship of fellow prisoners. Gerry's behaviour is further confused and complicated because there are no real walls. He often wishes he was back in there because then the way he feels would make sense; he would fit.[15]

Conlon's external world was almost as confused, convoluted and perhaps as frightening as his internal one. He had to adjust to a society in which he was viewed as both a lion and a jackal:

> My trouble now is that half the people I meet think I'm some sort of hero, which I'm not, and the other half think I'm a terrorist, which I never was. I go to pubs and clubs, and in lavatories everyone wants to shake my hands, and I don't know where their hands have been. I went to Glasgow for a Celtic-Rangers match and people I never knew were taking off their wedding rings and giving them to me.[16]

To complicate matters, the Guildford Four were still the targets of attacks from the British judiciary. In a pre-retirement BBC television interview, the Recorder of London and the Old Bailey's most senior judge, Sir James Miskin QC – the same judge who had said that the release of the Guildford Four was 'mad' – offered the ludicrous theory that the IRA could have bribed some young and hard-up policeman to 'cook up' certain documents to help free the Guildford Four. It mattered little to Sir James that, other than within the confines of his fertile imagination, there was no evidence of the existence of any such young and hard-up policeman. The possibility was there, and presumably, that would have been enough for him, had he been on the bench of the appeal court on 19 October 1989, to send the Guildford Four back to prison. The same man was no stranger to controversy: at a speech at a Mansion House dinner in London in March 1988, he told a 'joke' about 'nig-nogs' and said that he was engaged in a trial against 'murderous Sikhs' (one of whom he later sentenced to 30 years' imprisonment for murder).

A barrister, and Fianna Fáil member of the Irish parliament, David Andrews, said of Sir James's comments that he was 'very concerned that a mind like that can preside over a judicial system in any democracy. I feel a great sense of relief that Sir James is no longer in a position to adjudge cases.' Andrews went on to say that the comments were 'so right wing as to be almost fascist.'[17] Gerry Conlon said that the judge's critique was part of an ongoing 'whispering campaign' by the British judiciary against the Guildford Four. 'This has put our safety in jeopardy,' Conlon said. 'I would think that any kind of crazy character in this country could believe what Sir James Miskin has said, and, therefore, want to attack us, physically.'[18] Arguably, it was not in Sir James's nature to apologise for anything – certainly not to anyone he perceived to be an Irish terrorist – and he unwisely refused to express regret for his outlandish remarks. But nature and wisdom sometimes make incompatible bedfellows and, as the eminent eighteenth-century Irish parliamentarian, Edmund Burke, once put it, 'Never, no never, did nature say one thing and wisdom say another.'[19]

Despite the high-velocity pace of his life, Gerry Conlon did his best to enjoy his freedom. He was not shy and never lacked the confidence to walk up to a woman and strike up a conversation, with the intention of bringing her home to his bed. Nor was he one of those crusading bores who talked about nothing but the good causes that consumed his daily existence. When he was not 'working', he embraced life with the passion of one who felt that he had been denied it for too long. One of his many girlfriends was Dublin journalist Fiona Looney. She first met him six months after he was released from prison, though she didn't get to know him until a year later. She remembers that Gerry and Paul Hill were 'quite the rock stars' in Dublin in the months following their release.

> I think I first met him in The Pink Elephant nightclub in Dublin after an RTÉ *Late, Late Show*, but I really just shook his hand and wished him well. For what it's worth, I thought he was as sexy as

fuck! I had known Marion, Shane, Vicky, Siobhan, Louise Neville, and all The Pogues crowd for a few years, and I met Gerry through them. I spent some time with him over the course of a few months, but I wouldn't describe our relationship as a romance. He was a charmer, but there was also an innocence about him which I found really touching. When I knew him, he was incredibly forgiving and lacking in bitterness over what had happened to him. I was amazed at that – he honestly didn't seem to bear anyone ill will. On the other hand, he was like a child in a candy shop – and he helped himself to an awful lot of candy. He slept with dozens of women in the first couple of years after he was released and, like an adolescent teenager, he kept count. I think the count was around one hundred and fifty-six, and he was hoping I'd be the one hundred and fifty-seventh. Most women would be offended by that, but I thought it was funny and endearing. I remember him telling me how grateful he was to the IRA for taking him under their wing in prison; he reckoned it was the only thing that prevented him from being raped.[20]

Conlon started smoking marijuana at the age of sixteen and had sustained the habit in and out of prison. Occasionally he snorted cocaine and took ecstasy tablets, usually at a party or a rock concert. Frank Murray, the manager of The Pogues, has vivid memories of himself and Conlon hanging around together in Camden Town at the start of 1990: 'He was full-on, you know? Anything that he couldn't do in there [in prison], he was trying to do out here; he was trying to live the sixties, the seventies, and the eighties, all in one month. As a friend, it was very hard to go to Gerry and say, "Look, I think you're overdoing it a bit" because he'd been in jail for fifteen years and he felt he had the right and it was like, "Nobody's gonna tell me what to do."'[21]

On 29 August 1990, Kenneth Baker, the British Home Secretary, referred the Birmingham Six case back to the appeal court, on the basis of further fresh evidence becoming available. In this instance, the fresh evidence was of a forensic nature, which called into question the veracity of tests carried out by Home Office forensic scientist Dr Frank Skuse, whose original examinations indicated that, when arrested, four of the six prisoners had nitroglycerine on their clothing. It was the end of an era for Gerry and all those who had campaigned for this day. It was a victory, but even in victory there sometimes lurks the aura of defeat. At a stroke, gone was the *raison d'être* for Conlon's post-prison existence. The campaign was over, at least until the appeal was heard. What to do?

Tens of thousands of pounds in compensation was being sent to Conlon by the British government, and he spent it as if there was no tomorrow. The working-class lad from Belfast now had enough money to indulge practically any flight of fancy that engaged his imagination: an idyllic situation, many would say, but, for the emotionally disturbed Conlon, being given a pot of gold was the equivalent of an alcoholic being handed the keys of a bar and being told to lock the doors behind him on his way home.

Cut adrift from the cause that had consumed his life since he had come out of prison, Conlon now had time to seek a fair wind, and on his journey he found plenty of fair-weather friends. He wanted to fit in, to claw back those lost years, to be 'like the same fella I was when I went in'. He frequented Irish bars, chased women and generally tried his best to have a good time in the company of lads who reminded him of his own youth.

> It was an impossible situation. For a start, I had money and they were all on the sites or else on the dole, and I felt guilty as hell about that. I'd buy everything, all the drink, all the meals; the lot. It got to the point where I needed the hangers-on because I just didn't like being on my own. But, the strange thing is, I didn't regard them as hangers-on because I didn't feel I was deserving of anything more than they had. The only way to deal with that was to give the money away.[22]

He brought his friends to Manchester United and to Glasgow Celtic football matches, where he would have spent thousands of pounds on drink and drugs. He also brought some friends on holidays to Mexico, Jamaica, and other exotic locations and again footed the bill. Paddy Armstrong and he took a holiday in Goa, in western India.

One who was not a hanger-on but who was amongst the most prominent people in Conlon's life in the early years after his release was Joey Cashman – a Dubliner and the tour manager of The Pogues. In September 2015, sitting in an alcove of the Marine Hotel in Dublin's northside, Cashman raises his glass of vodka and Red Bull and says: 'To Gerry Conlon – the bollocks!' The glass does not reach his lips before an irreverent laugh erupts from him. Cashman has long grey hair that flaps over his left eye, a goatee beard, and he is dressed entirely in black, with winkle-picker shoes. 'I loved the guy,' he says. 'Me and him, man, we were best buddies; if I were to tell the stories … I'm off seven drugs, you know: crack, heroin, ordinary coke, weed, uppers, downers – hey, I'm even off nicotine. Got there all on my own. When I go to the clinic, I insist they take a sample every week.'

Cashman brushes the hair away from his left eye, looks around and turns back. 'Do you think he's listening in?'

'Who?'

'Gerry.'

'Course he is!'

'Hey, Gerry-man! You're still a bollocks!' Cashman bursts into another fit of unfettered laughter. He is clearly enjoying reminiscing about his buddy. 'I think, I can't be sure, but I think I met Gerry for the first time backstage at The Palladium in New York on the day before Saint Paddy's Day 1990, but I'd only time to shake hands with him and leave it at that.' Later they met in a pub in London and afterwards went back to Cashman's house off the Prince of Wales Road in Camden, where they traded stories all night. Cashman smiles when he talks about his friend from Belfast:

> We might have had a line or two of coke, but we didn't need it; we were both speedy people anyway. And me and Gerry, we clicked on so many levels, and then we became totally inseparable, so even when we were at different meetings, we'd still ring up during the day and make arrangements to go out that night. And if I could've talked for Ireland, he could've talked for the United Nations. But we'd some great laughs that night in my gaff. There was this one story that he thought was particularly funny.[23]

Joey explained that The Pogues had started working on their third album, *If I Should Fall from Grace with God*, in May 1977, and one of the tracks on the album was 'Streets of Sorrow/Birmingham Six', written by Terry Woods and Shane MacGowan. The idea for the song had come from Frank Murray, during a conversation with Shane MacGowan, and it was banned by the Independent Broadcasting Authority in April 1988 because it contained 'lyrics alleging that some convicted terrorists are not guilty and that Irish people in general are at a disadvantage in British courts of law.' Commenting on the ban, Murray said: 'The Pogues will continue to write about what they want and we hope every other artist does the same.' For MacGowan it was a challenge that he was more than willing to take on: 'Banned for what? It's straightforward police state repression of freedom of speech and its censorship.' For the free-spirited Pogues, the ban *had* to be defied.

On 12 November 1987, The Pogues were playing Queen's University in Belfast. Joey Cashman recalls:

> For some reason, Frank Murray wasn't with us, so I'm standing in for him. Anyway, I'm in my hotel room and I get a phone call, and a very stern voice says, 'Are you the manager of The Pogues?'
>
> Cashman's voice takes on a clipped Dublin tone: 'I might be,' I says. 'And to whom might I be speaking?' You see, I can be very polite when I want to be.
>
> 'I'm the Chief Constable of Northern Ireland,' he says.
>
> 'Oh, that's very nice. I'm looking after The Pogues tonight. So tell me, Mr Chief Constable, what are you expecting me to do for you on this fine day?' I'd half an idea what he was going to say, but I let him continue.
>
> 'I'll come straight to the point, shall I?'
>
> 'Please do,' I says.
>
> 'I don't think the band should sing the Birmingham Six song tonight.'
>
> There it was, wasn't it? Out in the open. 'Oh, you don't? And why don't you think the band shouldn't sing the Birmingham Six song tonight?'
>
> 'Because, in my opinion, if it were played, it could cause a riot and it might lead to, you know, fights and disorder.'

Cashman's eyes sparkled. He couldn't wait to get to the punchline:

> And I says to him, 'Well, I'll tell you something. I'll tell you what'll cause a riot and what'll start disorder, Mr Chief Constable: when I go out on that stage and I announce that you, the fucking chief of fucking police, rang me up in my hotel, and told us not to sing the fucking Birmingham Six song. So we *are* singing the fucking song and you can fuck off.' And I slammed down the phone and I felt like, wow! When do you get a chance to tell the chief of police to fuck off? I was expecting the cops to kick the door in, but I didn't give a fuck. Gerry loved that story. He must've laughed for fifteen minutes, easily.

Those who knew Conlon at this time speak of a generous, warm-hearted individual. Siobhan MacGowan has particularly fond memories of him. It was 19 February 1991, a crisp but sunny winter's day, Siobhan remembered. She and a female friend were having a cup of tea in a pub off Grafton Street in Dublin, when another friend, Mo O'Hagan, sauntered in along with Conlon.

> I didn't recognise Gerry. He had put some weight on since he'd got out. The guy was just standing there, smiling, with twinkling eyes, so I bought them a drink and gave Gerry his drink, and I said, 'There you are, Goat Face.' And he burst out laughing and exclaimed, 'Goat Face?' Then Mo said, 'This is Gerry, Gerry Conlon.' And I said, 'Oh, shit! I didn't know you were Gerry Conlon or I'd never have called you Goat Face.' We all burst out laughing after that, and we spent the whole day together, just the three of us, and we went back to Blooms Hotel. Mo left, and Gerry and I talked long into the night.
>
> The next day he said he wanted to see me again that evening but I had another appointment. He said he would sod off to London if I didn't see him, but I didn't believe him. I should have because the next morning he was gone. But I rang him in London and I arranged to go over for my birthday on 22 February. On the evening that I was supposed to go over, there were weather

problems and all cross-channel transport was delayed, and there were no mobile phones in those days. I found out afterwards that he was standing in Euston station with a bunch of flowers in his hand, waiting on me, and when I didn't show up he said he felt like a dick and dumped the flowers in a bin. We had a good laugh over that.[24]

Good laughs were plentiful in those halcyon days.

Four

Caught in the lights of a life over which he had little control, Conlon gravitated towards the eccentricity of The Pogues. The band was at its zenith. Two years earlier, it had released its celebrated Christmas song 'Fairytale of New York', which went to number two in the British pop charts. Their irreverent lead vocalist, Shane MacGowan, rarely appeared on stage unless he was holding a cigarette in one hand and a plastic cup in the other, which most suspected contained alcohol. Apart from the fact that he had liked The Pogues and had played their music while in prison, Conlon identified with the anarchistic MacGowan. The former punk rocker recalls that he was equally taken by Conlon.

The 2015 Dublin City marathon is in progress and large parts of the city centre are blocked off. The semi-detached house in middle-class south Dublin has a lived-in feel about it, a tousled order that makes sense to its free-spirited inhabitants. On the cluttered mantelpiece, a one-foot tall Buddha smiles down approvingly. Hanging above the Buddha is an ornate mirror on which is written disparaging graffiti about other Irish rock bands. An empty wine bottle awaits disposal at the side of the fireplace. In the middle of the room is a therapy bed and sitting on its edge is 56-year-old Shane MacGowan. He grimaces as he gingerly shifts his weight. Having broken his pelvis two months earlier, the slightest movement hurts.

'Are you in pain, Shane?' I ask. 'I can do this interview when you're better.'

'I'm okay, I am. I'm okay. It's sore down my left side, that's all.'

Shane winces. It's time, he thinks, for a sip of 'The Pogues' whiskey, which is brewed by West Cork Distillers.

Joey Cashman, sitting in front of the bay window, follows Shane's example. Cashman nods approvingly and runs his tongue around his lips, just to make sure he has captured every last droplet. 'Shane's broken every bone in his body, haven't you, Shane?' Cashman says as he holds up what little whiskey is left in the glass to the light. Shane grunts.

'So, Shane,' I ask, 'what did you think of Gerry Conlon?'

MacGowan's eyes instinctively light up. 'I thought Gerry was great,' he says in a rasping voice. 'Better than that: I thought he was brilliant, know what I mean? He was brilliant, fucking brilliant.' Shane has one of those infectious chuckles that sound like static on a two-way radio. 'I couldn't believe it when he came around to my place in London with my sister. I was expecting a guy at least two feet taller, like, snapping and miserable, like a fucking psycho, you know, and instead he was saying, "C'mon, let's go out. There's birds out there." And he was talking nineteen to the dozen, know what I mean, telling all these stories about the birds he'd already fucked since he got out.'[1]

Cashman shows MacGowan a photograph of Gerry, Johnny Depp, the events promoter Terry O'Neill and Cashman, which was taken in front of a poster advertising a music festival in Tramore, County Waterford, in 1990.

'Johnny looks like a fucking girl in that photo,' MacGowan says, chuckling mischievously. At that, 49-year-old Victoria Mary Clarke sweeps into the room from the back of the house and cheerily greets everyone. A successful writer and author, Victoria was only seventeen when she met and fell in love with Shane in a pub in London. It is beginning to get dark, so Victoria lights the candles, which brings a gothic tranquillity to the room. Then she asks Shane if he would like some patatas – a spicy potato dish popular in Spanish tapas bars. His reply to her is inaudible but it is enough to send Victoria to the kitchen. She soon returns and hands Shane his bowl of patatas.

Like Shane, Victoria recalls that Siobhan MacGowan had brought Conlon to their flat in London not long after he had been released. She was studying journalism at the time and needed a story, so she asked Gerry if she could interview him, and to her amazement he readily agreed.

> I was amazed. So I pitched it to the editor of the *Irish Post* and he said, 'Yeah, cool.' And it was great for me because it was an

opportunity to get a job. You see, me and Gerry got on really well, because he was very easy to get on with, and I remember saying to him about all the attention he was getting and so on, and he said, 'Oh, I'm just a wanker from west Belfast.' And I put that in the article, and when it came out, Gerry went mental and said to me, 'You bitch! You called me a wanker!' I said, 'But I didn't call you a wanker. You called yourself a wanker.' He taught me an important lesson: just because someone says something in an interview, doesn't mean you always print it.

The conversation turns to Johnny Depp, and how Shane had first met him. There is a difference of opinion. 'Johnny had arranged to meet Shane in the Centralia Café in Soho,' Victoria says. 'It was an Italian café. Gerry was there. Johnny was there. I can't remember who else was there. Shane was outside in the taxi and I went out and told him that Johnny wanted to meet him, and he said he wasn't getting out of the taxi—'

'I couldn't be bothered going in because there was no bar,' Shane quips. The room bursts into laughter.

'So I went back in and Johnny came out and Shane was in the back of the taxi, and Johnny shook hands with him,' Victoria says.

Joey Cashman seems a bit agitated at Victoria's story, which is probably why he feels compelled to help himself to another whiskey. He remembers Johnny ringing him up in London and saying, 'I want to meet Shane; I've got to meet Shane.' He tried to explain to Johnny that it probably wasn't the best time to arrange it:

I said to him that Shane was really fucked up at the minute and he was in a small recording studio in Camden. That didn't put Johnny off, so I brought him to Shane. And Shane was sitting on a pool table, barely conscious. He was swaying as if he was going to fall off, but he didn't. I went over to him and said, 'Shane, this is Johnny Depp.' Shane said, 'So fucking what?' And I said, 'He's a big fan and he'd love to meet you.' And Johnny came over and said, 'I love your stuff.' And Shane said, 'Yeah? So fucking what?' So I said, 'We should go now, Johnny.' And you know what? Johnny didn't want to leave! When we were outside, I said, 'I'm really sorry about that. Shane's going through a really bad time at the minute.' And Johnny turned around to me and said, 'Are you fucking joking? That was amazing, man! Fucking amazing!'

While Johnny Depp's recollection leans towards Cashman's account, there is also an element of truth in Victoria's story because, according to the film star, Shane did not remember meeting Johnny in the recording studio:

> The first time I met Shane ... he doesn't remember it. He was on a pool table, guitar in one hand, and a bottle of wine in the other. He was tired [Depp laughs]. Gerry Conlon was my friend. I've travelled around Ireland with him – don't like being in the States for too long – I like to stay in transit. It wasn't until two years later, when I was in Dublin with Gerry, that I met Shane. I was always a big fan of The Pogues and I think he's [Shane] one of the few poets around. Just hanging out with him is great. When he asked me to come round and play on his record; that was an honour, though I guess you could always cover it in the mix if I was shitty, right?[2]

Depp went on to compare Shane MacGowan with Marlon Brando, describing them as 'two guys who are completely true to their vision – non-conforming and uncompromising'.

Depp's holiday with Gerry Conlon had taken place in August 1990. Ten months had passed since Conlon's release from prison. His words had boomed and reverberated in the corridors of imperial and colonial power on behalf of the Birmingham Six. But during that period, it had played heavily on his mind that he had barely seen his mother and sisters: it was time for Conlon to rectify that error. He decided to bring his family on their first holiday together in almost twenty years. There was never really any other choice of destination: it had to be Ireland.

Conlon had had lunch with Johnny Depp two months earlier in New York and the pair had hit it off immediately, so it seemed natural for Conlon to invite Johnny to spend time with him in Ireland. The elder of the two Conlon sisters, Bridie, had made other arrangements which could not be broken. Her 32-year-old younger sister, Ann, had vivid memories:

> There was me, my mammy, and our David, who was a thalidomide victim. Now David had no arms but he was our driver; he drove with his feet, y'see. My daughter, Mary-Kate, who would've been only six at the time, was also there. We picked up Johnny in Dublin and we stayed in Sinead O'Connor's apartment; it was beside a big football stadium. And Johnny just loved my mother, and you know, he made such a fuss over her. He bought her the loveliest cardigan you ever saw, and he said she was so like his own mother. He spoke so tenderly about his mother. I've always admired him for that. Johnny was very, very down-to-earth – so similar to our Gerry. I swear to God, you'd have thought the two of them were brothers in their ways of kindness and decency.
>
> But sure, anyway, my ma couldn't stick it 'cause the Gerry fella was smoking weed and she hated that, and she insisted on David driving her back to Belfast and, once her mind was made up, that was it. Then David came back to Dublin and we travelled on down through Ireland. We went to Limerick and we stayed in a hotel there for a couple of days. Sure didn't Mr Gerry and Mr Johnny and our David go out on the tear? I don't know if they were looking for girls, or what – they probably were. And our poor 'oul David … they handcuffed him to the bridge.

When asked how it was possible to handcuff a man with no hands to a bridge, Ann exclaimed:

> It was his artificial hands! They handcuffed his artificial hands to the bridge. And when they came back to the hotel, the pair of them were giggling their heads off. You just knew they were up to mischief, and I said: 'Johnny Depp, where's our David? You'd better tell me where our David is.' And he said in his American voice, 'He's sorta tied up.' Then he and that Gerry one went into kinks, laughing. And I said, 'What do you mean he's sorta tied up?

Where is he? You'd better show me where he is, Mister Johnny.' And he did. David was on a bridge beside one of them big fancy hotels, and he laughed his head off when we came to get him, and all David wanted to know was where they were going for another drink.

After Limerick, the Conlon-Depp party headed to the picturesque town of Dingle, County Kerry, where they stayed for a couple of boozy nights. 'They brought the town to a standstill,' Ann said, a grin on her face. 'Johnny and Gerry were in this little pub and the whole town came to see them. You couldn't move in the place, and then everybody was stopping Gerry in the street and saying, "Aren't you him out of the Guildford Four?" I think the celebrity thing was getting to him in the end.'

'And then Johnny nearly poked my eye out,' Mary-Kate interjected. When asked how that had happened, Mary-Kate replied, 'We were out in this wee boat in the bay looking for Fungie the Dolphin and Johnny said, "Here, Mary-Kate, come on and see the dolphins" and when I leaned over, he accidentally stuck his finger in my eye. And he was so apologetic. Later he went out and brought me Levi shorts and a top, and he bought me a bodhrán. I still have it.'

'That's right,' Ann chipped in. 'He bought it when we stopped in Tipperary town.'

'We stopped in quite a few towns, didn't we, Mammy?' Mary-Kate said.

'Quite a few?' Ann cried out. 'Them pair of boys stopped in nearly every town we went through and had a pint. They were never sober, so they weren't!'[3]

Rumours were beginning to circulate in the press that a film based on the Guildford Four story was being planned and that Gerry Conlon and Gabriel Byrne were in regular contact. On 14 January 1991, both men told reporters that they wanted the Gerry Conlon film to be as authentic and as true to the actual events as possible. Both stressed that they were seeking to avoid the Hollywood glamour treatment: 'God knows,' Byrne said, 'they'd probably want to put Arnold

Schwarzenegger in it.'[4] Gabriel's suspicion that Hollywood would want to put Schwarzenegger in the movie was an obvious overstatement, but he had been around the movie business long enough to know that the studios would protect their investment and would have a decisive say in the proposed film on Gerry Conlon's life.

On 14 March 1991 the Birmingham Six were released following their appeal. It was a verdict that had been expected because the Public Prosecution Service had made it known they were not going to contest new evidence that had been made available to the court. In their summing up, Lord Justices Lloyd, Mustill and Farquharson concluded:

> For our part, we would say that in the light of the fresh scientific evidence, which at least throws light on Dr Skuse's evidence, if not destroys it completely, these convictions are both unsafe and unsatisfactory. If we put the scientific evidence to one side, the fresh investigation, carried out by the Devon and Cornwall Constabulary, renders the police evidence at the trial so unreliable that again we would say that the conclusions are both unsafe and unreliable. It is for these reasons that we allow the appeals.[5]

Amid scenes of rapturous joy, the six men approached the television cameras. Richard McIlkenny was the first to speak: 'It's good to see you all. We've waited a long time for this – sixteen years – because of hypocrisy and brutality. But every dog has its day and we're going to have ours.'

Paddy Hill, pale, thin-faced, with fiery eyes and volcanic energy, erupted: 'For sixteen and a half years we've been deprived and used as political scapegoats, for people in there [points to the Old Bailey], at the highest. The police told us at the start that they knew we hadn't done it; they told us they didn't care who did it; that we'd been selected, and that they were going to frame us – just to keep the people in there [points again to Old Bailey] happy; people who can't spell the word justice, never mind dispense it: they're rotten.'

Thirteen days later the judges gave their reasons for releasing the Birmingham Six. Paddy Hill attended the court proceedings. The appeal court judges, not unexpectedly, gave what the broadcaster

Ludovic Kennedy called a 'clean bill of health' to the trial judge and the earlier appeal judges. Paddy Hill summed up his feelings succinctly: 'Despite everything that had happened to us, not one policeman, not one prosecution lawyer, not one judge, had turned to the Birmingham Six and said: "We're sorry."'[6]

On 8 October 1993, three police officers whom the appeal court judges had named and accused of being 'at least guilty of deceiving the court' at the original Birmingham Six trial, had charges of perjury and conspiracy to pervert the course of justice dropped because the judge, Mr Justice Garland, did not believe they would get a fair trial, owing to the publicity given to the Birmingham Six case. In a statement, Paddy Hill judiciously observed that publicity had not stopped the Birmingham Six trial in 1975. And, unlike the Birmingham Six, the three detectives had no complaints when they walked out of the Old Bailey.

Three days after the Birmingham Six were released, Gerry Conlon was on a plane to Glasgow, where The Pogues were entertaining a St Patrick's Day crowd in the Barrowland Ballroom. Also on the flight were Siobhan MacGowan, Marion McKeone, Louise Neville and Victoria Mary Clarke. Spirits were high at the concert and Marion McKeone found time to rib Gerry.

> There were crowds surrounding him everywhere he went, backstage, and in front of stage, demanding autographs. I remember saying to him: 'As your lawyer, I advise you not to sign anything.' And Siobhan at the same time was yelling, 'For Christ's sake, Gerry, don't sign anything!' When a well-known musician came up to him at the backstage party after the show and self-consciously asked him to sign what looked like the back of a letter, I cautioned Gerry to remember what had happened the last time he had signed a piece of paper he hadn't read first. I think the musician was shocked but Gerry roared with laughter.'[7]

Siobhan MacGowan also remembered the good-natured banter: 'The craic was ninety and after advising him not to sign anything, we started to call him "Lucky Conlon" because he'd been so fucked-over by the system. Gerry thought that was hilarious.'[8] Conlon tried to give as good as he got but, as a gambler, he should have known that at odds of four-to-one, he had little chance. However, he was not the type to take a ribbing lying down, as Marion McKeone found out: 'Victoria, Shane, Siobhan and I all knocked about together in a big unruly group that travelled between London and Dublin. In those early days, Gerry was catching up on everything at breakneck speed, including partying. At times he was like lightning in a bottle, crackling with energy and life. He and Paddy Armstrong became part of our group pretty much as soon as they were released.'

Marion, a barrister, journalist and international human rights lawyer, went on to say:

> When Siobhan first brought Gerry to meet me in the Bull and Gate pub in London, I was wearing an old Astrakhan coat I'd picked up in Camden market for a few quid. I was also wearing Doc Marten boots, and when Gerry saw me, he burst out laughing. 'Fuck me!' he exclaimed, 'It's Granny Clampett!' (the crabby grandmother from the *The Beverly Hillbillies*). And he was right; I probably looked like some demented old bat, even though I was only in my twenties. Afterwards I just got used to being called Granny Clampett. But he never forgot the slagging I gave him in Glasgow and, not long after that, we were all in the Hyde Park Hotel and an announcement was made over the hotel loudspeaker for 'Granny Clampett' to go to the reception, and, without thinking, I went. When I glanced over my shoulder, Gerry, Shane and Siobhan were looking around the corner, and they were in a heap, laughing.
>
> It was around that time when Hollywood actors were lining up to play Gerry. Of course we all had great fun with that one. Johnny Depp, who was a fan and friend of Shane's, came to London for a stint to meet Gerry and talk to him about the role. He spent quite a bit of time hanging around with us all. Depp is a decent, generous guy, who seemed back then to have little or no ego. He and Gerry got on very well, but, compared to Gerry, who had such a big personality, Johnny was much shyer and more diffident.

McKeone recollected that she had advised Conlon to get counselling because he was having panic attacks. 'He would freeze and panic over things as mundane as crossing the road. He found the traffic so much more menacing than he had expected. Things like cash-dispensing machines, even a drinks machine in a hotel lobby, would make him anxious.'[9]

Siobhan MacGowan remembered the morning after The Pogues' St Patrick's Day concert. She and Conlon were sitting on the banks of the River Clyde, at the back of their hotel, and talking. Siobhan described the sun shining on the water. 'It was lovely,' she said. 'There was just the two of us. I don't think he was ever truly happy. He was doing the very best he could do.' A story she told to illustrate Gerry's emotional impulsiveness involved the flight back to London. He was firing plastic cups at her. Feeling tired and irritable, she told him to 'piss off'. He jumped up and said, 'Goat Face, Goat Face, here.' And he took a ring off his finger and said, 'My aunt got me this when I was in prison and I've worn it all these years, and I want you to wear it.'

Siobhan refused it, but he went on and on and in the end she agreed to wear it. The last time she spoke to him was when he was with 'Spider' Stacy, an original member of The Pogues, and Louise in Belfast a couple of years before he died. They were talking on the phone, and she said, 'I've still got your ring, Gerry.'

'I know,' replied Gerry. 'You're keeping it safe.'[10]

Finola Geraghty, film producer, director and actress, also hung out with this group in 1991/92. Like Marion McKeone, she noticed Johnny Depp's shyness:

> It was really a great mix of people, nice people, but not necessarily the most 'sorted' bunch. And we were trooping around the West End in a long line, with Johnny Depp and his friend trailing at the back. No one was talking to him – they were shy and so was he. We stopped at a club called The Milky Bar, which was a doorway in a wall that was plastered with pictures of Johnny Depp in his last film. But the people on the door didn't let us in. They didn't recognise Johnny, and no one said anything. We all went back to the Camden Palace instead, and I remember Gerry

and Mario sending me over to Johnny to ask if he wanted a drink, and he was looking at Gerry with admiration and he said: 'He is art, living art.'

It was in this galaxy of words – written, sung and acted – that Geraghty's talent found expression. She was part of a theatre company called Trouble and Strife, which had been formed in 1987 at Cambridge University. She said, 'Gerry was very supportive of our work. Our third play in 1991, *Never Had It So Good*, was about an Essex Salvation Army mother-and-baby home in the 1950s; not as much was made of them as the Irish laundries, but the principle was the same – punishment of unmarried mothers. Gerry said the setting reminded him of prison. He and Kirsty MacColl even wrote a letter of complaint to *Time Out*, when the magazine described the play as "Trauma, not drama".'

Commenting on some of her more memorable times with Conlon, Geraghty said: 'There would be incongruous moments with him, like Daniel Day-Lewis in the Archway Tavern; Robert Kennedy's daughter in the Drum and Monkey Pub, Archway. People and places you wouldn't normally put together.'[11]

A trip here, a trip there: there was always a trip to somewhere, anywhere where the lash of self-hate had no sting. The Greek island of Crete looked like such a place. Crete is a mountainous island with lush valleys and fertile plateaux. On 18 April 1991, Gerry Conlon, Paddy Hill and his son Seán, Paddy Armstrong, Joey Cashman, and a friend called Mario McGovern decided to holiday in the resort of Malia in the north-east of the idyllic island. For Paddy Hill it was an opportunity to further cement his relationship with his son.

> It was the first holiday I'd ever taken with Seán. The weather was superb, and we were having a great time driving around on mopeds or just lounging around the hotel swimming pool. We went out each evening for a meal, but then I would usually go back to the hotel while Seán and the other lads went off to nightclubs. Seán and I were not like father and son, but more like two men who were becoming friends – men who liked each other but were not entirely comfortable in each other's company.'[12]

It was probably the best that Paddy could expect, given that he had not been around Seán for sixteen years. To complicate matters, Paddy was laid low with food poisoning. 'I was bad, believe me,' Hill said. 'The doctor gave me an injection and he said, "If this doesn't work within the next two hours, you're on your way: there's an army helicopter in the army base down the road and they're flying you directly to the American naval base."'[13] Dr Monolis Katsouris, who treated Hill, confirmed the seriousness of Hill's illness: 'He was in a terrible state to begin with. In the course of one hour he had to go to the toilet thirty times. He was suffering from dehydration and high blood pressure.'[14]

With Hill feeling sick and miserable, Conlon prepared for a night out with Joey Cashman, Mario and Seán. Paddy Hill remembered: 'We were only in Crete a few days and Gerry took a handful of ecstasy tablets this night.'[15]

Cashman summed up events after the men left their hotel and headed to the most popular bar on the island:

> None of us were getting anywhere with the women. Remember, we were all young, single guys. Anyway, Gerry moved in on this English bird and he seemed to be getting somewhere. And then, for some reason, the girl asked me to take her home, which, of course, I did. But nothing happened. No sex; nothing. But, when I got back to the bar in the early hours, Gerry was screaming and shouting, and I asked him what was he going on about, and he said: 'As if you don't know, ya wee fucker ya.' As far as he was concerned I'd knocked off his girl – which I hadn't. But she wasn't his girl anyway, you know? All he'd done was try to chat her up and buy her a drink. And on the way back to the hotel, there was this long wall of lights, and Gerry smashed every light. When we got back to the hotel, he picked up these glass tables and threw them into the pool, and then he threw every chair into the pool, as well. It was after that that Gerry started calling me 'The Sniper'.[16]

Paddy Hill was in excruciating pain and this was the last thing he needed. 'I heard this hullabaloo and Seán came in and told me the cops were taking Paddy Armstrong away.

Paddy hadn't been out that night, so whatever had happened had nothing to do with him. So I got on me clothes and told the cops that Paddy had been with me and had done nothing wrong, and they let him go.'[17] In the meantime, Conlon had paid in full for any damages and the hotel management persuaded the police not to pursue the matter any further.

Twenty-five years later, Joey Cashman had an understated attitude to that night's shenanigans:

> So we were thrown out of the hotel. It was no big deal: I was used to being thrown out of lots of hotels. We just went to the nearest town and booked into another hotel. Paddy Joe Hill, Seán, and Paddy Armstrong went home the next day. In the new town, we found out that the year before an English guy had killed a barman. That was none of our business, but the next night we were walking past a bar and someone shouted, 'Drunken English bastards!' and I shouted back, 'We might be drunken bastards, but we're not English. We're Irish!' But they thought we were shouting 'Fuck off' and about ten Spanish men started coming towards us. So we were standing at a taxi rank, and I said to Gerry and Mario, 'Quick! Get into the taxi and close the doors!' As they did that, I opened the boot of the taxi, took out a wheel-brace and started running towards the men, yelling like a madman, and they turned and ran away. You see, I know about psychology and that. And then, well, then some clever dick amongst them must've realised that there was ten of them and only one of me. So they sorta stopped and looked around at me, and I sorta stopped too. Then they charged, and I turned and bolted back to the taxi. I jumped into the back of the taxi, and then a guy with long hair, in a brown leather coat, opens Gerry's door and grabs him out by the hair. I was sitting behind Gerry, and I jumped out of the taxi and hit the guy so hard, I broke my hand. All I heard was, 'You've hit a policeman!' and I'm shouting, 'I didn't know he was a fucking policeman!' and they all jumped on me and kicked the shit out of me. There was blood coming out of everywhere – and I mean everywhere. When we got to the police station, the cop I'd hit cleaned the blood off me. I was

so badly beaten up that they decided not to press charges against me for hitting the cop. The next day I went to the hospital and the doctor pulled my little finger back into place. I have never had pain like that in my life. I mean, there were tears in my eyes.[18]

When Conlon, Cashman and McGovern returned to London, they were surprised to find that their exploits in Crete had made the headlines in *The Sun* newspaper. Cashman, Gerry and Mario were in the Archway Tavern when somebody showed them the paper. The headline read, 'SHAME', and the sub-headline was: 'Guildford Four pair and Birmingham Six man are booted out of holiday hotel'. At first they thought it was a joke, that the paper was a fake, but they soon realised it was real. A consequence of the article was that Paddy Hill, Gerry Conlon and Paddy Armstrong issued libel proceedings against *The Sun*.

After the undignified fiasco in Crete, Paddy Hill came to the realisation that his friend Gerry Conlon was in freefall and was chasing ruinous highs. 'I came down to London,' Hill said, 'and we went out: me, Gerry and Paddy Armstrong. Before we'd even left the flat – it was a Saturday night – he must've smoked a quarter ounce of Bush [marijuana]. And unbeknown to me, he was sniffing coke in the toilet, and he'd dropped a couple of E tabs. So we're out anyway, and he's bubbling like fuck, bouncing, and over the period of the night he must have snorted a couple of grams of coke, and he must have dropped five or six E tabs. He was smoking weed as well, and drinking like a fucking fish.'[19]

Things went from bad to worse when, on 25 May, Conlon and some friends met in Bar Gansa in Camden. Soon after, the company split up, leaving in different cars to go to a twenty-third birthday party on a pleasure boat on the River Thames. Spirits were high and the occupants of Conlon's car hoped to get even higher at the party. Then, on Pentonville Road, north London, the car in which Conlon was a passenger was stopped by police. Travelling with him were Joey Cashman, Paddy Armstrong and Seán Hill. After a search, police discovered that Conlon had 1.4 grams of cocaine in a jacket pocket, and that Armstrong had 505 milligrams of cocaine in a cigarette packet.

The four men were arrested. On 27 May, the *Daily Mirror* headline read: 'BACK IN THE CELLS', and the sub-headline said: 'Guildford Four two locked up for twelve hours after drugs arrest'.

In London's Clerkenwell Magistrates Court, on 5 September 1991, Conlon and Armstrong pleaded guilty to possession of cocaine and ecstasy, were ordered to pay £30 court costs and were conditionally discharged for two years.

For Paddy Hill, enough was enough. A profound friendship, formed in the claustrophobia of prison and in a shared quest for justice, had to be expunged: Hill now believed that Gerry was a bad influence on his son. 'I told Seán,' Hill said, "get the fuck out of there [Conlon's flat]. You're not staying with Gerry anymore. You're coming with me." And it was around then that Gerry and me fell out, and we didn't talk for the next fifteen years.'

Few people would quarrel with Hill's wanting to take his son away from a drug-fuelled environment. Fewer still would disagree that Gerry was playing fast and loose with his life. Even before the friends parted company, Hill had made a desperate plea to Gerry's mother to intervene, telling her that her son was on the road to disaster and, if not rescued, would 'end up in the gutter'. As it turned out, his prophecy was not far off the mark, in that Conlon's drug habit did get progressively worse and would sap both his physical and mental health, and his money. But if Gerry Conlon had proved anything, it was that he was a survivor, the type of person whom Oscar Wilde might well have been thinking about when he said: 'We are all in the gutter, but some of us are looking at the stars.'[20]

Five

'On the grounds that the possibility of innocent contamination cannot be excluded, and on this basis alone, we think the convictions of all appellants are unsafe and unsatisfactory.' With these words, the appeal court judges in London, on 26 June 1991, overturned the convictions of the Maguire Seven.

The narrowness on which the appeal was allowed made it a far from satisfactory verdict for those who had been falsely accused. The judgement ignited a firestorm of revulsion in Conlon, who was quick to unleash his wrath outside the court: 'It's an evil court; it is not a vehicle for dispensing justice.' He went on to say that the court's ruling was 'a damage limitation exercise' and 'a political decision', and that, 'If they had dealt with any of the other grounds of appeal properly, it would be proven that the British judicial system murdered my father. That is what they are afraid of – that the whole world will know that British justice let an innocent and sick man die in prison.' The vitriol was remorseless: 'Those judges should have nightmares every night. They have given the most atrocious decision in this country. There is no British justice when it comes to Irish people. It's like being a black man in South Africa. We, the Irish, are black South Africans when it comes to dealing with British courts, British police, and forensic scientists.'[1]

Annie Maguire was more subdued in her condemnation of the limited reprieve than Conlon had been, but she was no less disappointed: 'I still hoped that British justice was going to be completed today. I suppose I was hoping for too much.' With extraordinary humility, she further commented: 'I have always said I wouldn't let bitterness get hold of me. You only end up being a very sick person. Bitterness could be something like cancer and it spreads and spreads to every part. Giuseppe Conlon died in prison which he shouldn't have done and I'm sure he'd agree with me – if some good comes, if others in the future are spared – we will accept that suffering as a gift from God, a cross to bear.'[2]

At the grave of Giuseppe Conlon, in Milltown cemetery, Belfast, Sarah Conlon reflected on the judgement and on her late husband's death in prison. 'His last wish has finally come true. Nobody lies when they are dying. Giuseppe knew he was an innocent man.' After expressing delight that Annie Maguire and her family had been exonerated at last, Sarah mirrored Annie's lack of bitterness: 'If I were bitter, I couldn't live with myself. I always trust and hope in God. But maybe those judges couldn't admit they did a wrong thing – putting innocent people behind bars.'[3]

Given the scale of the horror that had been visited on Annie Maguire and Sarah Conlon, and their respective families, these two ladies' faith in their religious beliefs and their lack of rancour is all the more remarkable.

The British Labour MP Chris Mullins said: 'It's an utterly incredible judgement and I can't believe anybody of intelligence will believe a word of it. I've got used to stupidity on the part of senior figures in the legal establishment but this one takes the biscuit.'[4]

The Irish government said it was 'deeply concerned' by the judgement and that it was 'imperative that consideration of this case should not end with the narrow grounds on which the appeal was allowed'.

At the end of a damning condemnation of the Maguire Seven appeal court verdict, Kevin McNamara, the shadow Northern Ireland Secretary of State, stated: 'It is not possible to say if such miscarriages of justice will happen again.' McNamara then asked 'Who guards the guardians?'

Guarding his own historical legacy was something that had, and would continue, to tax Conlon's mind for a considerable time.

By mid-1991, Conlon was becoming increasingly frustrated that the film about his life had not progressed as quickly he would have expected and, along with Joey Cashman, who had already worked on four feature films, he began trawling around film companies, looking for financial support.

Impatience, by its very definition, is irrational, and Conlon was suffocating on his own impatience. In his opinion, Gabriel Byrne, the man whom he believed held out so much promise, had delivered so little. But was this fair? The starting point for all films is an idea, which can be a true-to-life experience or a piece of fiction. After that, someone needs to write a script. Byrne had set that process in motion when he approached Belfast-born screenwriter Terry George in the Sin-é bar in Manhattan's East Village (the same bar where Gerry and Gabriel had first liaised with each other in 1990) and asked him if he would write a screenplay about Gerry Conlon and the Guildford Four, based on *Proved Innocent*. George had agreed. Byrne had also contacted the Irish director Jim Sheridan to direct the film. So the wheels were turning; the process was underway. Had Conlon expected too much, too soon? It usually takes anything from three to five years for a film to be made, and that is more often than not *after* a script goes into development. In Conlon's amateurish estimation, Byrne had been inattentive; he had missed a penalty kick. Byrne was certainly busy: he was preparing to produce and star in an Irish film called *Into the West*, and at the same time, he was getting ready to act in *Cool World*, along with Brad Pitt and Kim Basinger.

The question inevitably arises: what value could be placed on the one dollar gentleman's agreement between Conlon and Byrne in light of the former's disillusionment with the latter? The short answer is very little. It was still, at that stage, Conlon's project and he was in no mood for what he saw as dithering on Byrne's part.

Perhaps out of loyalty to Gabriel Byrne, Conlon had been initially reluctant to talk to Jim Sheridan about producing the movie. Yet the two men genuinely liked each other. It is hardly surprising that each man was taken with the other: they were both supercharged characters with immense energy and drive, and they were both natural communicators. Moreover, Sheridan had more than demonstrated that he had the ability to light up the silver screen with the Guildford Four man's story.

Although a relative newcomer to the film-making business, Sheridan, known to his friends as 'Shay', had directed the financially successful *My Left Foot*, starring Daniel Day-Lewis, in 1989. That film was made for £600,000 but grossed over £14 million at the box office. *My Left Foot* also received five Academy nominations, including best director for Sheridan, with actors Daniel Day-Lewis and Brenda Fricker receiving Oscars for best male actor and best female supporting actor respectively. Then, in 1990, Sheridan directed the big screen adaptation of Irish playwright John B. Keane's *The Field*, starring Richard Harris, who received Academy Award and Golden Globe nominations for his role. But while the film was artfully produced and directed, it had limited appeal and was a box office flop.

During meetings with Sheridan in London and Dublin, Conlon and Cashman listened attentively to his proposals. They were surprised to hear Sheridan express views that were very close to their own. They nodded to each other as Sheridan laid out his vision of *The Conlon Story*, the film's working title. Of particular interest to Conlon and Cashman was the fact that Sheridan said Daniel Day-Lewis was interested in working on the film, but would not act in it. Film studios like star power and Day-Lewis had it to spare. The potential involvement of Day-Lewis, the son of the Anglo-Irish poet laureate Cecil Day-Lewis, helped in no small way to convince Conlon that Sheridan was the right man for the job. But for the movie to reach its full potential, Day-Lewis had to be persuaded to take on the role of Gerry Conlon.

Now that Conlon had secured Sheridan's pledge to co-produce and direct the film, there was the unenviable task of telling Gabriel Byrne that Sheridan had stepped into his shoes and had taken overall charge of making the film. Joey Cashman recalled travelling to Los Angeles in the spring of 1991 with Conlon to meet Byrne:

> So me and Gerry are in this girl's house. Her old man is the owner of Mitsubishi, the Japanese electronic and car company. But she has no money. That wasn't a problem. On our last day over there, Gabriel turned up and he and Gerry took a walk down by the swimming pool, which, I may add, was full of slime. I don't know what was said between the two of them, and Gerry didn't say much afterwards, but it seemed to me that Jim was in the driving seat in regards to the movie, although Gerry did say Gabriel was still very much involved.[5]

The deep breath had been taken. Conlon undoubtedly would have preferred to be in the driving seat himself, but pragmatism and inexperience dictated that he give way to others. Still, that did not mean he was going to walk away from what he saw as *his* film. To do that would have stripped his life of discipline and purpose, which his life *had* to have. This reluctance to let go was not missed by those who knew Conlon in 1991: 'Getting the film made was very important to Gerry,' Ann McKernan said. 'It wasn't about money for him; it was about getting the truth out. And it was about keeping busy, as well. He needed to be doing something, something positive.'[6]

Conlon's psychotherapist Barry Walle explained this alternative *raison d'être* as 'displacement activity' and said:

> Without a strong reason to keep going, he would go into meltdown, and getting his film made was highly motivational. But any appearance of personal organisation was really accidental, or limited: where would he have learnt it? A lot of arrangements for travel were made by, or with the help of others. He was quite clever at covering up this difficulty, a bit like illiterate people, only he was far from illiterate. A major fear was appearing stupid, so he didn't like asking questions of strangers to navigate around places or organisations in case people thought him a numbskull, and again, he was far from a numbskull. He attributed other people with knowing how to do these things, and it was only people like him that didn't. He remembered the travel as a good time, an adventure, his purpose in trying to sell the film – an enabler perhaps. He certainly met a lot of interesting people he wouldn't otherwise have met. There may have been 'control' reasons wrapped in there, in that, having only loose control of his life, he didn't want to lose control of his story.[7]

Walle summed up succinctly part of the damage that fifteen years of wrongful incarceration had done to Gerry Conlon. Crucially, in the two years since walking free from the Old Bailey, he had received no treatment for the psychological malaise that was afflicting him and, given that his deep mental trauma was never going to magically cure itself, what emerges from Walle's analysis is that, despite his outwardly confident persona, Gerry Conlon was holding on to his sanity by his fingertips.

Despite all the body blows that life had dealt him, Conlon remained an idealist. Unfortunately, idealists are not always the best judges of human nature simply because they always tend to think the best of people. He had convinced himself that he could persuade the patriarchs of the film-making business of the merits of his real-life story, yet it appears that he had little or no grasp of the fact that wholesome stories of survival against great odds do not always translate into commercially profitable films. In the same vein, it does not seem to have crossed his mind that his story might need a hefty shot of artistic licence in order to attract investors *before* it could be turned into a successful production.

Conlon and Cashman were not without contacts: 'I met with a guy called John Patek from the William Morris Agency, who offered me an outrageous amount of money for the option, but I wanted somebody who would understand the situation. I didn't want John Wayne coming in and releasing people. I wanted the story to be told. I wanted people to understand it – when terrorism happens, when bombs go off, when innocent people are killed, that the reaction of the press and the police is to, "Get someone. Get anyone."'[8]

Cashman remembers the two visionaries setting off, 'with undying optimism to Ireland, the USA, and, of course, the UK. We met producers, including the president of Warner Brothers Films, who helped us but said the movie wasn't for them, directors, actors, agents, lawyers, accountants – and a lot of bullshitters,' Cashman recalls. 'One of the first things we learned was that Hollywood film companies might buy one hundred scripts but only turn ten or so into films. All the others sit on shelves in the company's storerooms. If they hear that a rival company is interested in a script, they will buy it just to stop the competition from making the movie.' Cashman explains that this resulted in their first decision: 'We would deal only with a company that signed a legal document to make the film.'[9]

Finola Geraghty remembered: 'Gerry went through an awful time with his film. He said he got through fifteen years in category "A" prisons intact, and it was dealing with the movie business people that gave him a nervous breakdown.'[10]

Throughout 1991, Terry George struggled manfully to avoid a nervous breakdown. He had to put together a script, but it was essential to get to the essence of Gerry Conlon, and that was never going to be easy because there were several Gerry Conlons, as Terry recalled:

> The book *Proved Innocent* was very anecdotal. Gerry had a phenomenal memory and his sense of Belfast folklore and his outrage came across. But I didn't have the structure I needed for a film. I had the sense that some stuff was too painful for Gerry to talk about. Because he's such a whirlwind and wants to get out, and party, and drink, it was hard to sit him down in one place at one time. I got exasperated and put him into a car, and we drove down from New York to Key West. That's a three-day drive, and I taped everything he said on the way down. I put him in a little moving cell, and the price for sitting still was two days' fishing in Key West. I was then able to get the father-son relationship.

Terry did not get the father-son relationship and, if indeed he did, it was not reflected in the film. When asked about the extensive use of dramatic licence in the film, Terry George was unapologetic: 'Inevitably, you are going to compress and manipulate and stretch and invent – at least to some degree – to make the story work as cinema.'[11]

For his part, Sheridan saw the father-son relationship, rather than the scale of the injustice perpetrated on the Conlons, as the dramatic thrust of the film: 'I wanted to tell the father's story most of all. I didn't really want to do the story of all the injustice. I knew the central father-son story could be universal.'[12] It may be that Jim Sheridan, producer, director and businessman, had a wary eye fixed on the reaction of the press when he expressed this sentiment before the première of *In the Name of the Father* in Dublin on 27 December 1993, almost six weeks before the film was released in Britain. Perhaps he anticipated that the film would be slated by the British press as being pro-IRA, hence this playing loose with the miscarriage of justice element in the film. It may be that he really did believe the father-son relationship was the core theme of the film; he said as much in a press interview in 1999: 'I was accused of lying in *In the Name of the Father*, but the real lie was saying that the film was about the Guildford Four when really it was about a non-violent parent.'[13] Whatever it may be, the fact remains that if the Conlons had not been victims of a miscarriage of injustice, they would not have been in prison, and there would have been no father-son relationship theme to explore: one could not have existed without the other. Having turned down 'an outrageous amount of money' from the William Morris Agency because he did not think their views about the film reflected his experiences, it is challenging to see why Gerry Conlon would have involved Jim Sheridan in the making of a film about his life if he had known that Sheridan viewed the injustice perpetrated against Giuseppe and himself as being of secondary importance.

While the tumult surrounding his film was playing out, Gerry plunged into a serious relationship with a young lady he nicknamed 'Minty', a striking 20-year-old English camera assistant, whom he met on a film set in 1991. Although there was a seventeen-year age gap between the two, in terms of psychological development it was much less than that because prison seldom affords inmates opportunities to mature, and Conlon, like so many ex-prisoners, had not really left his pre-arrest emotional base camp. Coupled with this, the dietary and social constraints of prison life ensured that he had kept his Peter Pan looks. For her part, Minty found Gerry intoxicating:

> He had the ability to make every single person feel incredibly special, like they were his confidant. Even in places with hundreds of people in it, he'd find you in a darkened corner of a club or wherever you were, indeed, whoever you were, and he'd huddle up close, look you deep in your eyes – pin you with his eyes – and start talking, weaving the magic web he had with words around you, sharing his emotions, his turmoil, whilst still making you laugh. He was magic, a gifted orator. No one was immune (most especially women), no one was ignored. Children grew four inches with pride (and attention) in his presence. It was like he walked around sprinkling feel-good fairy dust on people – whether they were highfalutin politicians, movie stars or naive little girls in over

their heads like me. In a world of glitz and glamour, lots of drugs and mostly all bollocks, Gerry made it real and made you feel special, which I think is all anyone wants at the end of the day. He understood that very well and used it. All anyone wanted to do in response was make him feel good, and we all tried very hard. Gerry was deeply loved by all our gang. His attention and focus was real. No matter who you were on the surface, he saw the person below.[14]

By January 1992, Minty and Gerry were living together in his Tufnell Park flat. Minty had a calming influence on Gerry and this pacifying effect was noticed by Siobhan MacGowan, Marion McKeone, Finola Geraghty and other members of the gang: the artistic friends with whom Gerry shared his deepest thoughts and trepidations. At the start of their romance, Minty found Gerry a delight to be around:

Being on the receiving end of Gerry's 'romantic' love was mind-blowing and intense. Imagine being that kind of focus for someone like him, at twenty years old. It was ferocious and passionate. I've never felt so cherished or precious. There was never any question as to how he felt at that point. It was in the tension of his arms when they snaked out and grabbed you and reeled you in as you walked past, in the burning of his stare across a room, or how he'd throw you over his shoulder and stalk off, not a care who saw him or what they said – in the way he hung on to you whilst he slept.[15]

Yet, no matter how blissful this relationship was in the beginning, its survival was always going to be a test of stamina, given the severity of the dislocation that Conlon was experiencing. For a start, he was driven by an overpowering emotional need to be unrestricted: after his imprisonment, boundaries of any sort were anathema to him. Accordingly, he was out of the home quite often – sometimes without Minty – travelling abroad, trying to sell his story to film producers and touring with The Pogues. This freewheeling pattern was hardly conducive to a lasting relationship. Then there was his old-fashioned idea of what constituted a loving union.

Born in a staunchly Catholic area of Belfast in 1954, Conlon had grown up in a society where, in many families, the man of the house ruled the household like a miniature feudal chieftain and where the wife's primary purposes were to accommodate her husband, rear their children and keep a tidy home. Conlon's stretch in prison had not dented this anachronistic outlook, but Minty came from a different age and perspective. On 17 March 1992, she recorded in her diary: 'Got home from work today. Gerry thinks it's all basically down to me thinking the cleaning and cooking is below me and that if he's paying the house bills, I should do all that without thinking and any other woman would do it and be grateful. He says I need to see a shrink more that he does and he is more honest than I.'[16]

What was emerging was a schism brought about by Gerry's adverse circumstances and the couples' age disparity. Gerry wanted a stay-at-home, do-as-you're-told partner while Minty wanted much more:

> He expected me to keep house and iron his shirts, furnish the house, and stay in it and wait for him. I'd been galloping full-tilt like a bolted horse since I left home at fifteen, and I was fresh off the plane from living in the United States on my own. I was looking for a partner in crime to embark on adventures and realise ambitions with. Gerry wanted me at home where he could control me. He used to bring up marriage and kids all the time, but I am sure it was only another method of control.[17]

Something else that put a chokehold on the relationship was Conlon's need to be surrounded by people – it did not matter who. While he undoubtedly liked the idea of keeping the party going – irrespective of cost – fear played a significant role in his choice of friends. Put bluntly, the man was terrified that 'someone' would murder him – and with good reason. Shortly after meeting Minty, he was walking close to the tube station in Chalk Farm, an area of north-east London, when he was confronted by a gang of skinheads, one of whom shouted: 'Look! That's Gerry Conlon! Get him!' Conlon took off running as fast as he could, with the skinheads in full pursuit. The skinheads followed him all the way to Camden Town and part of the way back to Kentish

Town. After taking quite a while to recover in his Tufnell Park flat, Conlon told friends that during the chase all he could think of was, 'My shoelaces will come undone. Oh, God, don't let them come undone, don't let them come undone.' Later he was accosted by a man wielding a machete who chased him for his life through Camden and who was shouting that he was going to chop off his head. So who could blame Conlon for seeking the protection of tough guys, close friends from his years in prison who would offer him some form of protection? But everything has its price. The tariff that Conlon paid for this shield was significant. His friends from the creative arts were spooked by his latest choice of companions. 'The gang were all professionals and they had full lives,' Minty said. 'When we were with them, it felt good. No one was there because of who the other was, but purely for the pleasure of each other's company. Real friends.' Minty explained how this changed when he started clubbing: 'The calibre of the people around him dropped significantly – lots of hangers-on only there because of who he was and what he could give them. Dishonest people. He'd bring them back to our home at the end of the night to carry on. I went down to 90lb in weight and started sharing his panic attacks with him!'[18]

While she may have shared his panic attacks, Minty nevertheless did not go Dutch with Gerry's frantic rush to get his film produced. On 28 April 1992, Minty prophetically wrote in her diary: 'I wonder if doing this film with Sheridan will help you resolve some of those feelings, Gerry? I think you're going into battle unprepared.'[19] When asked in 2016 what she meant by this, Minty said, 'He still hadn't come to terms with everything. It [his arrest, conviction and prison experience] was still as raw as it must have been when it happened. I always felt he'd paused his life while inside and then didn't know how to un-pause it when he got out.'[20]

On 29 May 1992, Minty wrote, 'Gerry's going to have such a shock when they make this film.'[21] She explained this insightful entry in 2016:

> When your life is being interpreted by people who weren't there and who are glamorising it – when the world is looking at it, dissecting it – he wasn't ready for it. It was too close and too

painful, and film-makers cheapen it in a way. It's their livelihood. It's not yours anymore – they take it and own it. I think that's what I was talking about. He didn't realise. Mostly he didn't realise he wasn't ready. He refused to even look at how raw it still was. It was as though it had only happened yesterday. It chokes my throat just writing this and remembering how much pain he was in on a daily basis. How can you hand that over to Hollywood and be okay? As lovely as everyone was who worked on it, in the end they were still 'in the movies'.[22]

The friction between the two was becoming unbearable and in a last-ditch attempt to mend their fractured romance, Gerry persuaded Minty to go on a private holiday with him. Everything was on course. Then, a week before they were due to leave, Gerry received a telephone call from 'Carl' to say he had just been released from prison after serving an eighteen-year sentence for grievous bodily harm. His release put Gerry in a predicament because Carl had been a true friend from prison, so close, in fact, that he had often written to Gerry's mother while he had been incarcerated. Now that he was out, Carl had no means of supporting himself and nowhere to stay: a not uncommon phenomenon for ex-prisoners. Minty said that Gerry wanted to take care of his friend and felt obliged to bring him with them on holiday. In truth, Carl did not have to go with them: Conlon had enough money to put him up in a hotel, on full board, until he and Minty came back, after which he could have helped Carl, but that option was not taken up.

Predictably, the tension was exacerbated when Conlon allowed Carl to live in the Tufnell Park flat after coming back from the holiday. While the former prisoners were genuine friends, this was above and beyond the call of duty, especially given the delicate state of Conlon's relationship with Minty. Predictably, Carl became Conlon's minder. 'I used to try to persuade Gerry to travel to remote places with me, to show him a world far away from politics and anything he knew,' Minty said. She thought it would give him a rest and some peace and was convinced it would heal him. She also used to argue that she wanted to do more with her life than clubbing and taking drugs. On many occasions, his response was that his needs came first. 'Within a year of breaking up with him, I was living in a tiger research station in Nepal, taking stills, and had regained my health and sanity, whilst he was still partying and doing the same thing. He should have come with me,' she added.

When the break-up came in the autumn of 1992, there was no long-drawn-out quarrel, no finger-pointing, just sadness: 'I got a job away which I knew would give me the strength to finally leave him for good,' Minty said. 'I will never forget his face when I went. I picked up my bags at the front door and looked back at him, and he said: "You aren't coming back, are you?" and there was such sadness and resignation etched there. That was when we acknowledged that it was over.'

Despite the break-up, Minty and Gerry met each other regularly. On 11 January 1993, Minty recorded: 'Gerry started to talk about marriage and babies again.'[23] When asked how often Gerry had proposed to her, Minty said, 'He did it a lot. Makes me choke again thinking of it. But mainly I can remember him with his forehead on mine telling me how much he loved me and "I want to marry you and have babies with you."'[24]

Five years later, speaking of the possibility that he might eventually get married and have a family of his own, Conlon said:

> It's now getting to the stage where I'm gradually accepting these things are never going to happen to me. There were two women in my life, one was a journalist and the other was a camera assistant. Two beautiful women and I know my mother wanted me to settle down with either of them, but – and it wasn't because I didn't have feelings for them – it's just that the feelings didn't feel like love. Although I was extremely fond of them and the relationships were working and I think once they started to work I started to want it not to work and that, I think, is one of the symptoms of long-term imprisonment.[25]

That he started 'to want it not to work' is the self-denial of happiness, the rejection of deliverance from misery. If this is accurate, Conlon was once again flogging himself, declaring himself a sinner, and proclaiming that he was unworthy of God's forgiveness or a woman's love. A more discriminatory view could be that, as Minty pointed out, Conlon's needs came first. It is noticeable that in this and future interviews Conlon never named the women with whom he had had intimate relationships.

In 1992, Dr Adrian Grounds of Cambridge University carried out psychiatric assessments on eighteen men (including Conlon) who had been wrongfully convicted and sentenced in British courts. In his 1996 report, Grounds compared the mental state of miscarriage of justice victims to that of 'brain-damaged accident victims, or people who had suffered war crimes.' Grounds added that, 'It often made them impossible to live with.'[26] Was Conlon impossible to live with? He told Siobhan MacGowan as much: 'He said afterwards he couldn't be with anyone. He couldn't commit; he wasn't able. He had too much going on, too much un-worked-out stuff.'[27]

While Conlon had a talent for retaining friendships with most of his former lovers, he had little or no talent for staying in relationships. Marion McKeone observed: 'When his relationship with Minty ended, he was heartbroken. He really felt it, and it seemed to launch him into a downward spiral of drink and drugs. But he didn't want to get help. I think he was terrified of what would happen if he tried to deal with the pain and the guilt of what happened to his father. So he ran away.'[28]

Forlorn, out of control, fleeing from help, Gerry Conlon was at large in a world of trouble.

Six

On 4 December 1992, it was reported in the press that Daniel Day-Lewis would be playing the role of Gerry Conlon in the forthcoming film. Day-Lewis's agent, Julian Belfrage, said: 'We are in the middle of settling the deal at the moment, but he is definitely going ahead with it. It will be a controversial film, but that is the sort of role Dan is attracted to. He knows Gerard Conlon; they have met several times and talked a lot, so it will be very realistic.'[1]

It was no secret in the movie-making industry that Day-Lewis did not want to act in any more films. Indeed, he was resisting acting in *The Conlon Story*, so persuading him to take on the role had probably been Jim Sheridan's most significant achievement during the pre-production period. If, back in early 1991, Gabriel Byrne had visions of Johnny Depp or himself playing Conlon, Sheridan, who had a three-film deal with Universal Pictures, had eyes only for his left-footer. At face value, it seems that nudging Day-Lewis over the line was a carefully choreographed dance, orchestrated by the maestro.

In a press interview in the immediate aftermath of the film, Day-Lewis explained how the come-hither had been put on him to take on the role: 'I was knackered, and I made the mistake of coming to crash out in Shay's house for a few weeks. Shay started to tell me the Gerry Conlon story. At that point I needed to make another film like a hole in the head. But Shay's not a bad storyteller at the best of times, so within a few minutes I remember thinking, "Please don't tell me any more of this story," because I could feel the nagging compulsion beginning to drag me close to the story. Within a day or so of that, Gerry himself turned up. By that stage, even though I was still very, very tired, I realised I couldn't see any way of avoiding getting involved in the film. That was the beginning.'[2]

Day-Lewis later revealed, 'I spent quite a bit of time with Gerry before it had been decided between us that I was going to work on the film. Even if I had chosen to work in a different way, that choice had almost been taken away from me because Gerry's a very vivid character and he makes a strong impression.'[3]

Embarking on a film of the magnitude of *The Conlon Story* was a mammoth undertaking for Jim Sheridan. How, for example, did he ever hope to keep all parties to the actual drama happy? To Irish republican and nationalist purists, here was clear-cut evidence of Perfidious Albion once more crushing Irish innocents underfoot, and any dilution of British culpability would lead to Sheridan being condemned as a British apologist. Alternatively, to the British – especially the English press – Sheridan was making a pro-IRA film while the IRA was still planting bombs in towns like Warrington, where, on 20 March 1993, two children, Jonathan Ball and Tim Parry, were blown up in an IRA bomb attack. In his quieter moments, Sheridan must surely have grappled with questions that could soon be cascading his way: why did you invent a scene in the film in which an IRA leader firebombs a prison officer, or, why did you let the British government and judiciary off the hook? And then, from the opposite direction, what about the innocents of Guildford and Warrington, Jim? Where's their movie? It mattered little that Gerry Conlon had spoken out repeatedly against IRA violence: large minds are hard to find in the middle of a dirty war. And, if all that was not enough to tax Sheridan's brain at night, there was the not inconsequential problem of persuading Daniel Day-Lewis to sign on the dotted line.

Terry George had already demonstrated the benefits of long road trips when he had virtually imprisoned Gerry Conlon in his car, while they drove from New York to Key West. Afterwards George said that he had been 'able to get the father-son relationship'. Could that mechanism work again? Jim Sheridan may well have thought it worth a try.

Joey Cashman recalls being in Sheridan's house in Dublin with the film producer and Conlon in September 1992:

Jim's a force of nature, a driven man, and some people don't like him for that. I'm not one of them; I think he's great. He's a very clever guy and clever guys sometimes court jealousy. Daniel didn't want to do any more movies. He was finished with acting, but he wanted to be involved in it as a producer. He was a shoe-maker in Italy, did I tell you that? I love him; he's a real free spirit, you know? Where was I? Yes, Jim, this is really, really smart. Jim says, 'Why don't we drive over to where I made *The Field*? Just the four of us. We'll rent a car and drive over there.' Later, when he and I were on our own, I said to him, 'Why the fuck are we driving? Why not just take a train and relax in first class?' He said, 'Joey, what can you do in a car?' I shrugged and said, 'Talk, I suppose.' Jim said, 'Exactly. And if we go in a train, or meet in a hotel, someone we know is going to come over and sit beside us and fuck up the conversation.' So we hired a car, and Daniel, Jim, me and Gerry drove across Ireland to County Galway and stayed in The Great Southern Hotel in the centre of Galway City.

Cashman describes a pleasant trip, during which they visited Daniel's sister's cottage on the Atlantic coast. They also visited locations in the village of Leenane and then Aasleagh Falls, a scenic waterfall on the River Erriff, near where *The Field* was filmed, as well as Ireland's only fjord in Killary harbour. Cashman also recounts an altercation that occurred at a small, well-known hotel frequented by anglers:

Dan kept on about this hotel that his family had been using for years, and when we got there, me and Gerry were bursting for a piss, so we went into the reception and the receptionist gave us permission to use the facilities. When we came out, the owner stopped us and said, 'What the hell do you think you're doing, using my toilets?' And I politely told him we'd asked his receptionist for permission. The guy screamed at us to get out. So we went back to the car, and Dan saw that Gerry was upset and asked him what the problem was. Gerry told him what had happened and you could see Dan getting redder; he was going fucking bananas. And he pointed and said, 'Don't anybody get out of the car.' I did get out, but I hung back and didn't let Dan see me when he walked into the hotel.

I stood at the front door. Dan was confronting the owner. I heard him saying, 'You know who my family are. You know me. I'm gonna tell every fucking person I know about how badly you treated these people, and get them to tell every fucking person they know.' Then he said to the owner, 'Have you any idea who you've just insulted? Well, have you?' The owner shook his head. 'That was Gerry Conlon. Of the Guildford Four.' Then Dan shook his head and I headed back to the car before he saw me. You could see the anger in him when he came out. He drove up the road like a maniac.

A few miles down the road, I couldn't hold it and burst out laughing, and I said to Dan, 'I thought you were going to kick seven shades of shit out of that fucking obnoxious bastard!' Dan stopped the car in the middle of the road and looked at me. 'What? You saw that?' And I told him I did. It was one of those situations, you know, where you don't know what's gonna happen next. 'Seven shades of shit? Why seven?' Dan said. I wasn't going to give him a lecture on shades of shit, so I just shrugged my shoulders. Then he burst out laughing. I don't know why we all laughed, but once he'd started, we couldn't stop.[4]

When the four men returned to Dublin after more than a week on the road, Day-Lewis was ready to sign up to play the lead role in *The Conlon Story*.

For Conlon, the blurred concept he had three years earlier was coming into focus. Or was it? He saw this film in terms of black and white, a straightforward rendition of his life with little or no regard being given to the complex political and social undertones that permeated his story. Others had a different view.

Acutely aware of the nuances of making a highly controversial film, Jim Sheridan and Terry George saw a lot more to *The Conlon Story* than Gerry Conlon. Sheridan had had to persuade Universal Pictures that his film would make the studio money or they would not have parted with a penny. Yet Sheridan and George were convinced that the miscarriage of justice element of the story was not structurally strong enough to carry the film to box office success. Conlon, on the other hand, believed differently; he thought that the miscarriage of justice constituent *was* the heart of the film and that, accordingly, it would stand on its own two feet. And therein lay the difference between the professional filmmaker and the idealist. Moreover, Conlon made a fundamental error of judgement in thinking this was *his* movie and therefore he could influence its direction when, in fact, Universal Pictures had completed their deal with Jim Sheridan, not him. Sheridan had control of the script, not Conlon. It was Sheridan's film, not his.

For the next four months, Gerry Conlon was Daniel Day-Lewis's best friend as the actor familiarised himself with Conlon's accent and mannerisms. Daniel and Pete Postlethwaite, who was taking on the part of Giuseppe Conlon in the film, accompanied Gerry to the Falls Road in west Belfast, where they met the rest of the Conlon family. While in Belfast, the pair received voice coaching for their roles.

The Conlons have fond memories of Pete. They also found Daniel charming and respectful, and he kept in contact with Gerry's mother, Sarah, long after the film had been released. Gerry too remembered Daniel with considerable affection:

> I went into jail when I was just turned twenty, so when I came out at thirty-five, I still had that twenty-year-old mentality. I wanted to party all night. I wanted to go out and do things a twenty-year-old did, even though I was thirty-five. I would be coming back from the pub at five or six in the morning with a crowd of Irish guys, just to have another few scoops, and Daniel would turn up and just sit and watch. But he was such a great, great guy, you know? He was just a lovely human being. You know Gabriel [Byrne] had a vision of Johnny Depp playing the part because he was so close to Johnny Depp – they had the same agent in LA – and I met Depp when I went out there: an absolute gentleman you know, and still a good friend.[5]

Conlon also said that he felt he could tell Day-Lewis anything: 'I haven't even told my mother the real story about prison, but I felt so secure in his presence that it just came flowing out of me. He's extremely shy until you get to know him; then he can be quite a character. He was quite proud of being a member of 'F Troop' at Millwall [a violent

London football hooligan gang]. We used to go out and have a few beers, and suddenly he just used to let out this roar, 'WALLAH', just something he invented.'[6]

Day-Lewis is renowned for absorbing the character of the person whom he is acting. It was reported that in Michael Mann's *The Last of the Mohicans* he had lived off the land for six months and learned to hunt and skin animals. In order to experience what Gerry Conlon had gone through during his interrogations, Day-Lewis insisted that he be locked up for three days and nights with only meagre food and water in a cold and empty room of the then defunct Sir Patrick Dun's hospital on Grand Canal Street, Dublin, and that he be interrogated by real-life Special Branch officers. He also requested that he be deprived of sleep and continuously verbally abused. In addition, he lost thirty pounds in weight so that when the film was released he would look more like Conlon.

For Day-Lewis, meeting and acquainting himself with Gerry Conlon, absorbing his Belfast accent and mannerisms, was business – not altogether unpleasant business – but business nevertheless. From a professional viewpoint, there was always going to be a closing of the account: 'There comes a point when you have to go your separate ways,' Day-Lewis said, 'and maybe even more so for me because Gerry's presence, so to speak, in my company, was a constant reminder to me of the fact we were not the same person.'[7]

It is possible that Gabriel Byrne was gifted with the forbearance of a saint. On the other hand, he may well have been smouldering – arguably with some justification. He had been Conlon's first contact with the film industry in March 1990 and had been instrumental in getting the project off the ground. Byrne had assumed that this would be his film and he would be one of the leading actors. Now it was Jim Sheridan's film, and Byrne had been relegated to the relatively minor role of psychotic IRA prisoner Joe McAndrew.

At the pre-production reading of the script in March 1993, Gabriel Byrne walked off the set, never to return. While self-respect and honour may have been the driving forces behind this drastic course of action, Byrne's departure was nonetheless a surprise to everybody, not least Jim Sheridan, who, insiders say, was fuming at Byrne's peremptory departure.

Did Byrne see his meagre involvement in the film as a comedown and could he not bring himself to accept it? According to Byrne, his non-appearance in the film was a matter of schedule adjustment:

> I felt the story had the makings of a great movie. It's a story of incredible injustice which forced people to look at what is justice. It is also appalling that Giuseppe Conlon's name had not been cleared, and I thought it would help if there was a movie which told the truth about what happened. Harold Pinter expressed great interest in writing the screenplay, but I had met Terry George, an Irish writer who lives in New York, and who knew Gerry Conlon, and I asked Terry to write the screenplay. When it came to a director, I thought immediately of Jim Sheridan, whom I'd just finished working with on *Into the West*. Jim and I agreed that we would produce the film together.[8]

As the shooting of the movie was coming to an end, Byrne diplomatically explained that all through the pre-production period Sheridan and he had been busy getting the logistics in place. He went on to say that there was an understanding that he would not be acting in the film because he had committed to another project, *Prince of Jutland*, the schedule of which conflicted with *The Conlon Story*. But if Byrne thought there had been an understanding, Jim Sheridan thought differently: up until the moment of the walk-out at the actors' pre-production reading, he had believed that Byrne was playing Joe McAndrew.

Filming began on 8 March 1993 in the Sheriff Street area of Dublin. It was an exhilarating time for all concerned. For Jim Sheridan, it was a return to his roots: 'It was great to work down there because my mother and father used to bring all the kids from Sheriff Street down to the baths.'[9]

Gerry Conlon was on fire, the blood in his veins bubbling with excitement. He wanted to be on-set to savour his triumph, and he was hammering away at Joey Cashman to drive him to the film location. Cashman was wary and tried to dissuade his friend from his intended course of action. He told him it is standard practice that if you are not working on-set, you should not be there, and if by some chance you do end up there, you should not, under any circumstance, speak to the director or the actors. But Conlon was impulsive and dismissed Cashman's advice. Not go down to the set of *his* film? Was Cashman mad? Without *him*, there would be no film. Without *him*, there would be no set. He was going – with or without Cashman.

The film crew had been shooting a scene that was based in working-class Belfast in 1973, where local women were bashing bin lids against the concrete ground to alert the IRA that the British army were in the district. By the time Conlon and Cashman arrived, there was a lull in the filming. Gerry and Joey stood behind the set for a while, but then Gerry quickly got bored, walked onto the set and started talking to everyone – especially the make-up girl. Jim Sheridan did not like that. Neither did Daniel Day-Lewis.

Day-Lewis had been in-role even before the shooting of the film had started: he was constantly speaking in Belfast slang, and his traits reflected those of Conlon's. Then the real Gerry Conlon shows up and, being his usual effervescent self, makes his presence felt. It was off-putting for Day-Lewis and a distraction from the serious business at hand.

A row broke out between Conlon and Sheridan over the former's behaviour. For Sheridan, this was a determining moment: either he was in charge of this film or Gerry Conlon was, and if it was the latter, there was not much point in him remaining on the set. Writ large, Sheridan could not tolerate anarchy on his film shoot. Left with little choice, he dramatically threw down the script and trotted slowly off the set, pursued by Cashman. Conlon remained.

Out of Conlon's earshot, Joey Cashman, in what was possibly his finest moment, stopped Sheridan and said to him, 'This film is not about Gerry Conlon; it's not about you; it's not about me. It's about miscarriages of justice – full stop.'[10] It was a strong message that carried with it an inherent plea to continue with the production. It was a message that Sheridan was eager to hear because, facing a loss of control of his set, he knew that he was in a precarious position: how could he, for example, simply turn his back on a multi-million-pound film? He would have become unemployable in the film industry.

According to Cashman, Sheridan looked at the ground as if he was making a tough decision, rubbed his chin, and said, 'Yeah, yeah.' Finding himself thrust into the role of a mediator, Cashman told Sheridan that he would persuade Conlon to leave the set. When Cashman returned to the set, he quietly said to Conlon, 'Can you get in the car, please?' Knowing that he had upset Sheridan and disrupted the film shoot, Conlon acquiesced.

The weight of what had just occurred between Conlon and Sheridan led to Cashman's car becoming a no-talk zone for a time. Then, while driving around Dublin city centre, the diet of silence was thrown out the window and Cashman blurted out: 'You fucking asshole! You can't do that.'

'Course I can,' Conlon retorted. 'It's my fucking film. It's about *me*! Me! Fucking me! Don't tell *me* what I can and can't do about *my* film.'

'I don't give a fuck if it's about your granny,' Cashman snapped back. 'You still can't go up to a fucking director and give off to him like that.'[11]

If Cashman expected Conlon to show contrition, he was gravely mistaken. Once again, Conlon asserted that *In the Name of the Father* was *his* film and that without *him* there would be no film. And yet, in the cut and thrust of argument, Cashman detected a change in Conlon's tone: a subtle realisation that the world, as he had known it, had been altered. In forcing Conlon to leave the set, Sheridan had asserted his absolute authority over all aspects of the film. Demonstrably, in the struggle for power, Conlon's ethical mandate had been eclipsed by Sheridan's practicable one.

Later, Sheridan, Conlon and Cashman met and the director explained that Daniel was concerned about the effect that Gerry's being on-set would have on the other actors. Day-Lewis was being tactful: the reality was that there was no room on-set for two Gerry Conlons. According to Cashman, the real Gerry Conlon understood, or at least said he did. Sheridan offered that, since Cashman was an extra in the film, he could be Conlon's 'eyes and ears' and report back to him what was happening. He also offered Conlon nightly viewings of the 'rushes' (the scenes shot on that particular day). In another conciliatory move, Sheridan said that Conlon could come on-set, as long as Day-Lewis was not in the scene. Here was savoir faire on a scale that the great statesman Klemens von Metternich would have appreciated – Day-Lewis was in just about every scene in the movie!

Jim Sheridan may well have had many sleepless nights during the making of the film. He must surely have realised that he had to be careful not to push Conlon too far because the Belfast man had the potential to undermine the film, perhaps fatally. The nightmare scenario for Sheridan was that, for whatever reason, Conlon would go public and declare that the film was riddled with factual errors and it did not depict the true story of what had happened to him and his father while they were in prison, or the relationship they shared. In that situation, the film would lose its moral authority and would be depicted as no more than a piece of fiction. On the other hand, Conlon was well aware that if Sheridan walked away from the film, no one else would make it. So each man needed the other.

To his eternal credit, Sheridan managed to keep Conlon on board, although Conlon would later say: 'I'm bitter about the film basically because I was excluded from the making of a film about my life. Everything was pulled out of me beforehand. I had to make myself available to Terry George, Jim Sheridan, and Daniel, all picking my brains all the time. I was almost like a commodity, this disposable thing.'[12]

Irony is seldom a stranger to great drama, and the absence of Gerry Conlon and Gabriel Byrne must have haunted the set of *In the Name of the Father*. To their credit, neither of the men who had first come up with the idea of the film in 1990 aired their grievances in public at the time.

At London's Bow Street court on 11 June 1991, three of the police officers who had interrogated the Guildford Four – former Detective Chief Inspector Thomas Style, former Detective Sergeant John Donaldson, and former Detective Constable Vernon Attwell – were acquitted of conspiracy to pervert the course of justice. Not only were they acquitted, but the magistrate, Ronald Bartle, issued a gagging order on the press to the extent that all they could report were the names of the defendants. The next day's *Daily Mirror* editorial was scathing: 'He [Magistrate Bartle] gave his reasons [for the gagging order] in an argument that we in the *Daily Mirror* think outrageous, disgraceful and a travesty of justice that will make Britain the laughing stock of the world.' The editorial went on to say: 'It is very difficult not to have contempt for a system of justice that is not only blind but dumb as well. God knows, we have suffered enough from the fools of law and order who have brought us to this humiliating position. Who will judge the judges?'[13]

In January 1992, the High Court reversed Bartle's decision following a judicial review taken by the Public Prosecution Service, and the charges against the three former detectives were reinstated. However, they were again acquitted at the Old Bailey on 19 May 1993. Trial judge Mr Justice Macpherson made it clear that he wanted to see an end to any further enquiries into the treatment of the Guildford Four at the police's hands: 'It seems to me that maybe the public and certainly those involved on the legal side would not wish to gaze at the entrails of the case further.' Outside the court, the solicitor for the former police officers, Scott Ingram, said: 'My clients are obviously grateful to the jury for its verdict, the right verdict.'[14]

In such a high voltage trial, opinion was always going to be at variance, no matter what verdict the jury brought in, and this was illustrated by Alastair Logan, the solicitor for Paddy Armstrong and Carole Richardson, who commented: 'The only chance the police had was to put Armstrong and Conlon on trial. That's what they have done. It was a nonsense of a criminal trial. It is a con-trick, a dirty lousy con-trick. It is an attempt to rewrite history, an attempt to reconvict the Four.'[15]

Paddy Armstrong was equally scathing: 'It was a whitewash from start to finish. I sometimes wonder why they bothered to go through the motions.'[16] Armstrong's contempt for the proceedings was heightened by the fact that the former police officers chose not to give evidence on their own behalf, or to offer any explanation for fabricated, handwritten notes of interviews which had formed a crucial evidential link in the convictions of the Guildford Four in 1975. The same discredited notes had also formed part of the basis of the Four's successful appeal in October 1989.

That same day, Kenneth Clarke, the Home Secretary, was speaking at the Police Federation's conference in Blackpool, and he echoed

Justice Macpherson's sentiments, saying that he welcomed the verdict, at which point the delegates, whose federation had funded the former detectives' legal costs, burst into unrestrained applause. Clarke then pressed home the government's line: 'I am glad to see innocent people acquitted. It enables everyone now to get that particular incident back in proportion. I hope now we can put this whole unhappy episode behind us.' Clarke's was wishful thinking: the Guildford Four case was about to go stratospheric.

Things were far from going stratospheric for Gerry Conlon by the end of the summer of 1993. He was once again directionless and, as ever when life turned sour, he was looking enviously at his ordered existence in prison, even going so far as to strip his flat of modern furniture to the point where it resembled a prison cell. Then there was Giuseppe: the very name haunted him. Friends reported that Gerry had started smoking 100 cigarettes a day for no other reason than that he 'wanted to get emphysema and suffer as Giuseppe had suffered.'

Meanwhile, Jim Sheridan was showing sterling leadership on-set. Emma Thompson, who played Gareth Peirce in the film, said of the producer/director: 'Working with Jim was just great because he's got the writer as well with him on the set, so everything changes all the time. So, therefore, because it's in a state of constant change, Jim is a kind of constant bubbling, flowing volcano. You know, it's like having a baby volcano on the set.'[17]

Shane MacGowan had written and submitted four songs for the film. Sheridan was not particularly keen on MacGowan's songs, but the title of one of them, 'In the Name of the Father' resonated with him: 'I liked the title *In the Name of the Father* because it implies "and of the Son". The idea behind the film is that the father figure becomes a kind of decimated symbol when you have a crushed culture. Once you destroy the father figure, the figure of authority, then you haven't got a society. It's about trying to restore a man who believes in non-violence and peace and will suffer rather than inflict suffering.'[18] Clearly Sheridan wanted to transform Giuseppe into a Christ-like figure, one who was innocent of any charge and who carried his cross with great dignity to his Calvary. It was powerful imagery that should have gone far to counter the accusation that this was a pro-IRA film. But, even before the last scene had been shot, the British Establishment and press were on the attack. Leading the charge was Tony Judge, spokesman for the Police Federation in Britain: 'This is an incident which is in the public eye. Anyone can make a film about a miscarriage of justice. It is a free society. But the film should not be a simple propaganda exercise, which could work to the benefit of terrorists. It should not overlook the horror that led to the police investigation.'[19]

On hearing this, Jim Sheridan, in what was possibly *his* finest moment, retorted: 'They said that about this film? My reply to that is: "We'll handle it more carefully than they did their prosecution." It's definitely not a film that condones terrorism.'[20]

The London *Evening Standard* had already fired a salvo at Oscar-winning actress Emma Thompson: 'It is not, perhaps, the wisest decision a British actress could make, coming in the wake of her Oscar. Given the recent spate of IRA bomb outrages, it is being suggested that she has been naive in taking on such a provocative role.' The malicious attacks against Thompson would become a feature of the British press after the film was released.

By the end of November 1993, the editing and cutting of *In the Name of the Father* had been completed. The film had taken fourteen weeks to shoot, five more than expected, and it came in over budget at $13 million. Would *In the Name of the Father* be applauded or denounced? The answer is – both.

Seven

Lauren Bacall, Carly Simon, Naomi Campbell and Spike Lee were amongst an audience in New York's Museum of Modern Art where the film was previewed on the evening of 3 December 1993. Other viewers told reporters that *In the Name of the Father* was 'overwhelming', 'powerful' and 'incredible'. Jim, Daniel, Pete Postlethwaite and Gerry were in attendance. Conlon told reporters that he was 'very happy' with the film.

Shortly before the preview, Conlon and Cashman had a private viewing of the first edit of the film in a London cinema. Conlon was nervous. A scene which Conlon found particularly harrowing was where Giuseppe had only recently been charged with possessing explosives and had then joined his son in a prison cell for the first time. In *Proved Innocent*, Conlon tells of how the prison authorities had turned down his application to see his father, and that he saw him only a week or so after arriving in Winchester Prison, during a court remand hearing. Gerry wrote that during their brief conversation Giuseppe had asked him, 'Is there anything to this, son?'

'I haven't done this. I'm innocent, Dad. I'm as innocent as you.'[1]

While Sheridan and George do relate this exchange in the film, they go much further by creating a scene in a cell in which Gerry launches a vicious verbal attack on his father about whether or not he had 'fouled the ball' during a game of soccer. From the outset of the film, Sheridan had made no secret of his intention to lay bare the generational and ethical gap between father and son, and in this scene he weaved his enhancements into an imperfect tapestry, with Gerry berating Giuseppe: 'I walked into the dressing room. You followed me in there and said again, "Gerry, did you foul the ball?" All the fathers were there and they were laughing at you, calling you "Poor Giuseppe".

And I ran out, and I hid, and I wrote your name on the ground. Your stupid Giuseppe fuckin' name. I wrote it in the dirt and I fuckin' pissed on it. I pissed on it!' Gerry's relentless denigration of Giuseppe in the scene continued: 'And then I got Holy Communion, and I thought I was eating you alive.' This was followed by Gerry saying: 'When that mad bastard out there [outside the cell] threatened to shoot you, I was happy. I swear to God. Honest to God, I was happy. I was delighted. You know why? Because finally it was all over. It was over!'[2]

When Gerry Conlon saw this scene, he was horrified and left the cinema, with Cashman following in his wake. He was very distressed. He had known this scene was in the film because he had received several copies of the screenplay, one of which is dated '20/02/93', two weeks before filming began. On the inside cover of this script, in red felt-tip pen and in Gerry's distinctive handwriting, is written, 'Pages 47–49'. Nothing else is written on the green cover. Those exact pages contained the scene that caused him so much anguish. Demonstrably, even before the filming had started, Conlon recognised that this was a scene that warranted his close attention. While both Jim Sheridan and Gerry Conlon admitted to having rows over the film, the 'pissing' scene was not rewritten to take in any concerns that Conlon may have expressed.

To understand Sheridan's portrayal of the father-son relationship, it is important to realise that the director had a strained relationship with his own father, Pete. When asked at a later date how his father had reacted to *In the Name of the Father*, Sheridan said: 'It's very interesting 'cause he was always the very negative guy in the movies, like *The Field*, the father ["Bull" McCabe] was bad. In the plays I wrote, sometimes I put my own father's name in it and my mother would go to the theatre and say, "That's him!"'[3] Did Jim Sheridan see the deification of Giuseppe and his demonisation of Gerry as an act of personal atonement, a reversal of his earlier depictions of his father? What was the truth; what exactly was Gerry Conlon's relationship with his father?

On 23 November 1979, two months before he died, Giuseppe, who was in Wormwood Scrubs, received a letter from Gerry, who was in Winchester Prison:

Dear Dad,

I was very glad to hear from you again. I hope by the time you get this letter that you are out of hospital. I know you don't like it there and I know you did not want to go in. They took you in, didn't they? Don't worry as they are going to come unstuck.

I hope that your chest is a bit better and you are keeping alright. I'm doing alright, so don't you worry, okay? Dad, the only reason that I would go back to the Scrubs is you, otherwise I'm not interested as it's finished there and I'm not going to take any more shit off them. You are all that I'm interested in, nothing else.

Dad, have you had any word about the parole? I'm praying very hard here that you get it. Dad, everybody knows we are innocent including those dirty stinking shitheads at the Foreign Office. Don't worry, the truth will come out in the end. What makes you sick is the way they try and run down other countries like Russia and China for jailing people, when these animals are doing it all the time – these rats have more faces than Big Ben.

Dad, Roy Walsh [former IRA prisoner] was moved the week before I went to Wandsworth. A guy told me that he went up to Hull. He's a great lad. Dad, have they still got them locked up all day? Are they not giving the wing any association yet?

I had a letter from Mum the other day along with your letter. She must still think I'm in Wandsworth, as that is where the letter is addressed to. Dad, I wrote to her from here over a week ago. I hope she got my letter. I will be writing to Mum after I'm finished writing to you, and you know that I always write to Mum every week without fail.

Dad, you know how much I love and miss you and I would do anything for you, you know that. Dad, don't let it get you down, we have got to keep fighting to prove our innocence and we will, so keep your chin up, okay?

Dad, there is not a single day goes by without me thinking of you. You are the world to me. No one could have had a better dad. As long as I can breathe then I will do everything I can to prove our innocence. I love you more than life itself, you are everything to me.

Dad, is anyone giving you any sort of bother? Dad, can you find out if my gear is still in my cell and if so can you check it to make sure it is still alright, as I still don't trust the screws, especially after what they have done – know what I mean?

Dad, tell everyone that I was asking for them, especially The Doc, Liam, and Billy. I hope they are keeping alright. By the way, has anybody new come since I've been gone? Let me know.

Dad, I love and miss you with all my heart and I'm praying for you, that you will get parole this time. Let me know if you get any word – don't forget. I love you.

Good night and God bless,

Your loving son,

Gerry

P.S. Write soon Dad.

Shortly after receiving this letter, Giuseppe went on hunger strike, having been refused parole. Gerry said:

We wrote to each other, and I gathered he had been taken into the prison hospital on hunger strike. I was frantic with worry. I wrote home to my mother telling her to tell my father not to be silly and to come off it right away. My father had gone on hunger strike as he was at his wit's end at being turned down for parole again. I kept desperately trying to tell him to come off, that everything would be all right. Suddenly I lost my reason. I smashed up my cell, made a pile of everything burnable on the mattress and set it on fire.[4]

The distressing effect that the pissing scene had on Conlon did not go unnoticed by some of his friends. Siobhan MacGowan had been pencilled in to play the part of Gerry's girlfriend in the London squat in the film, but passed on the offer because she was working for Van Morrison at the time and had to go on tour with him to America. Siobhan remembers Gerry's reaction to the film's release:

Gerry was excited when they were going to make the film, but he was pretty distraught before it came out. The scene that really upset him was the one where he was pissing on his father's name. He was absolutely distraught about that. He cried on my shoulder for two hours. I don't think they took it out. He was telling me about it before the movie was released. I think he thought when the movie was going to be made, in all the excitement of it, he saw it as having a purpose or something, but when it actually came out he saw it as not a true reflection and he knew that things had been put in. He was hanging out with Hollywood characters, and you get caught up in the high. He started taking a lot of drugs, and I think then the crash was huge. I think the crash, going from the lowest of the low, to the highest of the high, and then BANG. Real life sets in. The film hadn't solved the problems. It hadn't solved the deeper issues for him and that's when he came face-to-face with them.

When asked why Conlon had publicly endorsed the film if he believed that it was not a genuine manifestation of what had occurred or of his true relationship with his father, Siobhan said: 'Gerry was always the diplomatic type; if it was for the greater good, he would do it. He spoke to people he didn't like. He did things that were anathema to him, but they had to be done. He always said to me: "It's about the bigger picture."'[5]

Another scene that greatly disturbed Conlon involved the prisoners watching, appropriately enough, Don Corleone counselling his son Michael in *The Godfather*, in the prison canteen. Amid shouts for prison warders to stop walking in front of the movie projector, IRA man Joe McAndrew set fire to a prison officer with a makeshift flamethrower. In the film, Conlon doused the prison officer's burns and then confronted the IRA man: 'That was a good day's work, McAndrew. That was a good day's work.'

'Get away from me,' McAndrew had answered tersely.

'Will you not look me in the eye when I'm speaking to you?' Conlon said. 'I know how to look people in the eye without blinking as well. In all my godforsaken life, I've never known what it was like to want to kill somebody until now. Ah, you're a brave man, Joe. A brave man.'

The Joe McAndrew character in the film was based on Joe O'Connell – the IRA leader whose unit had carried out the Guildford and Woolwich bomb attacks. In real life, Gerry Conlon acknowledged to anyone who was interested that Joe O'Connell and the Balcombe Street IRA men had done everything in their power to put things right. In *Proved Innocent*, Conlon said of O'Connell:

> So I survived Durham and then found myself in Gartree. On the first day I arrived I met Joe O'Connell standing in the corridor talking to all the Irish prisoners. A very strange moment. This was the guy who'd led the Balcombe Street unit who'd bombed Guildford and Woolwich for which we were serving sentences. I spoke first and I said to him: 'I'd like to thank you for all you've done to help us and telling the truth.' Joe said to me, 'We told the police the truth. We told the truth at the appeal court. But you know yourself, Gerry, this is just an example of British justice in relation to Irish people. But if there's anything I can do to help in any way, I'll do it.'
>
> I'd just like to say that I know a lot of people would find this strange, but I found Joe O'Connell to be a nice guy. At times I could see that Joe was suffering, knowing myself, Paddy, Carole and Paul were serving life sentences for something we didn't do and he had done.[6]

In the Name of the Father had its Irish première in the Savoy Cinema in O'Connell Street, Dublin, on 16 December 1993. As the stars, production crew and guests made their way into the nearby Gresham Hotel for a champagne reception, a jazz band played *When the Saints Go Marching In*. Having marched in, the saints were addressed by the then Minister for Arts, Culture and the Gaeltacht, Michael D. Higgins, who hosted the reception. Paddy Armstrong and Paul Hill were there. Bono and U2 were there. Gerry Conlon had flown in from Jamaica, where he had been on holiday with his new Brazilian girlfriend, Liz.

Sitting demurely in a corner was Sarah Conlon with her daughters, Bridie and Ann, and some guests from the Lower Falls, including Roy Walsh, who had been sent to the punishment block in Wormwood

Scrubs in 1979 because he noticed that Giuseppe was having breathing difficulties during a heatwave and had refused to allow the prison officers to close Giuseppe's door. There, alongside them, was Sister Sarah Clarke, who had worked tirelessly on behalf of Irish prisoners in British jails. Also in attendance was Don Baker, who had taken over the role of IRA man Joe McAndrew from Gabriel Byrne after 'unresolved problems with Jim Sheridan caused him to withdraw from the project'.[7]

When questioned by reporters on the way into the cinema, Gerry Conlon said that his father would have approved of the film and that the film 'had no heroes, including the English judiciary'. It did not take long for the £100 cinema seats to fill up, although Gerry Conlon's seat was vacant for most of the screening; he spent most of the time in the foyer rather than in the auditorium.

When the credits had finished rolling at the end of the film, Jim Sheridan took to the stage to tumultuous applause. This was Sheridan's moment and he was entitled to the kudos, given that he had produced and directed a powerful and important movie. With the applause ebbing, he began calling up people to the stage. He called up his father, Pete. The film-maker's eyes followed the elder Sheridan as he made his way to the stage. His memory of this moment remains vivid:

> He's coming up on stage, and he walked up, and he got a big clap, and he hugged me, and in this ear [points to right ear], he said, 'I love you.' I pushed him back and looked in his eyes 'cause I'd never heard that before. I just looked at him for a while, and the audience kept clapping. Pete Postlethwaithe told me he was crying at the back. The audience went … it went that far [makes a hand gesture], the emotion … that's fuckin' 500ft. And he was dead two weeks later [clicks fingers], like that. That's mad.[8]

Soon the stage began to fill with film stars and rock stars, designers of varying hues and celebrity ex-prisoners. Three of the Guildford Four – Gerry, Paddy Armstrong and Paul Hill – took to the stage. The fourth, Carole Richardson, had refused an invitation to the film, as did Paul Hill's and the Maguires' solicitor, Alastair Logan.

After the showing, limousines brought the guests to none other than the state rooms of Dublin Castle, the seat of English rule in Ireland for 800 years. Given the subject matter of the film, somebody had a sense of humour.

Amid the fine food, the expensive wines, the clink of celebratory glasses, the pats on the back and the discreet lines of cocaine, stood the Conlon entourage. Gerry's sister, Ann, a down-to-earth, working-class Belfast woman, was not overly impressed by the 'faces' and the grandeur: 'I was starving 'cause the meal at the reception was only fish, and I don't like fish. And there were no spirits, only wine and beer. I only drank vodka at that time, and I wanted a half-bottle.' They decided to go back to David Loughran's room in the Gresham Hotel, where Liz, Gerry's girlfriend, inquired about David's arm. Rather than explain thalidomide, he told her it was blown off when he had to throw a bomb for the IRA. Horrified, Liz asked about his other arm, and David explained that that too was blown off three months later when he threw another bomb. With his girlfriend suitably distracted, Gerry sneaked out in search of friends and substances.

Ann said: 'David kept ordering drinks and every time a waiter came up with the order, David insisted they take a drink, and it ended up that he left no fucking waiters downstairs to do the room-service – they were all in David's room, blocked – singing their heads off. The next morning we were all dying and hung-over, and when the lift came down, Yasser Arafat and his bodyguards were in it. And I said, "Can we go up to the penthouse with you, Yasser?" But he just smiled. I don't think he understood a word I said. When I told the Gerry fella about Yasser, he didn't believe me, and then he cracked up when he found out it was true. He'd have made it his business to run into Yasser. He was like that; he liked meeting interesting people.'[9]

While in Ireland, Arafat addressed the Joint Oireachtas (the legislature of Ireland) Committee on Foreign Affairs and, in a clear message to those involved in the embryonic peace process in Northern Ireland, he said: 'Peace can solve all the issues. All the wars didn't solve anything in the interests of the people. For every revolution there must be an end.'[10]

To no one's great surprise, *In the Name of the Father* broke box office records in Ireland, grossing £306,351 in just seven days. In the United

States, in just four cinemas over a five-day period, the film grossed $165,801. By 7 January 1994, the press was reporting that the film was being nominated for a host of Golden Globe awards, including Best Motion Picture.

While many people found the film riveting, others were critical of it. Michael Dwyer of *The Irish Times* was one of the disappointed. In a review entitled 'In the Name of Truth', Dwyer wrote: 'I saw this film not once, but twice. On the first occasion I left the cinema almost speechless with anger. This reaction was provoked not by the tragic story which had just been acted out on the screen, but by the fact that a film, which purported to show how the suppression of truth had led to a truly terrible miscarriage of justice, could present as the truth an almost wholly fictional account of what had happened.' While Dwyer went on to sympathise with Sheridan's dilemma of trying to compress a fifteen-year story of injustice into a two-hour film, he was nonetheless relentless in his criticism: '*In the Name of the Father* managed to change almost everything, from the personal story of the relationship between Gerry Conlon and his father to the events that led to the Guildford Four's release. If this is poetic licence in the name of art, well, it makes me feel better for journalism.'[11]

Tom McGurk, the RTÉ presenter who produced *Dear Sarah* and who had made a television programme highlighting the injustice meted out to the Guildford Four, was scathing on RTÉ's *Pat Kenny Radio Show*:

> The film is riddled with inaccuracies and omissions. The profound reason for making this film is that it's a true story. It's a short step from the inaccuracies to the implications of the film. At the moment in Britain, in many established circles, the word is that of course these people were guilty but they got off on a technical argument.
>
> The real depth of the conspiracy is not represented in the film. At the end of the day this conspiracy, which lasted fourteen or fifteen years and involved hundreds of people, at the end of the day you say a couple of bent coppers put this together. The message of this film will be most welcome in the very places this conspiracy emanates from. They got off very lightly.

Gerry Conlon, also on the *Pat Kenny Radio Show*, rebutted McGurk in no uncertain terms: 'My whole family is happy with the film. I don't know why Tom is defending British policy and the British judiciary.' Tom was not defending either, and Gerry's strident defence of the film is challenging, even in the context of him sagaciously looking to the 'greater good'. No one knew better than he that the film was 'riddled' with inaccuracies, which, in some instances, were tearing out his heart. And yet he stood up, sword drawn and defended the movie.

In a later interview with Emer Mullins of *The Irish Times*, Conlon expanded on his support for the film, saying that his family 'loved the film'. He also answered an attack that had been made on him by his uncle, Paddy Maguire, of the Maguire Seven, who said that Gerry Conlon 'should be put back in prison for what he has done to my family'. Maguire also blamed Conlon for his family's incarceration. Conlon's response was that this was 'victims attacking victims. I think Paddy Maguire and his family have become very bitter about the whole situation. They have continually blamed me, which is true to an extent, but I mentioned their names after they were already mentioned and they were going to prison anyway. I think in some way they are bitter this film has been about me and my father, rather than about them.'

When asked about his relationship with Jim Sheridan, Conlon replied, 'We had several arguments at different times but everything worked itself out.' At the end of the interview, Conlon said: 'For the past four years I've had nightmares. But when the movie was finished, it was like my father's ghost said to me, "You've fulfilled your promise." It was like an exorcism had taken place.'[12]

But the nightmares were far from exorcised. How could they be? Conlon later admitted: 'Barring the premières I attended [where he spent most of the time outside the auditoriums], I've never really sat down and watched it from start to finish. You see, Pete Postlethwaite is so like my father; every time he turned to the camera it was like my father was looking into my soul.'[13]

Speaking to reporters shortly after the film was released, Paul Hill was both supportive and critical of it: 'I don't mind the poetic licence. It's something you have to accept. It is Hollywood after all, and these things have to be done. That doesn't mean it isn't legitimate to do a movie about these innocent people having been put in prison. But I would have been harder. I would have highlighted the roles of the judiciary, the DPP and the prosecuting counsel. They are the people who have come out of this whole sorry saga scot-free.'

Jim Sheridan wasn't getting away without brickbats either. If he had hoped that he could nullify any potential criticism from the British press by including the scene where Joe McAndrew torches the prison officer, he was mistaken. Many of the major newspapers, especially in England, pointed to the acquittal of the three former police officers in the Guildford Four case and then asked if the many inaccuracies in *In the Name of the Father* did not call into question the innocence of the Guildford Four.

The esteemed broadcaster and author Robert Kee, who had written a book called *Trial and Error* which championed the cause of the Guildford Four, said that the film 'tells so many lies that it makes its central proposition about a miscarriage of justice questionable'. Kee's change of tack was damaging because it represented an intellectual stab in the back to the cause of the Guildford Four.

Kee's volte-face aside, the most controversial critique appeared in the *Sunday Times* on 13 February 1994. In this article, entitled 'Like Father, Love Son', columnist Julie Burchill lashed out at, amongst others, the citizens of the United States, about whom she wrote: 'Despite the fact (or because of it) that the US, like no other nation, was built on genocide, it just loves to point a wagging finger at big bad England for oppressing cute liddle Oirland. This is very strange when you consider the historic lack of willingness on America's part to grant any real or lasting independence to the countries in its "back yard". But then logic was never America's strong suit.' Ms Burchill then pointed her own wagging finger at several people involved in the making of *In the Name of the Father*, starting with Jim Sheridan, who had explained the importance of the father-son relationship. Ms Burchill contemptuously dismissed Sheridan's lengthy exposition in four words: 'Thank you, Dr Freud'. The journalist then described Sinead O'Connor as, 'Sinead "I Am An Abused Child Of Ireland" O'Connor.'

What had Ms O'Connor done to incur Ms Burchill's wrath? On the face of it, the Irishwoman's crime was that she had recorded songs for a film that Ms Burchill did not like and had described as a 'failure'. Still, compared to the bile that Ms Burchill fired at leading actress Emma Thompson, it could be said that Sheridan and O'Connor got off lightly: 'But oh dear, oh dear. There's always one who has to spoil it for everybody else, as the teacher used to say at school, and that one is, you guessed it, Emma Thompson. Fast becoming the most mannered, irritating, actress since Meryl Streep, her performance is a national scandal. Questions should be asked in the house. As the saint-like lawyer who wins the Guildford Four their freedom, she seems like an amateur actress auditioning way out of her depth.'

She may not have realised it at the time, but Julie Burchill was dangerously close to being way out of *her* depth when she wrote of Gerry Conlon: 'His awe-inspiring pacifist father never forgave him for implicating him in his forced confession (which Gerard doesn't do here) and he died before there was a reconciliation. They didn't stay in the same jail, let alone the same cell.'[14] If this was hyperbole, it was also potentially libellous hyperbole because Gerry Conlon had *not* implicated his father in the Guildford or Woolwich bombings; he had no idea that his father would be coming to London to find him a lawyer. Unfortunately for Ms Burchill, Gerry was an avid reader and such was his ire at the tone of her article, he took a libel action against the *Sunday Times*.

Also reading Burchill's article was Terry George and he responded in the 7 March issue of the *Los Angeles Times*: 'Surprise, Surprise! Some British lawmakers don't like *In the Name of the Father*.'

Perhaps because they did not have the same emotional investment as their British counterparts, reporters in the United States tended to be more sympathetic. *Time Magazine* reviewer Richard Corliss wrote, 'By the end of the movie, whether or not you're a member of Sinn Féin, the Brits' brutality towards the Conlons will get your Irish up.' One of the most insightful reviews came from Candice Russell of the *South Florida Sun-Sentinel*: '*In the Name of the Father* is a deeply stirring film that lessens the moral authority of the I.R.A., English soldiers in Ireland, the British police, and the British government.' In the dramatic title, 'The Good Guys, The Bad Guys, And The Irish Guys', reviewer Francis X. Clines of *The New York Times*, wrote: 'The film ... takes on not just official British justice but also some of the sociopathic excesses of I.R.A. combatants; not merely injustice, but relative injustice as it glints on the modern cutting edge of a struggle rooted in centuries of Ireland's campaign to be free from English colonialism.'

Gerry Conlon had made the most of his fifteen minutes of fame after his dramatic exit from the Old Bailey in October 1989. But that all changed with the release of *In the Name of the Father*. Now he was a 24-carat, 24-hour-a-day celebrity – the bearer of a face that would be instantly recognisable wherever he went. And if Gerry thought he had problems before the film, they were as newly hatched butterflies on the wing in comparison to what lay in front of him. He didn't know it then, but a gluttonous monster was beating on his door.

Eight

In 1974, Conlon had gone to London to get away from the chaos that was enveloping Belfast and Northern Ireland. With the prospect of sleeping rough on the streets beckoning, he broke into a prostitute's flat in Bayswater and stole £700 cash. Reflecting on this night of thievery, Conlon said: 'I am not proud of what happened that night. Exactly one year and one week after the break-in I was convicted by an English court on five counts of murder, of causing explosions and of conspiracy, and handed a sentence which the English judge said should be not less than thirty years. In reality breaking into a flat was the most serious crime I ever committed.'[1] Another reality was that Gerry Conlon had never lost his adolescent appetite for reckless behaviour.

In October 1992, he and a group of friends were at a party in his Tufnell Park flat. Conlon recalled: 'I was back in at my flat with a whole bunch of people and these two guys were in the bedroom, with the tinfoil out, smoking. I remember one of them saying: "Walk away, Gerry, you don't need this. It'll fuck up your life." But I was cocky. See, after doing all that time in solitary, I honestly didn't believe that anything could be stronger than me. I was wrong.'[2]

The person who had tried in vain to persuade Conlon to 'walk away' said: 'I didn't want him to take crack 'cause I knew how fucking lethal it was. I pleaded with him to leave it out. I fucking begged him and I've never begged anybody for anything in my life. And he said, "If it's good enough for you, it's good enough for me." Then he asked me if I had any [crack] and I said no. I had some in my pocket but I wasn't giving it to him. I didn't want that responsibility. He found his way to it eventually, but not through me.'[3]

Four years later, reflecting on his drug addiction, Conlon said:

> I always sorta dabbled with ... I don't call them drugs, I call them ... I call them escapism. If you're not happy with yourself, if you're not happy with the environment you live in, you need an outlet, and after *In the Name of the Father*, I certainly needed an outlet. I couldn't handle the notoriety, the fame, the recognition. But it's also a very personal thing. I've touched hard drugs from time to time, and they have been my way of escaping from reality and the situation that I found myself in. It was almost as if I could levitate to a higher level, and pick my own little cloud, my own little space, to drift along and to come back with a different way of thinking. You know, it's like when you read a book and you close it, you think about what you've read. When you do drugs from time to time, you experience things and it leaves its mark.[4]

Gerry did more than do drugs 'from time to time'. According to Shane MacGowan, he 'was taking ridiculous amounts of crack. He used to put a big mould of it in his pipe, and you only need a tiny bit, you know, really. He'd have put two weeks' worth in one pipe and then passed it around.'[5] Joey Cashman said he bought crack 'by the block, cut it up, and gave it away to whoever was with him.' A man, known to Conlon and Cashman, said: 'He came to me one Friday night with fifteen grand and asked me to get him crack and after getting the fifteen grand of crack, he came back on Sunday asking for a loan. I gave it to him.'[6]

In a typically frank interview with reporter Seán O'Hagan in 1997, Conlon faced up to his crack addiction, saying that it brought him into contact with some very unsavoury people: 'Looking back, I can see that I wilfully put myself in danger. I'd go to the worst places where people had a crack pipe in one hand and a gun in the other, mad places full of low life, places where I didn't have to be because I had money. But I'd go in there and buy stuff and start handing it out free.'[7] The 'mad places' to which he referred were crack houses in Brixton, south London. It was as if he relished playing Russian roulette, as if death would be the final release from the prison of a self-deprecating, apocalyptic mind. But why? What was so wrong with his life? He had a hefty bank account; he had caring friends in London and the United States; he had a loving family in Belfast – so what drove Gerry Conlon to such recklessness? Conlon's psychotherapist, Barry Walle, said of his drug-taking and devil-may-care attitude: 'It appears to have many functions: it is ego restorative; he gets a fix for the way he feels; it confronts fear; it's an outlet for his rage; it's distracting and probably the closest he has come to feeling alive.'[8]

Conlon himself spoke of running around the streets of London with a McDonald's bag crammed with £30,000 cash as he sought out a dealer to buy crack. He knew he was in a mess: 'I was like every junkie. I became slippery, paranoid. I would go to the Bank of Ireland in Seven Sisters on a Monday and draw ten grand. On Thursday, I would take six grand out of the one in Finchley. One week, I ended up in the Bank of Ireland in Balham. That's how mad it got.'[9] What is astonishing is that Conlon's fellow addicts must have known he had access to large sums of money and that he frequently carried thousands of pounds on his person. Yet he was never mugged. Perhaps the addicts reasoned that there was no point mugging Father Christmas when you can get high with him.

Those who knew him best are convinced that Gerry's personality was his saving grace. Joey Cashman remembered a night in London, in 1994, when he heard a series of loud thuds on his front door. Peeking out the window, Cashman saw that it was not the police. When he opened the door, he was confronted by an enormous Yardie (a person of Jamaican lineage), complete with dreadlocks. In the giant's shovel-like right hand was a small white guy, whose feet were dangling in mid-air.

'Is this piece a shit yours?' the Yardie asked.

'What's he done?'

'Is he fucking yours, or not?'

Joey hesitated, not knowing whether or not to claim 'Juno', who was a close friend of Gerry's. 'He might be.'

The Jamaican jabbed Joey in the chest with his finger. 'Then *you* might owe *me* his seven fucking grand drug debt.'

Gerry, who had been standing listening, out of view on the stairs, shouted, 'Put him down, ya big fucker!'

In that instance, Juno was released and fell to the ground as the indignant Yardie pushed past Joey and marched up the hall.

Gerry exclaimed, 'Eddie-man!'

'Gerry-man!'

The two men hugged and slapped each other heartily on their backs.

Joey let out a sigh of relief. Juno contemplated making a run for it – until Eddie-man turned around and told him: 'Get the fuck in here, you little shit.'

A bottle of whiskey and a joint were produced, and the two ex-prisoners sat at a table, reminiscing about the good old days in Brixton Prison. The drug debt was left to another time.

Barry Walle could also see the strength of Conlon's personality and his ability to make friends:

> Gerard does, however, have considerable assets. He is a great wordsmith and raconteur. He has a lot of rich and coherent ideas in his head for poems, lyrics, scripts and stories. His phenomenal memory allows him to store them. He is knowledgeable about the production of films and popular music and knows a considerable number of the main players in the related industries.
>
> He is considerably concerned about others who are victims of injustice or prejudice, and he is a fervent anti-racist. He has been actively defending others and grieves for them when he can do nothing. Socially skilled, insightful and perceptive about others, he is actually a warmer, richer man to his friends and family than he knows or feels.[10]

It took Gerry Conlon only six weeks to work his way through the £120,000 he officially received for *In the Name of the Father*, the vast bulk of the money being spent on crack cocaine. Had he read the American critic and humorist Dorothy Parker, he would have realised that, 'Hollywood money isn't money. It's congealed snow, melts in your hand, and there you are.'[11] There he was, as energetic, engaging and as charming as ever. He attended openings of the film around Britain, smiled for the cameras, shook hands with and hugged the right people, gave very convincing press interviews, and to all intents and purposes, portrayed himself as someone in absolute control of his life. In private he was a ghost ship, an emotional wreck and a crack-user: a man who thought nothing of shaking hands with God and the devil at the same time.

Who would have thought, in March 1989, that exactly five years later, Prisoner 462777 Conlon would be attending the 66th Academy awards ceremony in the Dorothy Chandler Pavilion in Hollywood? Or that he would be the subject of a film that was in the running for seven Oscars?

In the Name of the Father had been a runaway success since its release, with audiences across the world flocking to see it. That it had been nominated for seven Oscars had surprised Conlon. That it would not win any Oscars did not surprise him because a leading member of the film crew had whispered in his ear, before the Awards ceremony, that the Academy was looking in another direction. Conlon could handle that: he was used to disappointment and he took this encounter with his old nemesis in his stride.

The film's entourage flew over to Los Angeles on the same plane: Jim, Daniel, Pete, Gerry, Joey, and other prominent members of the film crew, and they stayed in the Chateau Marmont Hotel on Hollywood Boulevard. While everyone else was put up in single or double rooms, Gerry was housed in a deluxe cottage. People may have differing opinions of Jim Sheridan, but he knew how to massage an ego. What he did not know was that neither Conlon nor Cashman had come prepared for the Oscars. 'We didn't have any dicky bows,' Cashman said, 'and somebody told us we wouldn't get in without them. This was the day before the show, you know, so we ran around L.A. looking for somewhere to hire out black suits. We went into this place, and the guy said, "I've two left." Those were the last two black suits in L.A. And we tried them on. They were okay; they fitted. We were lucky.'

On the night of 21 March, two limousines pulled up at the Chateau Marmont for the Irish contingent. Sheridan, Conlon, Cashman and Terry George climbed into the back of the same limousine. Knowing that they would never again be back at an Oscars ceremony, Conlon and Cashman were determined to make the best of it. As soon as the vehicle had taken off, Cashman asked if the driver would stop at a drinks store so he could buy Tequila. It would be surprising if warning bells did not ring in Jim Sheridan's head at Cashman's request. Giving these two boys access to bottles of hard liquor on the way to the biggest awards ceremony in the film-producing world? Prudently, Sheridan said he did not think that was a good idea. Predictably, Gerry sided with Joey: 'If Joey wants to stop at an offie, we stop at the fuckin' offie.' The limousine stopped at a drinks store and several bottles of Tequila were bought. Not too long after that the fun began. Conlon and Cashman stuck their heads out the top of the limousine, started shouting and waving to pedestrians in the streets and guzzled down their bottles of Tequila as if tomorrow was for saints and suckers. There was a huge queue of limousines waiting to pull up outside the Dorothy Chandler Pavilion.

Cashman said: 'We were off our heads before we even got there, and Jim was really embarrassed by it all. Just before we hit the red carpet, Jim managed to get Gerry down, and then he almost had to sit on him to keep him from going back up again!'[12]

Mustering all the decorum at their disposal, Conlon and Cashman got out of the limousine. While Sheridan was being interviewed by the press, no one was paying Conlon any attention, so he went up to the podium where only the top stars are interviewed and introduced himself to a television producer. Soon after, with his Tequila-drinking buddy standing alongside him, Conlon gave a very coherent interview during which he endorsed the film.

It was an open secret that it was going to be Steven Spielberg's night. His films *Schindler's List* and *Jurassic Park* had been nominated in fifteen categories between them, with *Schindler's List* the favourite to take the Best Motion Picture and best director awards. In the end, *Schindler's List* won seven Oscars, including, as expected, Best Motion Picture and best director. *Jurassic Park* won three.

The Oscars ceremony lasts for approximately four hours. Conlon and Cashman found the whole thing excruciatingly boring, so after two hours they retreated to the toilets for the remainder of the ceremony, where they wiled away the time smoking crack cocaine. Then, realising they were hungry, they left the building and searched the neighbourhood for a restaurant. People who had been desperate to get into the Chandler Pavilion could not believe their eyes: here were two people in black suits, with admission passes, and they were eating in a Mexican restaurant instead of attending the ceremony! Some offered the two Irishmen money for their passes, but they refused.

The two made sure they were back in the Chandler Pavilion before the ceremony ended – just in time to join the first of the night's parties: the Governors Ball. Cashman had fond memories of the event:

> Afterwards, you just walk out the door and there was a party in the building, or connected to it. It was really big, and the public had no access. There was loads of booze and champagne and all that. There was plenty of good stuff to eat there, you know, caviar, smoked salmon, grilled shrimps. I like that sorta stuff. So me and Gerry dug into that. I saw Bruce Springsteen and I asked Gerry if he wanted to meet him – which he did – of course he did. I'd met Springsteen before when The Pogues were supporting Bob Dylan in '89, I think it was '89, and Bruce and I were amongst a crowd who were backstage, waiting to meet Dylan. I don't know how, but Bruce knew I was with The Pogues, and he asked me for a shot of Tequila, which I gave him. Not a big thing, but he remembered when I reminded him of the incident, and he was only too pleased to meet Gerry.
>
> So then we gatecrashed the different parties for the rest of the night, and we ended up back in our hotel and all these women stripped off and jumped into the pool. I stripped off and jumped in, and Gerry jumped in after me. We'd great craic. I'll tell ya – it certainly beat going down to the local. Like, I can look back and if someone asks me, 'Where were you at the weekend?' I can say about that weekend, 'I was at the Oscars.' Know what I mean?[13]

Marion McKeone, aka Granny Clampett, had worked as a courtroom advisor during the filming of *In the Name of the Father* and had met Gerry in Hollywood. After the all-night partying, she spoke to him:

> He was nowhere near reconciling himself to what had happened to his father, and he told me the burden of guilt he carried was

exacerbated by a sense that he was 'cashing in' on what happened. Nothing could be further from the truth, but he was realising that the book, the interviews, the fame and the film, while they helped to raise awareness about the injustices that had occurred, weren't going to change what had happened to his father. He was always blaming himself, and he couldn't see that he was as much a victim of the police corruption and the injustice as his father was.[14]

Undoubtedly, Gerry Conlon was an achiever: he set himself targets and went about reaching them with almost evangelical fervour, but the one thing the son couldn't achieve was absolution for the death of the father because the only person who could give Gerry Conlon absolution was Gerry Conlon – and that was not an option.

The *In the Name of the Father* party flew back to Ireland the day after the Oscars. For Gerry Conlon, the party was over; the curtain had come down: the Guildford Four man had got his film made. Unlike Cashman, who clearly enjoyed the occasion, Conlon looked back on the experience with a sense of an ending and with heightened apprehension: 'I wasn't prepared for normal life outside prison, and I definitely wasn't prepared for celebrity life. It all came crashing down when I came home from Hollywood on the plane the day after the Oscars and I knew it was over. I was on my own again and I suddenly felt more alone than I ever did in prison.'[15]

Nine

On the day after the Guildford Four had walked out of the Old Bailey, the British government had appointed Sir John May to lead a public inquiry into the convictions of the eleven people charged with the Guildford and Woolwich pub bombings.

Sir John bared his teeth in July 1990 when he forwarded to the government his *Interim report on the Maguire Case*. In this report he criticised the trial judge Sir John Donaldson's handling of the Maguire Seven case and questioned the credibility of the forensic evidence that had been presented to the court. What is more, he recommended that the Maguire Seven case should go back to the court of appeal. When this occurred, the court of appeal quashed the convictions of the Maguire Seven, on 26 June 1991.

It was looking good for an even-handed report until, on 30 July 1992, Sir John met the Home Secretary, Kenneth Clarke, and the Attorney General, Sir Nicholas Lyell, and at that meeting a decision was taken that Sir John should not *publicly* examine the roles of senior police officers, lawyers and those involved in the Guildford Four convictions. The grounds put forward for this fundamental departure was that evidence, which may have been given in public to Sir John's inquiry, could have proved prejudicial to the defences of the three police officers who had been charged (and subsequently acquitted) with attempting to pervert the course of justice in the Guildford Four case. So, from being a public inquiry where evidence submitted by all parties to the inquiry was open to scrutiny, it went to a closed session, where only Sir John May could put questions to Crown witnesses and hear their responses.

Alastair Logan, the solicitor for the Maguire family, and Carole Richardson and Paul Hill, had always been highly critical of the move from a public inquiry to a closed court: 'The consequences of that [closed session] was that neither the defendants nor their legal representatives were entitled to be present or to know what evidence may have been given to him [Judge May].' Suspicions of an establishment cover-up were further aroused when the British government slapped a 30-year embargo on the secret evidence given to Judge May. Commenting on the embargo, Logan said: 'We have no explanation, firstly as to why it [the embargo] was changed [to 75 years], or any explanation as to why it should be embargoed anyway. After all, it was a public inquiry. I don't feel that justice is seen to be done if there are secret deals going on, secret parts of Sir John May's Inquiry, and secret documents held by the government.'[1]

Gerry Conlon believed that he knew why the embargo had been imposed and extended: 'The government knew, right from the start, that we were innocent. They knew we had nothing to do with the IRA, but they didn't care. That's why they have a 75-year immunity order on our case. Because they want all the people involved to be dead before they release our files.'[2]

Chris Mullins, the Labour MP who had campaigned on behalf of the Birmingham Six and the Guildford Four, said what many people were thinking, that Sir John's inquiry had been 'nobbled'.[3]

Amongst those who would not now have to face the court of public opinion were leading police officers Sir Peter Imbert, the then Metropolitan Police Commissioner, and retired commander Jim Nevill, both of whom had heard from the mouths of the IRA leaders Joe O'Connell and Eddie Butler, that their unit – and not the Guildford Four – had carried out the Guildford and Woolwich pub bombings.

On 30 June 1994, four and a half years after his public inquiry commenced in a fanfare of judicial piety, and two years after it mutated into a secret court, Sir John May held a press conference at which he announced the findings of his inquiry.

Historically, anyone involved in contentious cases and inquiries will know that it is not unusual for judges to find fault with the authorities in one breath and absolve them of fault in the next: and so it was with Judge May. There were failings, he said, but it was impossible to say whether or not Surrey police had used violence and deprivation to obtain confessions from the Guildford Four. He also condemned the Surrey police for twice arresting a man who had presented himself to police and had provided an alibi for Carole Richardson. The former appeal court judge criticised prosecuting lawyers at the original trial for withholding vital evidence from the court, the substance of which showed that Crown Counsel had signed off on a list of alibi witnesses, which excluded Charlie Burke and Sister Power.

In 2016, the BBC put in a Freedom of Information request for access to Sir John May's Inquiry papers, which had been withheld from the public since 1994. Surprisingly, 6 files out of 760 were released. One of the redacted documents (redactions are initialled) was written by Felicity Clarkson, an aide to Sir John. Entitled 'Note of Discussion 28 July 1993', Clarkson wrote:

> On the *Burke* alibi point, it seems clear that Crown Counsel proceeded from May 1975 onwards in the belief that the defence knew about *Burke* as a potential alibi witness. In May they concluded that it was 'probable' [Clarkson's initials] that the defence knew what *Burke* might be able to say but were not relying on him because they also knew that it was destroyed by *Peter Henry Vine* [Burke's work manager, who had contradicted Burke by telling police that he had been drinking with Burke on the night of 5 October [1974], when the Guildford bombings were carried out] hence the absence of *Burke* on the alibi notice. Crown Counsel apparently did not consider the alternative explanation that the defence did not know about *Burke* at all.

Ms Clarkson's use of the word 'apparently' denotes a degree of scepticism – and she was right to inject doubt into the veracity of Crown Counsel's position because, along with Burke's and Sister Power's, Vine's name was also omitted from the prosecution witness list. Of course, the Crown knew of Vine's existence, but they kept that knowledge to themselves because they realised that if the defence had had access to Vine's statement, it would have alerted them to Burke's value. This non-disclosure of material witness statements by the Crown throws up a crucial question: How could Crown Counsel presuppose that Conlon's defence knew that it (Burke's alibi) would be 'destroyed' by Peter Henry Vine's when they had made it their business to conceal Vine's existence from defence counsel? By offering Judge May's Inquiry this absurd excuse for concealing Burke, was Crown Counsel not ensnaring themselves in a web of deceit of their own making? And even if Conlon's defence team had been made aware by Crown Counsel of Vine's and Burke's importance, how would they have gained by not calling Burke to the stand? At worst, Vine's testimony would have been preferred over Burke's. At best, Burke's would have triumphed over Vine's. If the latter, Conlon would have walked out of court. It should be noted that Conlon had no credible alibi; he had been so drunk and stoned on the night of the Guildford bombing that he could not even remember speaking to Burke in the hostel or trying to borrow money from him, so he would have had nothing to lose in calling Burke. The Crown's threadbare argument to Sir John May's Inquiry – that Vine's evidence would have 'destroyed' Burke's – was further undermined by none other than Judge May himself, who said:

> There are two reasons for believing that as between Burke and Vine, Burke is more likely to have been accurate as to the date. First, he [Burke] specifically described it [his recollection of events on 5 October] as being the day when he left the hostel and went to new lodgings in Harvist Road. The hostel records show his departure date as 5th October 1974. Further, Sister Power confirmed this in her statement taken on 22nd January 1975, which was between the dates of the Burke and Vine statements. Secondly, Vine's statement that on the Saturday which he was describing, Burke talked about his new lodgings where he had been for five or six days. If this is correct, the [Vine's] description cannot have been of events on 5th October.[4]

Sir John puts his finger on the crux of the matter, and his logic triggers the question: is it feasible that the Crown prosecutors were so dumb that they could not have worked out the timeline for themselves – as Sir John had – and reached the conclusion that Vine's evidence, far from seeing Burke's evidence 'destroyed', would have augmented it and led to Conlon's acquittal?

So, if we are to accept Judge May's reasoning, Burke's alibi evidence would have held up in court. This would have demonstrated that Conlon's admissions about bombing Guildford were bogus, by virtue of the fact that he could not have been in his London hostel with Burke and in Guildford at the same time. This being so, the trial judge would have had no alternative but to acquit Conlon of the charges and, given that the Crown was saying that the Four had acted in consort, the self-incriminating statements of Armstrong, Richardson and Hill would likewise have become redundant, and they would also have had to be acquitted. Alas, Burke's, Sister Power's and Vine's statements were never sent to defence counsel and thus were never tested in court. Sir John was nothing if not a friend to his friends, and he put these two critical faux pas down to human error rather than to a deliberate attempt to pervert the course of justice. At the end of the 'Note of Discussion 28 July 1993', Clarkson recorded: 'A finding along these lines [human error, rather than calculation] is consistent with the JCS [Prof. Sir John Cyril Smith QC] paper and with Sir John's clear view that Michael Hill is a good, straight, forceful criminal lawyer with a high reputation which he is very concerned to maintain.'

In relation to the distortion of Douglas Higgs's forensic reports, Sir John said:

> On 24th January 1975 Mr Douglas Higgs of RARDE made a statement linking the Woolwich bombing with other throw bombing incidents. That statement was not disclosed by the prosecution prior to the trial of the Guildford Four. It should have been. It was overlooked by all concerned. Counsel had it in their possession at the very beginning of their involvement in the case but by the time questions of disclosure were being considered by them they lost sight of its potential significance.[5]

Once again, Sir John was disposed to believe that there was no intention on Crown Counsel's part to hide damaging evidence from defence counsel. However, this assessment was contradicted in the starkest terms with the release of the formerly embargoed Sir John May Inquiry files to the BBC, in 2016.

In one file a reference is made to the forthcoming trial of the Balcombe Street IRA men in 1977: 'After April 76: Manuscript note by Mr Mathew [the leading Crown Counsel at the Balcombe Street trial] indicates request to Mr Higgs to redraft his statements of 24-1-75 and 19-2-76 omitting Woolwich'.[6] This mind-blowing revelation left members of the May Inquiry nonplussed, and this incredulity manifested itself in one of the formerly embargoed files released to the BBC:

> Why was Higgs asked to take Woolwich out of his statements? Should Higgs have agreed? I think we need to write to --- about this. Even Judge Cantley let slip at the Balcombe Street trial that he wasn't impressed with 'because I was told so' as a reason given by a senior scientist! (20:180F) Why, particularly when it became clear what the Balcombe Street 'defence' would be, were Higgs's earlier statements not disclosed to their [the Balcombe Street accused] solicitors?[7]

Given that the Guildford Four defence teams were kept completely in the dark about Douglas Higgs's differing statements and that, at the Balcombe Street trial, attempts had been made by the Crown to alter Higgs's statements, it is not unreasonable to conclude that the concealment and tampering with Higgs's statements may have been attempts to pervert the course of justice. This view is further reinforced by the non-disclosure of Sister Power's, Peter Vine's or Charlie Burke's statements to the defence at the Guildford Four trial. So, did the Crown orchestrate a fit-up of the Guildford Four?

Sir John's boundless benevolence extended to the point where he found no calculated deception in the prosecution's silence in regard to Charlie Burke when the trial judge, Sir John Donaldson, while addressing the jury, said that, although Conlon claimed to have an alibi, he did not have 'an independent witness to support him'. The fact that there were two independent alibi witnesses – Sister Power and Charlie Burke – the existence of whom was known only to Crown Counsel,

Gerry with his sisters, Ann and Bridie, outside the Old Bailey in London, 19 October 1989. All photos courtesy of *The Irish News*/Hugh Russell unless otherwise stated.

Gerry with his sisters, Ann and Bridie, outside the Old Bailey in London, 19 October 1989.

Gerry at home in Belfast with his mother, Sarah, just after his release, 1989.

Gerry signing copies of his book, *Proved Innocent*, in Belfast, 1990.

Gerry in Belfast, 29 October 2012.

Gerry at the grave of his father, Guiseppe, just after his release, 1996.

Gerry filming *How Far Home*, 1998.

Gerry and Ann Maguire outside the Houses of Parliament, showing their letter of apology from British Prime Minister, Tony Blair, 2005.

Gerry shows the media his letter of apology from British Prime Minister, Tony Blair, 2005.

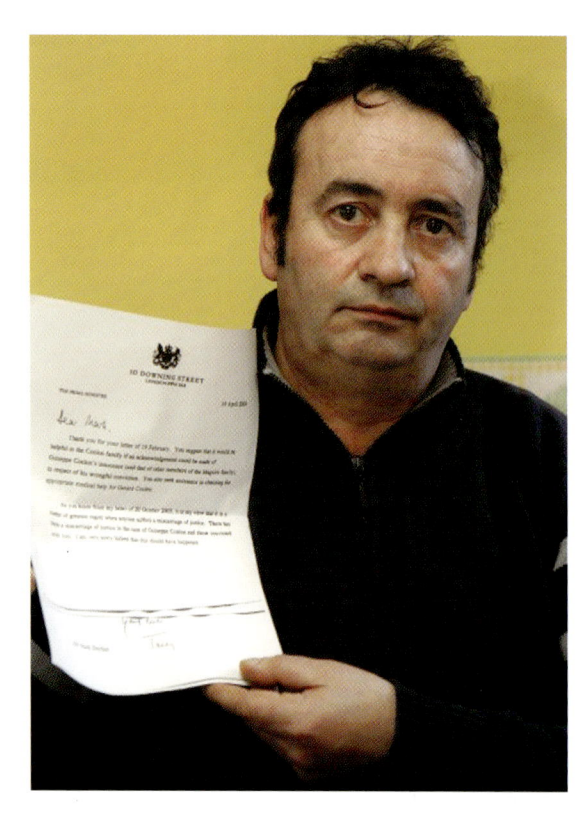

Gerry and Jim Sheridan meet before lobbying Irish Taoiseach, Bertie Ahern, to secure an apology for the Guildford Four and Maguire Seven, 2005.

Gerry with a photo of his father, Guiseppe, at home in Belfast, 4 January 2011.

Gerry in New York, 1990. Photo courtesy of the Conlon family.

meant that Judge Donaldson was misleading the jury, but the fault for that did not lie with him. Of all people, Lord Denning found fault in Judge Donaldson's approach to the May Inquiry. When asked if he thought it had been wrong for Donaldson not to appear before the May Inquiry, Denning said: 'I think he was wrong to do that. Oh yes, John Donaldson ought to have gone before the inquiry. In a way, by not doing so, the criticism is left unanswered.'[8]

There was an allegation that the judges who had presided over the Guildford Four appeal in 1977 did not give proper weight to the confessions of Eddie Butler and Joe O'Connell. Sir John dismissed this allegation as 'ill-founded', given that the appeal court judges had accepted the veracity of the IRA men's confessions. Judge May, like his fellow judges at the appeal court, deliberately ignored the contradiction in accepting the testimony of the Balcombe Street IRA men when they said that they had carried out the Guildford and Woolwich bombings, and then dismissed that same testimony when they professed that the Guildford Four were innocent. In his enthusiasm to absolve his fellow judges of any responsibility for the Guildford Four debacle, Sir John May deftly sidestepped some important questions: in light of the explosive new evidence from the IRA men, why hadn't the appeal court judges ordered a retrial of the Guildford Four in order to test the validity of the claim by the Balcombe Street IRA men that the former were innocent? And why didn't the appeal court judges order that O'Connell, Butler and the rest of the IRA unit be charged with the murders of the five victims in the Guildford and Woolwich pub bombings?

But Sir John was an understanding man. The septuagenarian exonerated the Metropolitan police for not investigating Butler's and O'Connell's claims that their IRA unit, and not the Guildford Four, had carried out the pub bombings. The judge said that it would have been better if the police *had* investigated the claims, before limply offering that he could understand their ignoring the confessions because Guildford Four man Paul Hill had admitted to having carried out the pub bombings. Obviously, Sir John thought it a tad irresponsible of the police to ignore credible confessions of mass-murder.

Finally, Sir John arrived at the crux of the matter: 'Nevertheless the miscarriages of justice which occurred in this case were not due to any specific weakness or inherent fault in the criminal justice system itself, nor in the trial procedures which are part of that system. I have no doubt that, contrary to the widely held view, there was no conspiracy to convict the Guildford Four or to maintain the conviction.'[9]

Alastair Logan said of Sir John's report: 'Four people spent fifteen years in jail for an offence they didn't commit and no one really knows why it happened.'

Chris Mullins MP said: 'It is a report that will satisfy only those responsible for creating the mess in the first place.'

Discordant voices could whinge and cry foul and lament about missed opportunities, but the judge had brought in the right result for the British Establishment. According to Sir John May, there *might* have been a few rogue police officers here and there, there *might* have been some prosecutors who had held back vital evidence in order to ensure convictions, but there was no 'specific weakness or inherent fault' in the British criminal justice system. The miscarriage of justice that saw four innocent people put behind bars for fifteen years just happened, and it was nobody's fault. And no one had been 'nobbled'.

Ten

While Gerry Conlon found refuge and comfort in the crack houses of London, his family suffered in silence. Ann McKernan knew her brother, and moreover, she was not afraid to confront him about his wayward behaviour whenever he periodically returned to his native Belfast: 'My mother was demented over him, whether he was in England or in Belfast, 'cause he went on benders and you didn't hear from him for weeks. I threw him out of our house in Albert Street. When he came in with the dark glasses on, I knew he was on the heavy drugs and I threw him out. My mammy hated him taking drugs. She was very, very worried about him and she used to say: "God forgive me – see when he was inside, I knew where he was. He's going to be found dead on me." And that was her whole worry.

'Gerry and my mammy hadn't a great relationship until later years. See, my mammy didn't know how to handle him, his mood swings, nor nothing.' When asked if Gerry was particularly moody, Ann replied: 'He'd have walked past my mammy in her bungalow and he'd have ignored her. And she came to me crying and she told me, and I said to him: "You can't do this to her. I'll make her put you out and you can come live with me." There'd have been none of that 'oul nonsense with me – and he knew it. It was terrible for both of them, and even more so because Gerry didn't know how to relate to his own mother.'[1]

Sarah Conlon did not deserve this angst. Neither, it must be said, did her son. Both had lived splintered lives, both had had to learn to live in relative isolation for fifteen years; both had changed. In his 1997 interview with Seán O'Hagan, Gerry explained the relationship he had with his mother: 'I've never been able to talk his [Giuseppe's] death through with my mother. I simply couldn't bring myself to do that. She's seventy-one now and, in a way, she has closed her mind to what happened. I can't do that, so it eats away at me.' Equally, Conlon found it difficult to speak to his sisters: 'I couldn't sit down and tell them about when I was in Strangeways, how they put glass in my food, how they ripped up family photos and urinated on them. I need to sit down with someone and have these deep-rooted feelings pulled out of me.'[2]

One person who had noticed the transformation in Conlon was Joey Cashman:

> When he started to take crack – I mean seriously take it, around about the time of the Oscars – he changed. At that stage we were beginning not to hang out because Gerry was starting to annoy me; he was starting to bring some awful fuckin' assholes – ex-cons, real scary bastards – back to his flat in Tufnell Park. And not only that, but he'd turned the place into a cell: his room had a bed, a table and a TV. I can't remember much else. It was like … if he couldn't go to jail, jail could come to him. Then I discovered I had a sex addiction. Gerry would come around but I was kinda like … anti-social. I never got out of bed for two years.[3]

While Joey was not going anywhere, the two men were nevertheless moving in different directions. It was almost as if Gerry wanted to dice with danger and court death, while Joey wanted to live and feed his burgeoning sex and drug addictions.

Shortly after returning from the Oscars, Conlon entered the most unstructured and destructive part of his life. He went to Belfast, where he rented a flat in Osborne Park, an affluent, politically neutral part of the city. Once again, he settled into his claustrophobic routine, rarely leaving the flat and passing his time dabbling in drugs, alcohol and gambling. But, of course, with the release of *In the Name of the Father*, things had changed. He could not go to the corner shop without being recognised and nowhere more so than in his native city. Whatever his reasons were for moving back to Northern Ireland, he was wise to be circumspect in Belfast because there were people living there, some of them paramilitaries, who would have regarded him as an enemy, and who would have had no qualms about hurting or even killing him. Looking back on this period of his life, Conlon said ruefully:

> It was almost like a dream and the dream was over and I was back in normality, but I was left with the millstone of *In the Name of the Father* around my neck. Every Irish person I met wanted to know was it accurate. I still walk around the streets of London, or Manchester, or Liverpool, and I'm still instantly recognised. So normality doesn't exist for me. I live in this crazy déjà vu world, where I float between the present and the past, and that's because people keep asking me about the past and when they ask me about the past it becomes very, very, vivid.[4]

While in Belfast, he was accompanied by Juno, the man who had been held up by Conlon's Yardie friend outside Joey Cashman's front door. Juno was a former millionaire who had lost his business, was smoking crack cocaine and was dependent on Conlon for his existence. 'Angie', one of Conlon's girlfriends, described Juno as 'a nice guy. One of those guys who'd come out smelling of roses if he fell into a bucket of shit. He had a successful call-girl agency in London and within a year of meeting Gerry, he'd fuck all! He lost his house and Gerry got all the girls! He used to say: "I had everything till I met Gerry; now I've lost all my girls to the crack and Gerry."'[5]

Conlon was not in the least domesticated, although some Yardies had taught him to cook Jamaican food when he was in prison. That said, he would barely bother himself to make a cup of tea, let alone lift the vacuum cleaner or put clothes in the washing machine. There is an argument that he suffered from an affliction not uncommon to pampered first sons: laziboneitis. In the absence of any attempt to cater for himself, his niece Sarah-Kate McKernan would come over to Osborne Park every day and clean her uncle's flat. She would also do the laundry, shopping and cook his meals. Occasionally Ann's former husband, Joe McKernan, would drop by to keep Gerry company at night.

For Conlon, living in Belfast was not altogether a penance. Slowly, inexorably, Northern Ireland was being given the kiss of life. Security restrictions that had been in place since 1969 were being eased in light of the IRA's cessation of military operations. People were starting to come out of their houses, out of their enclaves, out of their long winter of hibernation. The city centre, a depository for IRA bombs for over two decades, was opening up. Business people spotted opportunities. Gerry Conlon saw no reason to end his hibernation. He saw his father every time he shunted towards sleep. Belfast offered no more relief from the tyranny of his dreams than London.

Like most young prisoners, Conlon had been passionate about music while in prison; it offered solace and, after being released, it gave him a platform on which he could escape, albeit temporally, the pernicious voices that kept whispering in his ear. The annual Glastonbury Music Festival was a great draw for the ex-prisoner and, on 23 June 1994, he was getting in the mood by gorging on ecstasy tablets and smoking crack cocaine. Then he began to hyperventilate. Hypothermia followed. This led to a seizure which doctors diagnosed as a mild heart attack. 'I threw eight hundred quid's worth of gear out my back window and swore that I would never touch the stuff again. The next morning, I climbed over the neighbours' fence and got it all back.'[6]

On 8 September 1994, Conlon was due to attend an event to highlight the video rental release of *In the Name of the Father*, but this was cancelled when he was rushed to hospital with another minor heart attack. Conlon may not have known it, but cocaine and its derivative, crack, is a vasoconstrictor: it narrows arteries, including those to the heart, and when this occurs the heart tries to work harder, but it is not being given enough oxygen to function properly and it cramps up. Thence the heart attacks. Cashman put out a press statement saying reports that Conlon was seriously ill were inaccurate: 'This story's got completely out of hand. He was to do a tour of about seven cities, and now that's had to be cancelled. He's too ill to do it, but not seriously ill. It's just unfortunate it happened at this time.'[7] What was unfortunate, to put it mildly, was that Gerry had no guarantees, short of coming off crack cocaine, that this would not happen again. It did.

On 25 January 1995, the Dublin High Court ruled that a libel case being taken by Conlon against the *Sunday Times* should proceed to trial. At issue was the critique of *In the Name of the Father* that had been written by reporter Julie Burchill on 13 February 1994. The court heard that Gerry Conlon took exception to two statements in Ms Burchill's article about his father. Judge Murphy ruled that Times newspapers had not established that Conlon's case was unsustainable and said that it was a case for a jury to decide.

By February 1995, Conlon was in chronic disarray. He had no direction in his life, no cause to fight, no one to lobby, no female friend to pamper and no reason to get out of bed other than to escape from his nightmares. Then he met Angie in a bar in Kilburn. Perhaps it was because Angie was a crack addict, or it might be that he saw a part of himself in her, but he liked the convivial young lady who called everyone 'Darlin'' and spoke in an earthy Devon accent. She was down-to-earth, easy to talk to and, impressively, a good listener. What Gerry did not know was that Angie had the fire of Queen Boadicea in her belly – and a temper to match: no one, certainly not Gerry Conlon, would intimidate her.

Besides his flat in Belfast, Conlon also had a flat above a bookmaker's premises in Camden, and that was where the pair retired to after leaving the pub. Angie remembers that 'Gerry talked non-stop to me. I think it was because I got a raw deal and he could relate to that.'

During their all-night conversation, which inevitably entailed Conlon rehashing his experiences at the hands of the British Establishment, Angie told him that she could not look herself in the mirror. Conlon was aghast at this. In his worldly view – a view that would eventually stand him in good stead – the highest in society could fall by the wayside and often did, but that did not mean that person could not pick themselves up again. Angie gulped hard as she recalled Conlon's words:

'"What do you mean you can't look yourself in the mirror?" Then he took the mirror off the wall and held it in front of me. "Look at yourself." I couldn't. I turned my face away. See, I didn't like the person who'd be looking back at me. "I said, look at yourself." Nah, I wasn't going there. "Fucking look at yourself when you're told!" To shut him up, I glanced in the mirror. "What do you see?" he said.

'I told him straight: "A junkie. A worthless junkie."

"'What else?'

"'Nothing else. There's nothing else there.'

'Gerry had this stare. He kinda looked right into your eyes when he'd something important to say: "Hey, wee girl! You're better than most people. What the fuck's the matter with ya?" Then he told me I wasn't a worthless junkie: I was a junkie but not a worthless one. That seemed kinda funny. We laughed our heads off at that.

'He taught me a lot, he did. He took everyone at face value. It's a quality that not many people have. If he liked you, he liked you, and if he didn't, he told you to fuck off. But ... he built up my self-esteem.'[8]

And therein lay part of the conundrum that was Gerry Conon: he had met a young woman whose life was in turmoil, who was floundering in self-pity, and he stepped in with chivalrous gallantry to rescue her, telling her that she had worth, that she had a future. Yet he undeniably wallowed in his own despair and self-chastisement over the arrest and death of his father. This man was well read, his favourite book being *The Ragged-Trousered Philanthropists* by Robert Tressell (Dublin-born, Tressell's real name was Robert Noonan. His timeless classic is an exposé of the social inequality that existed in the town of 'Mugsborough', the fictional setting for the novel. The 'Philanthropists' are the workers, on whose backs the capitalists generate personal wealth). Moreover, Conlon had read the Bible several times in prison and could quote whole passages from it verbatim. Time and again, those who knew him spoke of Conlon's great sympathy for his fellow human beings. For the likes of Angie, he was a physician and a healer. Yet he chose to ignore the biblical proverb 'Physician, heal thyself'.[9] In the torture chamber of his mind, there was no room for self-healing or self-absolution.

Impulsive, given to trying to run before he had learned to walk, Conlon took Angie to Belfast the next day, where she stayed in his sister's house for two weeks. During her time in Bridie's house, Angie met the rest of his family. Ann McKernan was impressed with Angie's hard-boiled attitude: 'She went with Gerry for years. Every one of my girls, my mum: everybody loved Angie. She and him murdered one another, but Angie gave him as good as she got.'[10] When Ann was speaking of Angie during an interview, there was a smile on her face; it seemed as if she was proud of Angie for standing up for herself, for womanhood.

Throughout these two weeks, Angie visited Gerry's Osborne Park flat where she met Juno and where a few pipes of crack cocaine were smoked. It could have been worse.

Northern Ireland had always been spared the ravages of hard drugs because paramilitary groups, principally the IRA, saw the taking and supplying of drugs as deviant behaviour which must be eradicated – by execution if necessary. Thus it was, when the IRA announced a cessation of military operations on 31 August 1994, that the organisation turned its attention to drug dealers, and from 1995 to 2001, nine drug dealers were shot dead by an IRA front organisation called 'Direct Action Against Drugs'. There would have been few people in Northern Ireland taking crack cocaine, but Gerry and Juno were amongst them. While that would have been frowned upon by the IRA leadership, it is doubtful if it would have resulted in Gerry's execution, given his large public profile and the negative implications his murder would have had for the fledging peace process. But Juno did not share Gerry's glow, and he would have been at risk. Who on the island of Ireland, other than Gerry Conlon, would have given Juno a second thought if he had been murdered and dubbed a drug dealer? He would have been one more statistic amongst thousands.

With crack cocaine almost impossible to buy in Northern Ireland, Angie took on the role of supplying Conlon and Juno, making frequent trips to Belfast from England. She also sent crack across in the post! She was a central figure in what was a bizarre and sometimes violent relationship:

> It was a crazy time. We were taking so much crack. Gerry was seeing other women; he didn't hide it. And I was cool with that at the time; as long as I got crack. In London, he used to give me money to stay away, and he'd have been having a party round there, loads of girls, loads of sex. I used to phone him up and say down the phone: 'Running out of money, darlin'! Running out!' He'd say, 'Don't you come round here!' and I'd say, 'I'm on my way. Get one

of the girls to put the kettle on, darlin'.' Then he'd say: 'Don't you fuckin' dare come round here!'

I used to terrorise him, I did. I was his nemesis; I used to terrorise that poor man. He met his match with me. And every now and then, when he really pissed me off, I used to go around and smash all his windows. It was a mental relationship, but it was just how it was. My mum tried to get me sectioned 'cause I used to turn up at his house and wreck the place and rip all his clothes up.[11]

The madness of Angie was more than matched by Gerry's anarchy. Angie recalled: 'I came back one day and no one was in the flat. So I found out from a dealer that he was in a mate's house and I went round there and there he was with this Chilean call-girl called Beatrice. You must have heard of her: "Who's next, Beatrice?" No? Everybody knows her. I didn't mind him being with Beatrice, but I did mind that he tried to hide it from me.'

Conlon was a familiar figure for the call-girls of London. 'Sometimes you'd be sitting in the flat over the course of the day and it was like fucking Piccadilly Circus,' Angie said, 'there was that many call-girls coming and going. But he wasn't shagging them.' Surely that negated the whole point of sending for call-girls in the first place? Angie replied: 'Gerry didn't need to shag call-girls. He was a charmer; he could've shagged any girl he wanted. No. He'd bring them in, drive them mad with his stories, kick them out, and then bring in another one. My Gerry loved to talk, and we'd all heard his stories. I could've told you what he was going to say before he said it.'[12]

By 1995, Conlon had been awarded approximately £300,000 in compensation, most of which he had given away or spent frivolously. On top of that, there had been the money from his book deal and the £120,000 he had received for *In the Name of the Father*. Angie said of his spending:

> He was doing ounces and ounces of crack a day ... thousands and thousands of pounds. I remember one day he came home like the Pied Piper, with maybe twenty people behind him, and he said to

me: 'I'm buying them trainers in the morning. And I said: 'Fucking what?' They were a load of waifs and strays, people that looked like they hadn't been fed in weeks. He said: 'I'm taking them all out shopping and buying them clothes and trainers in the morning and I'm bringing them into McDonald's. Look at them; the poor bastards.' But that was just him; that was him. He wanted to give everything to everyone. Fucking hell, he was literally giving his money away. It was like he didn't really want it. He never passed a beggar in the street without dropping them a tenner – all the beggars knew him by his first fucking name! It was like he didn't really want the money.

When asked how Conlon could have spent £10,000 a day, Angie replied:

It's not that hard, believe me. When you're awake twenty-four hours – and Gerry tried to stay awake every minute of every day – and you've fifteen people in the house, and this one's saying she hasn't got enough money for her phone bill, and that one's saying he can't pay his rent and he's going to be evicted … people used to turn up with their tales of woe and their bills and he used to fall for the stories and hand out money as if he was Robin Hood. I used to go mad. When his money began to run out in London, before he got the final payment of his compensation, I said to him: 'Where are your friends now? We'll see who your friends are when you run out of money and you've got fuck all in your bank balance.' In the end, when all the money was gone, there was only me and him.[13]

That Conlon wanted to rid himself of the means to buy 'ounces and ounces' of crack probably made sense to him, and he said as much to Barry Walle. The problem with this strategy, if it could be called a strategy, is that not having access to tens of thousands of pounds does not guarantee that an addict will quit taking drugs; he or she may not take the same amount of drugs, but addicts usually find a means of feeding their habit. In addition to that, studies conducted by Dr Adrian

Grounds on miscarriage of justice victims discovered that the victims often received large lumps of money in compensation and that they gave significant amounts to family and acquaintances in an attempt to make up for the pain their loved ones had endured. Few if any of the miscarriage of justice victims had any appreciation of the value of money. Consultant psychiatrist Dr Paul Miller said that Conlon 'was given access to large sums of money when he lacked the mental capacity and emotional maturity to handle it'. The same could be said for all of the miscarriage of justice victims.

As Angie had predicted, when Conlon's money ran out in 1996, the hangers-on drifted off. Joey Cashman lent his friend £10,000. All that was left of the Conlon entourage was Gerry, Angie, Juno and another crack-user and friend named Alan. Money was too precious to be squandered on frivolities such as food. 'We lived out of bins for a while,' Angie said. 'Alan used to scour the hotel skips and supermarket bins of Mayfair for food. We actually ate very well but we spent all our money on drugs.'[14]

Crack takes no prisoners. Neither did Ann McKernan: 'He was home in Belfast and he tortured me for a chain my Uncle Hughie had given me. It was valued at £1,000. He tortured me and I let him have it, and he sold it for crack. He hated taking crack; he hated taking drugs, but he couldn't get off them at that time.'[15]

Angie felt that Conlon used drugs as an attempt to escape his nightmares:

> He had these awful nightmares. The whole time I knew him, the whole time, every night, horrible nightmares. He was haunted, he was, but he never really let anyone see that. I saw that because I was in the bed next to him. Even when we didn't have anything to do with each other, I'd still go down to Plymouth and get in the bed with him. The pillows would be green after a week or two. He'd need new pillows because he used to get such bad night sweats, and the nightmares were terrible: squealing, shouting out, 'Stop it!' and, 'Get off me!' All the time. All the time. But he never told me about it. He told me about the police station, what happened, about the gun and the police threatening to shoot his mum and

everything, but he never told me about the nightmares. I dunno, I think it was somewhere he couldn't go, but in his sleep it took him there without his consent. And I think that was what a lot of the drugs were about because then he wasn't sleeping, he was awake. He was haunted, bless him. He was haunted.[16]

Eleven

In January 1996, a reporter for *The Observer*, David Rose, wrote about the legal consequences of the Guildford Four convictions being set aside:

> To destroy what was left of the old regime in criminal justice required five words. They were uttered at the Old Bailey by the Lord Chief Justice of England at midday on 19 October 1989. The words were: 'The officers must have lied.' Lord Lane's comment on the Surrey detectives exploded like a depth-charge in a placid lake. His horror and cold fury were harbingers of tidal waves that have yet to subside.
>
> Inside the court, reactions were muted, despite the colossal implications of what had been said. But outside, in a street sealed off to traffic, came the tumult. The first of the four to come out was Gerry Conlon. He was greeted by ecstatic pandemonium, the hundreds on the road augmented by crowds clinging to scaffolding on a building site opposite the court.
>
> Someone had set up a little row of microphones. Conlon stepped up to it, his eyes shining with anger and delight. He raised his arm above his head. 'I've been in prison for fifteen years for something I did not do,' he said. He seemed to know this was not going to be an isolated event: 'Let's hope the Birmingham Six are freed.' There were some who, for a time, believed the damage in confidence in English criminal justice would be limited: that the system, by belatedly correcting its own malfunction, had proved it was still essentially sound.
>
> However, even at that early stage, other commentators grasped the enormity of what had transpired. In the Court of Appeal,

the release of the Guildford Four brought about an intellectual transformation. Judges who for years had solemnly expressed their reluctance to disturb the verdicts of juries suddenly had to recognise that police evidence might not always be true.[1]

In his revealing article, Rose quoted Sir John Woodcock, Chief Inspector of Constabulary, who coined the phrase 'noble cause corruption'. This is a credo which holds that it is permissible for police officers to use violent and degrading treatment against suspects, to manufacture evidence and to lie under oath in a court of law – criminal offences – in order to obtain convictions of those against whom there would otherwise be insufficient evidence to bring in guilty verdicts. In other words, it was acceptable for law enforcement officers to break the law whenever and in whatever circumstances they deemed necessary, providing *they* judged that it was in the public good. But to whom was it acceptable? Charles Pollard, chief of the Thames Valley force, provided Rose with the answer to that question: 'Everyone knew it happened like that, judges, magistrates, the whole criminal justice system had a sort of conspiracy. If you didn't do it that way, you couldn't actually convict guilty people and that needed to be done.'[2] Here was a freely given confession – no duress – from a senior police officer in which he admitted that during the 1960s, 1970s and 1980s it had been normal policing practice to fit-up suspects and, in case there is any doubt, the whole criminal justice system – including judges – had been in on the fit-up. This montage of judicial illegality was also laid bare by the Tory MP Sir Ivan Lawrence QC, who said that during the 1960s and 1970s 'The police made things up in a large proportion of cases. I defended villains, heavy villains, including the Krays. And they were always being verballed [the attribution of false verbal admissions to suspects], sometimes planted. You would get notebooks which had been refitted with different pages inserted; you knew because the staples had been put in the wrong way round.'[3]

Thriving like a malignant cancer cell within this Wild West ethos was the delinquency that made it so easy for the likes of the Guildford Four, the Birmingham Six, the Bridgewater Three and others to be falsely accused and convicted. It does not take a giant leap to imagine that within this judicial 'nudge-nudge, wink-wink' culture, judges would have swayed juries into accepting the perjured evidence of police officers, rather than that of the accused. Equally, noble cause corruption provided the template whereby appeal court judges could keep those suspects in prison and deny their appeals – sometimes in contradiction of very convincing evidence, such as instances where the real culprits went out of their way to admit that they, and not the accused, had carried out the offences.

It is doubtful if Gerry Conlon had ever heard of the term 'noble cause corruption' during his lifetime, but he knew what it was like to be on the receiving end of it, and he certainly would have been of the view that there was nothing noble in fitting-up innocent people.

On 21 February 1996, Gerry Conlon and Paddy Armstrong attended the High Court in Dublin, where the two successfully sued *The Sun* and were awarded damages and costs for the article that had been written about them in relation to their trip to Crete in 1991. In a statement read to the court, *The Sun*'s lawyers said: 'The article made certain allegations about the conduct of Mr Armstrong and Mr Conlon, which caused them offence, which it regretted ... An editorial in the same edition suggested that any sympathy for Mr Armstrong and Mr Conlon arising out of their wrongful imprisonment was misplaced ... *The Sun* unreservedly withdraws any such suggestion and also regrets the same.'

By the middle of 1996, Gerry was broke and was living with Angie, Juno and Alan in Dagenham, a sprawling, working-class suburb, nine miles or so from the centre of London. Dagenham was not dissimilar to Belfast in appearance, although it had none of the latter's sectarian and political tensions. Crucially, it was a place where Conlon felt at ease, where people would not look down their noses at him and judge him. He told his psychotherapist that he felt he 'fitted in' in Dagenham and that he felt less of an 'alien' there.

Angie's mother, 'Ellen', was described as 'a practical, problem-solving, yet homely sort, just the anchor that Gerry needed at that time.'[4] Ellen owned a home bakery and a café across from the flat that Conlon, Angie, Juno and two others occupied. Occasionally Conlon helped Ellen with the morning breakfasts in the café. He enjoyed working, even if it was only for a few hours a day; it gave him a sense of worth, a feeling that he was gainfully contributing. Moreover, for the first time since his release from prison, he felt a degree of security. Were he to try and settle in Belfast, he was convinced that his life would be in danger. At the same time, he had already been targeted by thugs on two different occasions in central London. Perhaps it was this sense of worth, and the idea of an ad hoc family structure, with values and inherent obligations, which gave Conlon his sense of sanctuary.

Despite his penchant for hard drugs and his volcanic relationship with her daughter, Ellen liked Gerry:

> My mum loved him to bits. When he never had no money, my mum used to come over to our flat and say: 'There y'are, Gerry. There's some food; there's some tobacco.' She'd never give me money 'cause she knew I'd spend it on drugs, but she'd have given Gerry money. She used to give him twenty quid a day when he was skint 'cause she knew he'd have spent it on the horses. Y'see, the horses were more important to him than the crack. I remember him coming out of the bookies with paper bags of cash, where he'd have won thousands and thousands of pounds. The bloke behind the counter would've said: 'Will you take a cheque?' and he'd have said 'No', and he'd have had two McDonald's bags full of money.[5]

On 30 May 1996, Conlon was back in Belfast and back in trouble. Never one to pass up on the chance of a blowout, Gerry and some friends were partying in a house in McDonnell Court in the Lower Falls area when police arrived at the front door and said that they had received complaints about rowdy behaviour and loud music. After receiving assurances that the music would be turned down and there would be no more disturbances, the police left. Not long afterwards they were back again after receiving more complaints. Things became tense when those in the party house spilled out on to the street. An argument started with the police officers, and Conlon and three women were arrested. In what was one of his more bizarre decisions, Conlon punched a policeman in a police station while waiting to be processed.

He was charged with assaulting a police officer and causing a breach of the peace. In court, the next day, he was remanded on continuing bail.

It could well be that this brush with the law was the elixir Gerry Conlon needed because those around him sensed he was becoming desperate to get off drugs. So were Angie and Juno. Angie needed to get off crack if she was to stand any chance of rebuilding the relationship with her estranged son; Juno wanted to get back the life he had lost to crack, and Alan, who had emphysema, knew that every time he inhaled crack, he was further damaging his already polluted lungs. There were informal discussions between the four friends, and there was a collective acceptance that they would never break away from crack cocaine while they were living in London: it was simply too easy to buy drugs there and, since Gerry was a gold-card punter, the dealers were more than happy to extend him unlimited credit. Unfortunately, at that stage, the discussions went no further. Conlon decided to go it alone.

Breaking free from the gravitational pull of crack cocaine was never going to be a gratifying stroll along a promenade on a bright, sunny day: crack is probably *the* hardest known drug to get off. At the end of his tether and frantic to regain control of his life, Conlon took a decision in August 1996 to go 'cold turkey', which is akin to riding a storm in the Drake Passage in a blow-up dingy. He did not seek medical or psychological assistance.

The comedown was every bit as horrific as he had anticipated. He told Seán O'Hagan that he was 'walking the floors, sweating, banging my head off the wall, raging. I'd wake up after a few hours' sleep and smell the drug. Then I'd get up and walk for hours and hours in the pouring rain, in the snow. But I never went back out looking for it again.'[6] Alas, he spoke too soon.

The problem for those trying to get off crack cocaine is that it is not just their bodies; their minds are also addicted to the drug and unless they change their lives, their friends, their circumstances and look for professional help, it is difficult, although not impossible, to break the habit. Gerry did none of those things and, consequently, that last boast that he 'never went back out looking for it again' was premature.

As evidenced time and again, Gerry Conlon had an eye for opportunity, and when, in 1996, he was asked to play a drug dealer in

Antonio Bird's upcoming film *Face*, he accepted the role. *Face* was a British gangster film, written by Ronan Bennett, about Ray (Robert Carlyle), a disillusioned socialist who takes up bank robberies for a living. He teams up with Dave (Ray Winstone), Julian (Philip Davis) and others to pull off what was to be 'the big one', a multi-million-pound bank robbery, after which they could retire to the good life. But the dream turns to violent recrimination when the big one turns out to be a small one. Conlon played the role of Vince, a drug dealer whose cash and stash is stolen by Ray and Dave. In the process, Dave beats up Vince. Conlon was very convincing in his role, primarily because he did get beaten up. 'I remember Gerry saying that he was crapping himself when Ray [Winstone] beat him up in the corner,' Angie said. 'If I remember right, Ray really did beat the shit out of him! Gerry used to laugh when he told anybody that story. He liked Ray; he said he was a gentleman. I think they went out for a drink a few times during the time they were shooting the film.'[7]

Possibly because the word was out that he was off crack, good things seemed to be happening to Conlon. People, who would not have entertained him while he was free-basing, were coming to him with business propositions. In November 1996, while filming *Face*, he was approached and asked to invest what was left of his compensation money in a chain of bars in America. It looked like a capital idea: Irish-theme pubs were popular the world over – and especially in America with its vast Irish diaspora. Newspaper reports at the time said that he was due to fly out to Connecticut to open the third of the Four Green Fields pubs, and he would be the chain's public relations person. There was the promise that leading Hollywood actors would be opening new pubs, and it had been planned that the Irish rebel band The Wolfe Tones would play concerts in some of the bars. Unfortunately for Gerry, his expectations were dashed and his involvement with the project did not proceed.

In January 1997, Gerry Conlon received £240,000 as a final compensatory payment from the British government. He later said he accepted the money because he needed to buy drugs and that he had acted against the advice of Gareth Peirce, who had told him not to accept the offer because he was entitled to more money.

The first thing Conlon did was to pay back his debts: £10,000 to Joey Cashman and £7,000 to Ellen, Angie's mother. That done, he promptly moved out of Angie's flat and into a three-bedroom house in an upper-class area of Dagenham. Angie had been visiting friends and when she got back, she learned Gerry had received his final payment and had moved out of her flat:

> Done my fucking head in, it did. It's funny now but it wasn't funny then. He moved into Spearpoint Gardens, a posh area, and never left word where he was. One call to a dealer was all it took to find him. We'd a big row over that. We'd lots of rows. We were two of a kind, me and Gerry – hot-headed. I remember I put a razor blade in his shoe one day. He was being really horrible to me, and I said: 'I'll show you, ya cunt ya. I'll sort you out, you fucker.' I put a razor blade in his shoe and nearly cut his toe off. When he put the shoe on, he didn't half take it off in a hurry. Then he found the razor blade and shouted: 'You fucking cunt! You could've cut my toe off! You did this.' And I said: 'I did not. I did fucking not. Not me.' But he knew it was me. It couldn't have been anyone else.
>
> I remember another occasion we was having this big fight. He'd pulled the hair out of me and he kicked me out. I'd packed all my stuff in this big suitcase and we was walking down the stairs. I remember saying to myself, 'You fucking cunt.' He was walking in front of me. He'd got down three stairs, and I chucked the big suitcase at him. It hit him on the knees, and I saw him rolling down the stairs. And I knew. I shouted: 'It slipped!' He was lying at the bottom of the stairs, his feet above his head, looking up, and he was in agony. The poor man could barely talk, and he kinda mumbled: 'You tried to kill me, you fucking bitch.' I said, 'It slipped. I swear. It slipped.' Y'know, when me and Gerry broke up, we were still great friends, and we used to have a laugh about our rows.[8]

On 20 February 1997, Gerry Conlon pleaded guilty in Belfast magistrates' court to punching a police officer. Magistrate Tom Travers said: 'If you don't agree to sign a bail bond to be of good behaviour for 15 months, then you will have to go to prison for 28 days.' Conlon signed the bail bond and was released. Outside the court, he told reporters: 'I very rarely come back here and rarely drink. It was one of those occasions when I met some old friends and had a drink. A party developed and people were having fun. The next thing, the police were at the door. I think that the circumstances of what had gone on previously triggered a reaction that need not have happened. Hopefully this type of thing won't happen again.'[9] It didn't.

'He got a quarter of a million quid and we spent the lot in about nine months, maybe twelve,' Angie said, 'and then we moved back into my little flat. The whole lot went on taxis, crack, girls, fags and booze. And he gave everybody everything.' Their vicious fights continued. Gerry had spent thousands of pounds on new clothes, all of which Angie cut up one evening because she discovered he had been with a woman she didn't like. On another occasion, she held Juno hostage with a knife one night because he had thwarted her from taking money out of Gerry's bank account. Gerry returned, threw her a grand and told her to fuck off. Despite all this, Angie knew they loved each other:

> Gerry should've killed me twenty-seven times over really. I think he didn't because I'd the balls to stand up to him. My attitude was, 'I fucking done it. So what? What are you gonna do about it?' With me, what you saw was what you got. I was hard work – I admit it – but so was he. In the end he always forgave me – and I always forgave him. That's the way it was with me and Gerry: we loved each other. How could we have done what we done without love?[10]

According to Angie, every minute of every day was a battle for Gerry Conlon. During his 1997 *Observer* interview with Seán O'Hagan, Conlon outlined his hopes for the future: 'I want to write. I want to get it all out. I think it's important to try to make some sense of my life, to find some sort of happiness for myself instead of wandering from one mishap to another. That's all it's been until now.'[11]

Twelve

Like most drug addicts, Conlon lived life in the minute; tomorrow was too far away to worry about, and besides, it always took care of itself. Above and beyond that, he was used to withdrawing thousands of pounds from banks whenever the notion took him, and it may well be that he expected everything would magically work out and that, come what may, he would survive in the comfort to which he had become accustomed. Yet, on more lucid occasions, he had told his sister Ann that he regarded having pocketfuls of money as 'a curse'. Furthermore, during sessions with his psychotherapist Barry Walle in 2000, he had expressed relief that the money had dried up. Whether or not he wanted to escape from the 'curse' of having too much money, he was looking at a bleak financial future by the start of 1998.

Now frantic to get off crack cocaine, Conlon looked around him for a pathfinder, someone who would lead him to a drug-free utopia, and he found that pathfinder in Alan, his one-lunged friend with emphysema. Alan was even more desperate than Gerry to break his crack habit and had fled London to take up residence in Plymouth. Word filtered back to Gerry, Angie and Juno that Alan had kicked his habit. A new, more settled order of things beckoned; there was hope where previously there had been none.

Angie was the first to follow Alan to Plymouth. 'I never thought I'd come off crack, never in a million years. I thought it was my life – it was my life at that time – I'd have done literally anything to get it.' With Gerry's money running out fast, Angie asked him for a deposit for a flat in Plymouth. She wanted to move there and come off the drugs. Gerry agreed, but only on the condition that she went to Plymouth first and then he would send the money. He was afraid that, like before, she would just take the money and spend it on crack. 'I was back and forth between London and Plymouth for a few weeks, but we were fighting hard to stay off crack. We were off it, on it; off it, on it. We both wanted the same thing, but the crack wasn't letting us go without a fight,' said Angie.[1]

As if to bid one final hurrah to London, Conlon and Angie decided that, before cutting their ties completely with the capital, they would exact some payback on the drug dealers. 'We knocked every fucking dealer we could for about ten grand each before we went to Plymouth,' Angie said, laughing. By any standards, they were playing a dangerous game:

> The dealers smashed up my flat and everything, looking for the money we owed them. They were looking for Gerry too, for sure. But I told them so many porkies. I told one dealer that Gerry was making a film in L.A., and he'd be back shortly, so if you just give me his ten grand with the gear, he'll square you up when he gets in. I told the same dealer I'd to pick him up at the airport on Friday – and all the time Gerry was in the bedroom next door. We did the same to the next dealer, and the next. They thought nothing of giving him tick. Had to be done. It had to be done. We knocked the dealers for tens of thousands.

In ripping off the crack dealers, what Conlon and Angie had effectively done, figuratively speaking, was to burn *The Bounty*: a permanent return to London was now out of the question.

When asked if the dealers would have hurt Conlon, Angie hesitated: 'I'm not sure. Maybe. I remember going into a crack house. Gerry was already there and he had these Yardies on their knees and they were all smoking … and Gerry was the centre of attention. It was like he was holding court. The Yardies fucking loved him. He could speak their lingo and all. And he went into some very dark places, y'know? It was almost like he wanted to face death. These things that he did, the places he went and the chances he took, it was like he wanted things to end badly, and people always admired him. Most people were so shocked by the front of him: the balls that he had.' Angie adds: 'He slept with a knife under his pillow. That was just the way it was. I think he did that even when he wasn't facing situations. I don't know how he didn't get killed; I don't know how he didn't. The dealers only ever saw pound signs.'[2]

For a few weeks after moving to Plymouth, Conlon stayed with Angie in her flat. Then he moved into his own first-floor, two-bedroomed maisonette at 16 Ashford Road. It was sparsely furnished, with two sofas, two chairs, a table and a television. Ann McKernan described the maisonette as a 'pretty drab place. It could have done with a lick of paint.'[3]

For a scanner like Conlon, someone who kept an eye out for potential enemies at every bus stop and street corner, Plymouth was a peculiar place to put down roots. From Elizabethan times it had been a major military port. In 1588, Sir Francis Drake had famously continued playing bowls on the Hoe, the cliffs overlooking Plymouth Sound, while the Spanish Armada sailed up the English Channel. And in 1620, the Pilgrim Fathers left Plymouth for the New World. More to the point, 42 Commando of the Royal Marines was stationed in Plymouth, and Gerry Conlon did not like to be around British soldiers in case they attacked him. He would later tell Angie that he would not have come to Plymouth if he had known about its military background.

Not long after arriving in Plymouth, Gerry and Angie both went cold turkey, but they failed to overcome their addictions. Luckily they had Alan, who was a constant inspiration and source of encouragement, while Ellen visited her daughter and Gerry on a regular basis, cleaned their flats, and provided whatever assistance she could in the circumstances. But practical help and advice, no matter how well-intentioned, went only so far, and the more Conlon looked around him, the more he retired into reclusion. At least in London he had gone out and socialised, but in Plymouth he did not really know anyone, rarely left his flat, lay all day on the sofa with the television remote in hand, chain-smoked, ate ready-made meals or sandwiches from plastic packages and peeked through the drawn curtains to see if some shadowy figure was lurking about in the street below.

Contact with his family back in Belfast was minimal and on the rare occasions that he did return to his home city, he felt the conversation with his mother was stilted and polite. It troubled him that they had never been able to have a deep conversation about Giuseppe, or had sat down and tried to make sense of what had happened to their family.

Madness travels, and the madness of Gerry and Angie travelled with them on the train to Plymouth. After some weeks, Conlon decided to return to London to meet some people for the weekend, leaving Angie in his flat on her own. Angie was not a patient woman and after four weeks and no sign of Gerry, she was getting very angry. He eventually returned with about £3,500. Full of ire, Angie waited until he was asleep and snoring before taking the money and getting a taxi to London, which cost £800, each way. There she bought two grands' worth of crack, most of which she smoked in the back of the taxi on the return journey. As she was sobering up, remorse set in and she asked the taxi driver to deliver what was left of the money to Gerry. Angie said: 'The driver didn't know Gerry but I told him what I'd done and he said, "You can fuck off, love. You can fuck off and face him yourself." I'd about forty quid left and about 300 quid's worth of crack. So I woke him up. He went mad, didn't he? He went fucking mad. I shouted back at him: "What are you cracking up for? I waited four weeks for ya." He raved and ranted for a bit and then he said, "All right; all fucking right. I was four weeks late getting back. Fair play to ya. That's it."'[4]

Despite all his woes, Conlon resolutely placed his bets on the horses every morning. Sometimes, when he felt up to it, he would walk the 700 metres to the bookies himself, usually very early in the morning when there would be few people about. Inside the bookies he would have as little conversation with the other punters as possible. When he felt low, perhaps after an exceptionally bad night's sleep, Alan would go to the bookies for Gerry, keep him company when he was particularly down, take him for a game of snooker on a Sunday night and generally look after him. The indefatigable Angie also looked after him – in her own inimitable way: 'He used to go mad at me for shoplifting. He used to call Toys R Us, "Toys R Angie" 'cause I moved down to Plymouth and I came off the crack and I needed something to replace it. There was no CCTV or anything in Plymouth when we moved there, so I decorated Gerry's flat, my flat, everybody's flat. And he used to say, "You're gonna bring the police to my door." Then, about six months after us moving there, they had CCTV everywhere and I got caught. I was so embarrassed.'[5]

Angie was not the only party who was embarrassed around this time. In November 1998, Gerry Conlon won his libel action against the *Sunday Times* for the article that Julie Burchill had written on 13 February 1994. A consequence of Conlon's victory was the *Sunday Times* agreeing to print a retraction: 'Our review of the film *In the Name of the Father* claimed that Gerry Conlon of the Guildford Four implicated his father, Giuseppe, in his forced confession, for which his father never forgave him. We are glad to accept that this was not true.'[6]

It was around this time also that Conlon reached his Thermopylae moment. There could be no more procrastination, no more retreating: he had to get off crack, and he reckoned that the only way to do so was to go cold turkey again. Fortunately, Alan and Angie, both of whom had come off crack by this time, were in Conlon's corner. Angie's trust and faith in Gerry was unflinching: 'He was a lion,' she said, emphasising every word. 'He was. He fought so hard to get off crack. There was a period when he was going up the walls for it; he said he could smell it everywhere. But he held on. He was always trying to get clean and he did it. He beat it.'

Joey Cashman, who visited Conlon in Plymouth at the start of 1999, said Gerry told him that breaking the habit had been the most difficult thing he had ever done in his life. Cashman, who has also beaten a crack cocaine addiction, said:

> I know guys who went on heroin, just to get off crack. People tell you that coming off crack isn't as difficult as coming off heroin, and that's right – to a point – you don't usually vomit, or get the shakes or anything like that, but by fuck, your head is pickled. All you can think of is the hit and usually that thought never leaves you; you could be off it twenty years and suddenly the craving smacks into you. You bring that craving to the grave with you. Fair play to Gerry. He did the business.[7]

The fight to come off crack took its toll on Conlon. He was sore all over from muscle aches, and he suffered motor impairment, which is a slowing down of the nervous system that leads to extreme fatigue. He had mood swings: one minute he would be very amiable and then he would erupt at the slightest irritation. 'We had this massive fight,' Angie says, 'over a tin of tomatoes 'cause I opened a tin of tomatoes and dished them up for breakfast. I dunno; I suppose it was because he was coming down.'

As well as giving up drugs, Conlon had to contend with Angie – the haphazard *enfant terrible* – which was quite a traumatic experience in its own right. 'I'd my own flat,' Angie said, 'just round the corner from Gerry's. He paid for me to have a separate flat to get a bit of peace, though I could go and stay in his flat anytime I wanted.' She remembered one particular night when she woke up in her flat to find it tipped upside down. She thought she'd been spiked and went over to Gerry to tell him:

> He said, 'Don't worry. You lie on the sofa. I'll be back later.' He went out, and I went to the kitchen. I lit a fag under the chip pan but didn't turn the gas off. Then I went into the front room and flaked out. When I woke up, there was no kitchen – I'd burnt the whole fucking lot down! He came home and he was ripping it. He got the fire brigade and all, but it was fucked. He said to me, 'You fucking idiot! You burnt my kitchen down!' And I said, 'Do you know what? I'm away home,' and I left him with his burnt-out kitchen. But yeah, he forgave me; he always forgave me. I was a fuck-up back then. I had a good teacher – Gerry.

No matter how many catastrophes or misadventures occurred during their relationship, Gerry and Angie remained together: both appeared to have a vast reservoir of forgiveness for the other. Angie was asked if they loved each other. 'Of course we loved each other. How could we have done what we done without love?' When asked if Gerry knew what love was, Angie replied: 'I think so. I think there was a lot of love between us, looking back. But it was never the same when the two of us came off crack. In the end we was like brother and sister, but at the start, yeah, we loved each other.'[8]

Besides having no kitchen, the problem for Conlon now he was clean was that he had no hiding place; the run-back to the House of

Oblivion had been cut off: cold reality and soul-drowning nightmares had to be stared down. Gerry had told friends and reporters: 'When I was on drugs, I didn't have to face the world.' The world that he faced in the absence of drugs was markedly more horrific than anything he had experienced beforehand. The nightmares became more real, more vivid: it was as if he was the director, leading actor and audience in his own nightly horror film. And while he had always been security-conscious, even when living in London, his sense of insecurity became so heightened that he turned into a virtual hermit. Added to this, there was his topsy-turvy relationship with Angie and the negligible contact that he had with his family in Belfast.

There were also suicidal thoughts. On one occasion he stood on a platform at Westminster underground station and urged himself to jump in front of an oncoming train, then berated himself for not 'having the balls' to do it when the train passed.

A major part of Conlon's problem was that he had not received an apology from the British government for the wrongs that had been perpetrated against him and his extended family. 'Half my battle is, half my grievance is, they've never said sorry. If you don't say sorry to someone, you don't think you've done nothing wrong to them.' When asked by an interviewer if an apology would help, Conlon said:

> Yeah. It would remove one strain of anger and rage and that's gotta help, you know. I deserve an apology. They took the best years of my life, the years that I should have maybe been a good builder's labourer, a good plasterer's labourer, a good brickie; having kids. All them years – wiped – meaningless: nothing there. What can I look back on? Fifteen years in jail; fifteen birthdays; another nine anniversaries for my father. People usually have the joy of watching a child being born, their first kid, you know? Nothing there; like window-cleaners, they wiped out a whole part of my fucking life, right out the window.[9]

Now that he was compos mentis, Conlon's mind focused on the amount of compensation he had received from the British government. When he did the sums, it worked out that he had been awarded £90 per day for every day of his incarceration. In a *Guardian* newspaper article on

19 October 1999, Gareth Peirce called the settlements in the Guildford Four case 'miserly', while Oliver Kelly of Belfast, Paul Hill's solicitor, said that the government's assessments for compensation 'fell far short of what a reasonable person would expect. In these cases, there should be no penny-pinching'.

Labour MP John McDonnell was sympathetic to the claims for more compensation:

> We can't find out at this stage how these assessments are made because you can't enter into discussion. It is not an open and transparent and therefore fair system. These are people who in many instances have been pressurised into settling for sums of money when they are in no fit conditions to make those agreements. There is no support for them when they come out of prison, so we are asking now for the Home Secretary to review the whole system.

Obviously Gerry was not going to argue with McDonnell's and the solicitors' viewpoints: 'What price do you put on someone who spent the best years of his life in prison, watched his family disintegrate and watched his father die in prison?'[10]

By the summer of 1999, Angie and Gerry were no longer a couple. Reflecting on the break-up of their relationship, Angie said: 'We didn't have a sit-down or a blowout, or anything like that; it was … our time had come and we both knew it. That's not to say we didn't still feel love for each other, but it wasn't the same love as before. It was kinda sad really, 'cause, despite everything, me and Gerry were great together. He treated me like a Queen, he did.'[11]

On 15 December 1999, at the request of Gerry Conlon's legal advisors, psychiatrist Adrian Grounds once again interviewed him. Given the flight path of Conlon's life from the last time they had met in January 1994, it is not a surprise that Dr Grounds saw a marked deterioration in his patient's demeanour. Conlon was a lot slower; his movement, his speech and his attention seemed to drift during their conversation.

Conlon told Dr Grounds that he rarely left his maisonette and likened this isolation to being locked up in a prison cell. The professor also noted that Conlon was filled with self-loathing and remorse, and would have welcomed death because he did not feel as if he was part of this world. Amongst the pages of this catalogue of misery, there were nonetheless flickers of hope. With remarkable lucidity for one who was depressed to the point of contemplating suicide, Conlon told Grounds that an apology from the British government would go a long way to curing his malaise.

Grounds's conclusion was that Conlon was neglecting himself and that he was in a state of severe distress. The psychiatrist subsequently wrote and spoke to Conlon's general practitioner, who referred Gerry to consultant psychiatrist Dr Geoff Tomlinson and his colleague, Dr Joanna Bromley. At the start of 2000, after speaking with Conlon, Drs Tomlinson and Bromley recommended that he be referred to psychotherapist Barry Walle, for cognitive behavioural psychotherapy.

Twenty-six years had passed since this innocent man was taken from his home in Cyprus Street, Belfast and imprisoned. Twelve years had passed since he had walked out of the Old Bailey into a world that was foreign to him. Shamefully, in all that time, the British authorities had not lifted a finger to help him. Gerry Conlon had treaded a frenzied and essentially lonely path and yet, astonishingly, he had not entirely caved in under the strain. Not only that, but he was still struggling for justice for his family. The father would have been proud of the son: he was weak and fragile, but he was still in the fight.

Thirteen

Although his father had been in the Royal Navy for most of his adult life, Barry Walle, known as 'Baz', opted to join the RAF and had served for six years. Walle was considered by his peers to be an expert in the field of post-traumatic stress disorder (PTSD): 'Inevitably, because of my background, a good portion of my work was with ex-military. I was just getting skilled enough to work with trauma by The Falklands; that, and being able to speak the lingo ensured they came to me. That largely unmet need shaped my career choices, I suppose.'[1]

Walle, soft-spoken and personable, first met Conlon on 24 March 2000 at Glenbourne, an acute hospital in Plymouth that catered for people suffering from mental health problems. The psychotherapist remarked that one of the issues that sometimes confronted him when working with patients was 'sense of control', and he commented that this was all the more pressing with Conlon, who was a strong character with a forceful personality. 'But he was ready to work on his problems,' the former RAF administrator said affectionately. 'He'd had enough, and, I have to say, he was very frank about his inability to hack it any longer.'

Their introductory meeting had been a mild affair, with the unassuming Walle giving Conlon literature to read on PTSD. Conlon felt comfortable enough to relay to the psychotherapist some of the intrusive thoughts and nightmares that were peppering his brain. The Belfast man also told Walle that the following week he would be attending a session with a trauma therapist in London called Helen Bamber. Walle thought it best that Conlon should concentrate on having one therapist, rather than two, and suggested that he listened to both before making up his mind which one to choose. Later Bamber phoned Walle, 'to check me out and Helen seemed happy to leave it to me to call her if I wanted any help.' Barry Walle would be Conlon's consultant, close friend and confidant for the next five years.

It was 23 January 2016, in Chandler's Bar and Bistro on Plymouth pier, and the dark clouds that had frowned all day finally shed their tears. Sitting at a table beside the glass-fronted bar, Walle ordered Calamari and salad. 'I used to bring Gerry here for lunch,' he said. 'He liked it here.' Walle continued:

> Even after I officially stopped working with Gerry in 2003, I still went around and picked him up and we'd have gone for walks around Jennycliff, or Plymbridge Woods, along the River Plym. Also Lopwell Dam on the River Tavy, and the Yealm Estuary. All these places were beside water, tranquil places, few people; I used to call them 'Recovery Places'. But you couldn't walk too far or too fast, a mile maybe two at the most, because Gerry's breathing wasn't great.'

In those earlier sessions, Walle encountered Conlon's remarkable memory for the first time:

> Gerard has an extraordinary facility of memory – virtually 100 per cent. He can do a roll call of all the prisoners and warders on every wing that he was on or who engaged in any activity with him, recalling face, name, key characteristics and events. If today is 'x', he can remember in great detail what he was doing on that day '74 through to '89.[2]

In another consultation, Gerry described in graphic detail his arrival in a top-security prison in 1976. Wakefield was a Victorian jail that housed 740 prisoners, 70 per cent of whom were sex offenders. Conlon despised sex offenders. He was also infuriated that they put up no resistance to what was a very harsh prison regime. If there was no fight in the sex offenders, there was plenty in Conlon, and Walle heard how he had been sent to the punishment block for throwing 'vile' food over warders. During their talk, Conlon outlined the layout of the punishment block, how many bricks were in a wall, how many footsteps it took to get from the outer wall to the cell door, and even the smell of cockroaches. Conlon's astonishing memory, Walle concluded, would seem to most people to be a gift from God, but in this patient's case, it could be a curse at times because Gerry could not switch off the terrible experiences. On many occasions he dual-functioned: in that he was partly in the present but mostly 'back there'. Tellingly, Walle remarked that Conlon perpetually rewound every snide remark, insult and injustice in his head: 'Again, this operates in all sense modalities, not just pictorial, and has emotional consequences.'[3] With most people, insults and injustice minimise in importance with the passage of time and distance, but with Gerry Conlon that did not happen: he could not let go. This *idée fixe*, the constant watering of hostile comments and behaviour, was one of the principal reasons why Conlon did not settle in Belfast when he was released from the Old Bailey in 1989: some people from his native city could not forget or forgive the fact that, when he was a teenager, he had been a petty criminal.

As early as their second meeting on 29 March, Walle introduced Conlon to Eye Movement Desensitization and Reprocessing (EMDR) therapy, a revolutionary treatment that was first discovered in 1987 by Dr Francine Shapiro, who made the chance observation that eye movements can reduce the intensity of disturbing thoughts. EMDR has eight phases: the first one is 'History and Treatment Planning' and the eighth is 'Re-evaluation'. At the end of the session, Conlon was exhausted. Walle would later report that the treatment 'involved EMDR with cognitive interweaves for the flashbacks. This was making some progress, and a small number were eliminated and others reduced'.[4]

Despite having a virtual 100 per cent recall facility, a continuous feature of these early sessions was Conlon's blocking out of the time he had spent with his father in prison, and of his father's subsequent death. Walle says that Conlon could not even bring up an image of Giuseppe, or his cell, yet he could tell you who was in the cells on either side of his father and the names of the prison wardens who worked the landing. The psychotherapist thought this was a very worrying phenomenon. Giuseppe, in his opinion, was central to Gerry's recovery: his imprisonment and death had to be confronted if Gerry was to salvage his sanity. Yet Gerry had imprisoned Giuseppe in the deepest dungeons of his mind. It was going to be a monumental task to secure the release of the elder Conlon.

Another anomaly that caught Walle's attention was Conlon's fixation with the absence of an apology from the British government: 'At the back of his mind is still the pressure for an apology'.[5] A feature of his personality was that he lived from one *raison d'être* to the next; life had to have purpose, or Conlon had the capacity to submit to negative behaviour. Thence, the fight for an apology from the British government was Conlon, consciously or unconsciously, adopting another reason for living: he was throwing himself a lifeline.

The pattern that emerged from the early engagements with Walle was Conlon's attempt to control the discourse; he wanted to dictate the pace and trajectory of the sessions, and, equally important, to avoid dealing with the issues that were at the core of his deep depression. Even when it came to taking medication, Conlon wanted and had the final say: 'He is averse to and declined psychotropic medication, having seen its application and effects in the prison system, and because he fears becoming addicted.'[6]

A major issue that Walle encountered was Conlon's antagonism and fury. Walle said: 'A considerable amount of time is spent simply absorbing his anger, allowing him to depressurise. Most sessions begin with an amount of this and it often takes over the whole session. It is noticeable that if I am away for a week of two, his anger is accumulative. Direct behavioural/cognitive work to mediate on the anger has been limited to suggestions and the occasional practice at containing it and putting it on one side'.[7] It was always going to be an uphill struggle for Walle to put a cap on Conlon's twenty-six years of pent-up acrimony and umbrage against the British authorities, and the psychotherapist knew that from the outset. Perhaps, at times, he subliminally felt that Conlon's rage was being directed at him. If he did, he did not confront Conlon with his suspicions.

Walle persevered and tried to prise open doors that had remained closed for over two decades. One that remained closed in that initial period was Giuseppe's cell door. On 30 May, he reported that Conlon was: 'Definitely in grief-mode/depressed. Can see his father's cell door with name card reversed – still can't see his face.'[8]

On 5 June 2000, a two-part BBC *Spotlight* programme revealed that the British prime minister, Tony Blair, had written to Paul Hill's wife, Courtney Kennedy-Hill, and said: 'I believe it is an indictment of our system of justice and a matter for the greatest regret that anyone suffers punishment as a result of a miscarriage of justice. There were miscarriages of justice in your husband's case, and the cases of those convicted with him. I am very sorry indeed that this should have happened.'

In a *Guardian* newspaper article the next day, Conlon said that he was 'delighted' with the news, but he also let it be known that he was angry with the belated timing of the apology and the fact that his family had received no apology. From an ethical point of view, Conlon's anger was perfectly understandable because Blair's apology was delivered in a private correspondence to Courtney Kennedy-Hill rather than to her husband Paul, who at the very least deserved his apology and thus a letter. What did Blair expect Hill's wife to do: apologise to her husband and the Guildford Four on his behalf? Did he expect her to use whatever influence she had to keep his apology out of the public domain? For some inexplicable reason, Tony Blair and his advisors failed to appreciate how insulting the Guildford Four and the Maguire Seven would have regarded this intervention to be. Conceivably he believed that by apologising privately, he would avoid having to do so in the House of Commons. If that were the case, he was very wrong.

Whatever his motives were, the prime minister had exacerbated Gerry Conlon's anger: 'We should have had an apology a long time ago, as well as proper compensation. It's been driving me mad that there has not been an apology so this thing can be put to bed. My mother in particular should have had one. I'm still going through a terrible time, getting dreadful flashbacks. My psychiatrist tells me that he has never experienced a worse case of post-traumatic stress syndrome, even worse than those soldiers in the Falkland's war'.[9]

During the *Spotlight* programme, Paul Hill was asked about compensation, and he replied: 'No one knows the monetary value you can put on fifteen years. I don't think there is anybody alive who can come out of that experience and not be scarred.' Paul later reflected on the day he was sentenced: 'I stood in the dock. I was numb. I had no feelings whatsoever. I wasn't sad; I was not depressed. And I think the most poignant thing was that the judge expressed regret that the death penalty was not an option.'[10]

On the day after his *Guardian* interview was published, Conlon had a very disturbing conference with Barry Walle, who reported that his patient 'looked almost like having a heart attack. Heavy central pressure, central chest. Covering general prison milieu at the time – no clear correlation to image flashback. Clearly body memory, but original source unclear.'[11]

On 7 July 2000, *The Independent* published an article entitled 'Down and Out'. In it, reporter Steve Boggan wrote:

> This was Gerry Conlon's moment. There he is, jumping for freedom, an innocent man who'd served 15 years for the Guildford pub bombings. Today he is a broken man. And the system that broke him has done little to put him back together again. For Conlon and the rest of the men who had been convicted of two pub bombings in Guildford in 1974, the past has been defined by corrupt police officers, complicit forensic scientists and gullible courts. They had endured beatings, isolation and despair. But on that day in October 1989, the future finally looked bright.
>
> Fast forward 11 years. Conlon is alone in a small flat on the south coast of England. His voice on the phone is desperate. 'I can see them, the men I saw die in prison,' he says. 'There was one who got some glue and cut up a mattress and glued bits to his body and then set himself alight. I can still smell the burning flesh. I can't get it out of my mind.
>
> 'I never had a single thought about killing myself in prison, but now I think about nothing else. I plan it; I buy things to do it. I have a knife and some rope and lots of pills. If not them, then I have my balcony. I keep it locked for now because I dream of jumping off it. Prison was better than this.'[12]

Conlon's downward spiral began to accelerate. On 30 August 2000, Barry Walle noted that he was 'not looking after self properly, poor, minimal eating – sleep pattern out – pains and aches, smoking too much (almost as if 'I want to go like my father with emphysema' as it would make retribution). Pain particularly upper thorax back that he described as half crown size and thinks it's his lung'.[13]

After their 12 September session, the psychoanalyst revealed that Conlon had been 'deep into initial interrogation, beating, torture, humiliation, degradation, abandonment, fear. "I shouldn't have done it" [signed the confession], "signed my life away", "killed my father", "other people in Northern Ireland were tortured – they didn't crack."' At the end of the engagement, Walle observed that Conlon was 'sitting there at table, broken'.[14]

On 3 November, Conlon told Walle of a nightmare in which his father was advising him how to commit suicide. In Conlon's alternative world, Giuseppe was introducing his son to a horseshoe-shaped contraption that could be fitted around an individual's head. It had a bolt across the open end that induced death when screwed tighter and tighter into a person's head. This dream was taking place in a ground-floor cell with only a curved window. It was dark, damp and miserable. Conlon could see 'this pair of boots, shiny black leather (à la prison guard) on someone he can't see. The yard is lit by one of those horrible yellow lights. Somehow he can see a block of flats opposite, nothing special, that is lit in sunlight and he can see the individual blades of grass'.[15] In a second apparition on the same night, Conlon told Walle that he was stuck in the middle of an Orange Order march with his mother (the Orange Order is a Protestant/Unionist organisation that orchestrates thousands of marches across Northern Ireland each year). Terrifyingly, he tried to get his mother out of the march, but every exit and means of escape was blocked by marchers and supporters. Conlon was wearing only a T-shirt and was desperately trying to hide a nationalist tattoo with his hand. At the end of this exchange, Walle recorded that Conlon, 'went on to do eloquent dialogue on changes that prison effects: "You become islands, you learn how not to deal with people, you swap compassion for harshness, love for hate, never able to love, receive love, you're in their face with threat – it's survival. When you come out, everyone, your family have got love – you haven't, you've lost that capacity."'[16]

A chink of light began to shine into the dark places. On 7 November, Walle recorded that Conlon looked much better, was sleeping more soundly, and had not had a repeat of the nightmares since he had brought them out into the open during their 3 November session.

On 1 December 2000, with a view to publishing his story at a future date, Conlon requested that Walle record their sessions because he thought it 'might be useful for him in the future if he does rewrite the book (*Proved Innocent*) properly without worrying about libel or Official Secrets Act etc'.[17] Walle noted that, in this exchange, Conlon made no mention of having suicidal thoughts.

Any cautious optimism that Walle may have harboured was soon dispelled when the nightmares returned with a vengeance at the start of 2001. One in particular centred on the outbreak of a third world war, where Conlon was in the Category 'A' wing of a prison, and 'executioners, masked and gowned, working their way through the blocks and the prisoners managing to organise some resistance but were convinced of the inevitable'.[18]

On 7 February 2001, 44-year-old Stephen Downing was released on bail, pending a hearing at the court of appeal. Downing had served twenty-seven years in prison for the pickaxe murder of Wendy Sewell, aged thirty-two, at Bakewell, Derbyshire, in 1973. The then 17-year-old had been convicted on the basis of confessions he had made to police, but it transpired that he had never been formally arrested, and had not been told he had a right to see a solicitor. Moreover, Downing had retracted his confessions before his trial, saying that he had signed them because he had been 'cold, tired, hungry, and in pain'.

No sooner had Downing's bail application been granted than Tony Blair told the House of Commons that he was 'happy to pay tribute to the work of the family' of Downing and to campaigning reporter Don Hale, who had fought on the former prisoner's behalf (Blair later nominated Mr Hale for an OBE). A barrister before he became a politician, Blair was careful not to apologise for a miscarriage of justice because Downing's conviction still stood and would remain safe until it was quashed on appeal in 2002. But to Gerry Conlon, secreted in his little maisonette in Plymouth, existing rather than living from day to day, this was Blair being disrespectful for a second time. The way that Conlon saw it, the speed with which Blair had rushed to side with Downing's campaign – on the day of his release on bail – was in stark contrast to the prime minister's approach to his own family. He had been out of prison for twelve years and during that time neither Blair nor any other prime minister had said anything that could be construed as comforting to his family – never mind giving them an apology. Added to that, Conlon would also have been furious at newspaper articles that reported that Downing would receive up to £8 million in compensation against government agencies and in an action against his original lawyers (these reports were wildly exaggerated and Downing received only around £800,000 for twenty-seven years' wrongful imprisonment).

On 16 February 2001, Gerry met Barry Walle in Glenbourne Hospital. Walle wrote in his report: 'Haven't turned the tide on this worsening episode yet. Suspect link to stress of being near an apology and the frustrating delay, as well as the obvious one he postulates, i.e. the release of Stephen Downing and the immediate apology to him and his family from Blair! And he still doesn't have one. I've decided not to push Gerry too far in order to ensure he's up to attending our meetings in the next few weeks.. Hopefully things can change a bit then.'[19]

Matters had not improved by 21 February. Walle recorded: 'Still stuck in the same circle. The only thing that is going to break us out is an apology. I can't help but agree with his reasoning about the delay being further insult and abuse since they [the government] seem to be so readily apologising to everyone else. All I can do is limit my goals to get us to that meeting. He is really stressed by it.'[20]

In some ways, Gerry Conlon was lucky. He had good seconds in his corner. Besides the unflappable Walle, there was Gareth Peirce, who worked feverishly in the background on his behalf. Meetings between psychiatrists and government ministers were arranged by Mrs Peirce's law firm, Birnberg Peirce and Partners, in 2001, but the administration's position was that Gerry had received all the compensation that was due to him, with the exception of minor expenses.

Arguably, a breakout from Fortress Conlon was always on the cards. All that psychological and emotional infiltration, the dismantling of that huge personality, the secrecy, the vigilance, the denial of self, the relentless boredom and the growing pile of losing bookies' dockets – The Plymouth One felt as if all the life had been sucked out of him. Walle recorded that Gerry cancelled their 6 March appointment because he 'went on a bender over the weekend'.

At their 9 March meeting, Gerry told Walle that he had gone to London and had visited crack houses in Brixton, where he had smoked crack. This was the equivalent of voluntarily jumping into a cobra pit because Angie and he had ripped off crack dealers for tens of thousands of pounds before leaving London for Plymouth. It also had the potential to undo all the hard work that Gerry had undertaken to get off crack. Was this his attempt to bring about the end of a life he did not think worth living, or was he so low that he just had to get high? Of Conlon's sojourn in London, Walle wrote:

> High-risk behaviour, crack of course, dealing with Yardies. Visited crack houses and had it delivered. Pinned three of them [Yardies] to a wall with a knife when they tried to short-change him, was going to strip them and send them out naked to humiliate them but backed off when he realised how terrified a pregnant girl who was with them was. Didn't get much of a buzz out of it; if anything, served to prove that he didn't fit there anymore either – must use that as illustration that he wouldn't fit in prison either. Recognised that he was an ace away from doing life. Got more out of that high-risk behaviour and restoring his 'respect' than anything else but can't be bothered with that any more. Doesn't think he'll go back there. Not bothered that anyone will follow him down here [i.e. Plymouth] to sort him out – they were too terrified.[21]

Fourteen

Sarah Conlon liked to look her best for Sunday Mass, so every Saturday Ann McKernan accompanied her to the hairdresser's. On 30 May 2001, while waiting for her mother, Ann felt tired and went upstairs to lie down on the bed, telling her husband, Joe, to wake her up when her mother arrived. Ann recalled: 'I remember getting into the bed and I don't know what happened but I remember going away back, as if I was going through a tunnel. I must have been trying to call Joe's name. The next thing I remember was Joe coming into the room and trying to waken me up.' She continued: 'He looked at me and realised I'd taken a stroke. Apparently when an aneurysm ruptures, it brings on bleeding in the brain, and that leads to a stroke. I was taken to the City Hospital and the doctors did a brain scan. That was when they found out I had three aneurysms in my brain and that I needed operating on.'[1]

By 3 April, Ann was getting feeling back in her right side, but she was still ill. Walle recorded that Gerry was very worried about his sister: 'May have to go over to Belfast, which he dreads, but is waiting to see how it goes.'[2] Conlon travelled to Belfast to visit Ann in hospital six days later. The two had always had a special relationship: 'From we were kids, we always covered each other's backs,' Ann said. 'Don't get me wrong, we had our arguments, but we never fell out. He was my world. When I'd the aneurysms, he got off the plane and came straight from the airport to hospital to see me. And I said to him: "What did you come over for?" and he said, "Aye, I know; you're my wee sister." And then he said: "C'mon and we'll talk." He was demented, he really was. He said to me: "Nothing better happen to you."'

Surrounded by his family, Conlon should have taken succour from being home, from being in the warm embrace of those whom he loved and who loved him. Yet he could not bring himself to open up to his mother. It was not all Gerry's fault. Sarah Conlon, despite her kindly smile and embracing charm, had had to develop Spartan-like discipline in order to hold her family together while their menfolk were imprisoned. During that time, Sarah had learned to conceal her feelings and to insulate herself from the travails of the outside world. As a result, intimate tête-à-têtes would not have come easily to her. According to Ann, her mother was 'a very, very hard woman to understand. See, the only two people she told everything to were her sister, Bridgie, and Bridgie's daughter, Moya. She felt that that was her worry, not her children's.'[3] Unsurprisingly, on this occasion she did not divulge her inner thoughts to Gerry, who was even more worried than usual; he thought that his mother was looking old and tired, and he was upset when she made references to dying. In the back of his head was the possibility that she would die before the British government had given their family an apology.

On 8 May, the *Sunday Business Post*'s Belfast-born journalist Niall Stanage visited Conlon in his maisonette. In a very instructive if tragic article, Stanage wrote: 'Gerry Conlon is likeable, articulate and fiercely intelligent. But he is also, by his own admission, devoid of self-belief. Several times during our interview he seems on the verge of tears. The brown eyes are narrowed, despairing. Many of his answers are preceded by heavy, quavering sighs.'

Barry Walle also spoke to Stanage, with Conlon's permission, and compared Gerry's symptoms to those of victims who had suffered 'very severe childhood abuse'. Conlon spoke of his mother and the enormous anguish she was experiencing: 'She is going through her own memories of that period. I think she is going through them on similar lines to myself, and I think she is frightened of hearing more bad news. But I would like to tell her that my father may have been small in stature, but he was huge in heart. He was a giant among people, in the way he carried himself, and his dignity was always intact.'

Conlon went on to say that he sometimes wanted to end it all: 'It's harder sometimes to stay alive than it is to die.' He also spoke candidly of his debilitating panic attacks, saying that the last time he got on a bus he 'started spouting leaks from everywhere'.

In an echo of interviews past, Conlon said: 'I don't know how to understand kindness or love. If I'm shopping and I see families together, it makes me feel a little disturbed. It seems that everyone has someone, or has a connection. I seem to be on my own, outside of all that pleasure, or ability to enjoy life.' When Stanage asked him if he had any memories of feeling happy, Conlon replied: 'None at all.'[4]

At this juncture in their interview, Barry Walle pointed out: 'There is quite a bit of evidence now to suggest that the brain actually grows new networks, new connections, and shears off old, disused ones. The consequences of that for Gerry is that after 15 years of hard time in jail, with no positive emotion whatsoever, most of his ability for positive emotion has gone. He knows no joy.'[5]

Conlon and Walle travelled to Cambridge University to meet Dr Adrian Grounds on 6 September 2001. Grounds said bluntly to Conlon that the science of treating PTSD victims was in its infancy and that his preconceptions of a full recovery might be too high. Initially, this was quite a shock to the ex-prisoner because he had been of the opinion that there was a cure for his affliction. Despite Grounds's gloomy prognosis, Walle later recorded that Conlon was 'feeling strangely calmer than he had for a long time'.[6]

In his subsequent psychiatric report on their meeting, Grounds wrote that Conlon 'looked very low in mood and highly anxious and fearful. He had difficulty in communicating because of long lapses of attention when he would stare ahead and become inaccessible and unresponsive to questions. After 10–15 seconds or more he would become aware of his surroundings again, look perplexed and ask what had previously been said. These appeared to be dissociative states.' Grounds, who had visited Conlon's maisonette previously, also wrote that he was neglecting himself and that his flat was similar to that of a prison cell. During their talk, Conlon told Grounds: 'I feel more guilty than the people who did this. If it wasn't for me, my father wouldn't have died and my mother wouldn't be the saddest person I've ever met.'[7]

Soon after, on 9 October, Dr Grounds interviewed the Conlon family, including Sarah, her daughters Bridie and Ann, and Joe McKernan, in the McKernan home in St Peter's Close, Belfast. In his report on the interviews, Grounds wrote:

The interviews with Mr Conlon's family revealed severe and long-lasting adverse effects on them, arising from his arrest and imprisonment. These effects continue and were not resolved by his release. His mother and sisters faced great personal losses. These included the imprisonment and death of Giuseppe Conlon, loss of the integrity and closeness of their family, and loss of the quality of their previous relationship with Gerry Conlon, who has become estranged and irrevocably psychologically damaged. They have suffered severe losses of their previous life opportunities and each has suffered severe and chronic stress.

Dr Grounds recommended that the individual members of the Conlon family receive 'individual supportive psychotherapy or counselling' and he added that 'the significant difficulties they have in communication and disclosure with each other may be reduced if they were assisted by a skilled family therapist.'[8]

On 17 January 2002, Conlon went to Belfast for Sarah's seventy-fifth birthday. Sarah Conlon did not like parties and she had made it clear that she did not want one for her seventieth birthday. Instead, the family went out to a restaurant for dinner. Gerry had been staying with his mother and, that night, for the first time since his release from prison, the name 'Giuseppe' was spoken aloud between them in the small bungalow. Tears were shed as each related to the other the real story of the calamitous events that had shaped their lives. Ann McKernan recalled Gerry coming into her house the next day:

> Gerry was over the moon 'cause he came up to me and said: 'Me and my ma had a good talk and it was good. Don't get me wrong – it was sad, but it was good.' He said: 'I think that was a big problem.' Gerry didn't want to open up to my ma or tell her what he was suffering. But she saw what his bed was like, you know, wet with sweat. And she understood him better. They did talk about my father, and that was the first time. He felt so close to her and he really protected her. He was very good to her. No matter what, from when he got out of jail, he was very good to my mammy. And later on, I said to her: 'Gerry said youse had a talk.' And she

said: 'Aye, we had a talk. He's all right.' That was my mammy. She wouldn't have said any more; it was between her and Gerry.[9]

Barry Walle recorded in his session notes: 'Good trip to Belfast. Hugged mum, told her how much he loved her, both burst into tears and had the most meaningful discussion ever, about feelings and Giuseppe, etc. Real buzz. Got him to label it – joy – and really acknowledge it. The first green shoots of positive emotion.'[10] Sadly, the green shoots withered.

Despite the fact that they were no longer lovers, Angie continued to visit Gerry and look after him by cooking his meals, changing his bedding, washing his clothes, and sometimes, if he was particularly jittery, even shaving him. She would still sleep in the same bed with him and help him through his nightmares and the panic attacks. On 14 December 2002, the two went to London to attend a party and, although drugs were readily available, neither took any, a measure of how far they had come since going cold turkey in 1998.

Sarah Conlon visited the chest clinic on Belfast's Lisburn Road on 17 February 2003. Ann McKernan recalled: 'They saw a black shadow on her lung and they wanted to keep an eye on her, and she had to go back because they saw a deeper one. We had to wait a lot of weeks to find out what it was.'[11]

On 12 March, Gerry flew to Belfast to attend to his mother. He found looking after Sarah to be cathartic and later told Barry Walle that he had never felt closer to his mother since his release from prison. In another development, Gerry told the psychotherapist that ministering to his mother had 'kept his thoughts off his own situation'. That he had registered the absence of his own paralysing thoughts during his trip to Belfast is profound. Had Gerry inadvertently identified the means whereby he could put a halt to his psychological collapse?

In the following months, Conlon made several trips back to Belfast and each time, on his return to Plymouth, he told Walle that he took great comfort in being able to help his mother. A corollary of Gerry staying with his mother was that, in the intimacy of Sarah's little bungalow, they were able to once again confide in each other and dismantle the wall of silence that had separated them. To the family's relief, it was later discovered that the matriarch did not have cancer, although she emerged from the experience a much frailer woman.

At the end of May 2003, Angie sat Gerry down and informed him that she was going back to live permanently in London. He hugged her and wished her well in her new life. But after Angie had left, Barry Walle recorded that Gerry was upset at her departure. This was hardly a surprise because these two swashbucklers had quite a history between them: they had stayed together when there was money to burn and when they were so broke they ate throwaway food from Mayfair's hotel bins; they fought, they fell out, they made up; they helped free each other of their drug addictions; she had climbed into his bed even after their love affair ended; he had restored her self-esteem, but now she was moving on. Angie recalled her wedding in 2006. She asked Gerry if he was coming, and he assured her he was: 'I'm running around all day looking for him and my husband was running around looking for me, and Gerry didn't come,' said Angie. 'I was really, really annoyed and I removed him from my Facebook. I was disgusted, and when I finally met up with him, he said: "I couldn't watch you getting married to someone else. I just couldn't." I cried for years over him. We just didn't know.'[12]

Barry Walle's treatment programme ended in June 2003 when he retired. Even though the treatment was over, their friendship survived, with Walle calling in on Conlon, sometimes three times a week, and taking him for walks in the surrounding countryside. In the final entry of his notes, Walle recorded: 'Managed in vivo [outside of Conlon's normal environment] supermarket shopping unaccompanied, but glad to get out so not so strongly reinforced.'[13] Conlon had a long way to go as far as his mental health was concerned, but in persuading him that he *could* go into a supermarket on his own, Walle had broken through a barrier. Walle's notes show that, while the nightmares persisted, there was a marked decrease in their regularity. Moreover, when Conlon first began talking to Walle in 2000, he had had little or no contact with his family for two years and had never candidly spoken to his mother. By 2003, he was regularly travelling back to Belfast to meet his family and had had several important conversations with Sarah.

Other people were having important conversations about him and Sarah, and one of them was Margaret Walsh, a Social Democratic and

Labour Party councillor from west Belfast. 'My husband, Gerry, knew Giuseppe because they both came from Bow Street, in the old Pound Loney [a demolished Victorian area of the Lower Falls], and Gerry said Giuseppe was a very nice man. And I remember me and my mummy having a conversation about the lack of an apology and her saying to me: "If you feel you have to do something about it, then follow your heart." And that's what I did.'[14]

In 2003, Walsh began the process that would eventually see the British prime minister, Tony Blair, deliver the apology that the Conlon and Maguire families had been seeking since their arrests thirty-two years earlier. The diminutive, softly spoken councillor's first port of call was her party leader, Mark Durkan, who agreed to meet Sarah and Gerry Conlon. Durkan said:

> I met Gerry in the bungalow beside St Peter's Cathedral. I spoke to him and Sarah, and it was separate conversations. Gerry seemed to be in a very dark and lonely place. He was describing what he had gone through, of how he never escaped the flashbacks. As well as the apology, he was also making the case for the quality of psychological treatment that he and others needed. He had his facts well-marshalled. And then he went from these very vivid, articulate and intense flows to staring into a teacup, almost folded over in the chair, just lapsing into silence. And then there was an impish smile and he was back. That was one thing about Gerry that always struck me: whoever he was meeting, he always had you well-taped. He could colour in a whole set of characteristics about who was at the meeting, and who had rank and who hadn't. And he could read a room, and of course he played it: he could turn on an outburst, and find out who had written the brief for the meeting; his antennae were amazing.
>
> What was coming across in the general sense was that Gerry wanted the apology for Sarah, she wanted it for Gerry and both wanted it for Giuseppe. Gerry was also mindful of the Maguire Seven and he was saying that the Maguires needed their apology too. And when I brought this up with Blair, he said: 'Okay, tell me more about this.'[15]

On 19 April 2004, Tony Blair sent Durkan a letter in which he wrote: 'As you know from my letter of 20 October 2003, it is my view that it is a matter of greatest regret when anyone suffers a miscarriage of justice. There has been a miscarriage of justice in the case of Giuseppe Conlon and those convicted with him. I am very sorry indeed that this should have happened.' This letter was almost an exact reproduction of the letter that Blair had sent to Courtney Kennedy-Hill in 2000. During the three intervening years, Blair had given no indication that he was prepared to issue a public apology to the Conlons and the Maguires. Clearly he preferred the idea of offering half-baked sentiments of regret through third parties, in the hope that that would be the end of the matter. Like others, he underestimated Gerry Conlon.

On 23 January 2005, the Conlon family attended a special Mass in St Peter's Cathedral in west Belfast to mark the 25th anniversary of Giuseppe's death. Afterwards, in an interview with *The Irish News*, Sarah Conlon said: 'There's not a day goes past you don't think about some part of it. It's just something I have never got over. It's something that happened that should never have happened. You will be going to your grave with it. I just couldn't believe it. Everything fell to pieces.'[16] Speaking to the same reporter, Gerry Conlon eloquently relayed his trauma and the guilt that he still carried: 'Our lives are always going to be empty because the most important person has been taken from us through medical neglect. It leaves you so devastated. So empty that it's hard to get up and face the days. The family is deeply distressed in their own heads. I come home and look at my sisters and mother and I feel so guilty. I shouldn't feel guilty. It should be those that fabricated it, the British government, the police.'[17]

Margaret Walsh saw an opportunity. 'I came up with the idea of a petition,' she said matter-of-factly. 'I contacted the *Irish News* and they were very enthusiastic about it. But it wasn't just me; Mark Durkan and Brian Barrington [a personal advisor to Seamus Mallon MP] did a lot of the work. And so did Joe McKernan; Joe did a mountain of work on his own.'[18]

On 25 January, *The Irish News* officially declared its support for the Conlon family by launching a petition for their readers to sign and send to Tony Blair. With a photograph of Giuseppe Conlon in the top-left corner, the petition said: 'We, the undersigned, call on the British prime minister, Tony Blair, to issue a public apology for the miscarriage of justice which saw Giuseppe Conlon die in jail for a crime he did not commit. We also call on Mr Blair to ensure that the Conlon family, and those who have suffered similar miscarriages of justice, receive the care and counselling they require to recover from their traumatic ordeals.'

In the Shelbourne Hotel in St Stephen's Green, Dublin, on 27 January, Gerry Conlon and Jim Sheridan threw their arms around each other. It was an emotional reunion for both men. Adding his name to the petition, Sheridan said that an apology would restore 'a level of respect'. The film producer added: 'One of the tragedies of war is that families can get split apart and it is time to repair these things. It's an old wound and it's time to let it heal up properly.'[19] Afterwards, Sheridan, the Conlon party of Sarah, Gerry, Bridie, Ann and her husband Joe, along with Mark Durkan and Margaret Walsh made their way to Government Buildings to meet the Taoiseach, Bertie Ahern.

The meeting began at 4.30 p.m. in the Sycamore Room in the prime minister's department. Mark Durkan was moved by what happened next: 'And I remember going to Government Buildings to visit Bertie, and Sarah getting down on her knees and kissing his hand. It was like an old-fashioned image of people kissing the bishop's ring.' When asked what the Taoiseach's reaction was, Durkan said: 'He was touched; he was embarrassed; he got her up, and later on they were walking out and he had his arm around her and gave her a hug. And I think in the hall on the way out, she whispered something in his ear.'[20] After the meeting, Durkan told reporters that the Taoiseach was 'absolutely with us on the need for a public apology directly and sincerely given to the family'.[21]

Within days of launching the petition, *The Irish News* reported that it was being 'inundated with hundreds of messages from across the world in support of the campaign to secure a public apology for Giuseppe Conlon'.

On 1 February, Bertie Ahern met his British counterpart, Tony Blair, in 10 Downing Street. Mark Durkan met Mr Blair separately and said that the prime minister was 'very quick' to say he would make a public apology as soon as possible. Margaret Walsh had the pleasure of telling the Conlons of Blair's willingness to publicly apologise. The family were ecstatic.

On the morning of 9 February 2005, all roads led to Westminster. Despite Angie having bid Gerry farewell before going back to London, they had kept in close contact. Gerry tried to settle his nerves by making breakfasts in Angie's mother's café in Dagenham. Soon Barry Walle picked up Angie and him and brought them to the Houses of Parliament. Other members of the Conlon family travelled from their hotel to Westminster by train. The trip evoked heart-rending memories. The eldest of Gerry's sisters, Bridie Brennan, captured the mood: 'As soon as I got on the platform, it just felt as if I was going on a visit. I have sad emotions. I'm thinking about Daddy. I am bringing myself back thirty years. It's frightening.'[22]

Contact between the Conlon and Maguire families had been non-existent ever since their arrests in 1974/75, and the tensions that had divided them were still relevant thirty years later. How would the families cope with being side-by-side, receiving the same apology? And if the ice was to be melted, where, and in what circumstances, would the thaw take place? Patrick Maguire, who had been only thirteen years old when he was wrongfully convicted of possessing nitroglycerine and sentenced to four years, recalled the vital conclave:

> The night before I had decided that it was time to let go of my hatred for Gerry Conlon. For a long time, I had been very angry with him for having volunteered our names to the police. For a long time I would have killed him without thinking twice had I bumped into him – or so I believed. However, now I'd come to realize he wasn't the only one to blame for what had happened – there'd been many others – and he'd been a victim too. For these reasons I'd decided I'd talk to him, which I hadn't done since he told the police we were bombmakers. I would do it, not for my peace of mind, but for his. I hadn't told my family I was going to do this.
>
> As we moved along a corridor, I saw him. I walked towards him with my hand out so he would not misunderstand my intentions.

FOURTEEN

Then it was done, and it was good, and more followed. He spoke to my Mum too and she spoke to him.

For me, that was the best part of the day.[23]

The arrangement had been that Tony Blair would give the apology at Prime Minister's Questions, after a question posed by SDLP MP, Eddie McGrady. However, parliamentary procedure meant that questions to the prime minister were drawn in a ballot and could not be prearranged. Therefore, the apology would not be given from the floor of the house. When Gerry Conlon heard this news, he broke down in tears and was comforted by his sisters.

The Conlon and Maguire parties sat stunned in the 'Strangers Gallery' after Prime Minister's Questions had finished and Tony Blair had left the chamber. Was that it? Was it for this that Giuseppe Conlon had died? Was it for this that the Conlons and Maguires had been so cruelly treated for all those years? The party walked down the steps from the gallery, dejected and profoundly disappointed, but all was not lost. An aide to Tony Blair approached and informed them that they were to meet the prime minister in his private office in the Commons where he would personally apologise to them. The mood lifted when the aide escorted them, about twenty in all, to Blair's office.

Standing at the open door, Blair first shook Gerry Conlon's hand. It was a warm handshake, the greeting of a man anxious to present an image of sympathy, someone who was taking responsibility for putting right a terrible wrong. The party filed into the prime minister's stately office and stood around an oval table. There was a tripod stand with a television camera in the corner.

Gerry spoke to Blair about the suffering his family had endured. The prime minister listened intently and put his arm around the west Belfast man as they spoke. It was a tender and sincere gesture. Then a very dignified Vincent Maguire spoke of his family's torment, of how he had spent his childhood years in prison. Tony Blair listened as the Conlon and Maguire families told him their harrowing stories. Finally the moment that the families had been waiting so long for was upon them.

Standing in front of the families, Tony Blair read out a prepared statement in which he appropriately expressed his sadness at the appalling loss of life in the Guildford and Woolwich pub bombings. Then he said:

> There was a miscarriage of justice in the case of Gerard Conlon and all the Guildford Four, as well as Giuseppe Conlon and the Maguire families and all the Maguire Seven. And, as with the others, I recognise the trauma that the conviction caused the Conlon and Maguire families and the stigma wrongly attached to them to this day. I am very sorry that they were subject to such an ordeal and such an injustice. That is why I am making this apology today. They deserve to be publicly and completely exonerated.

There was an intense silence as the majesty of the prime minister's words swirled around the room. Then there came an eruption of applause and emotion. The families joyously hugged one another, the old antagonisms buried beneath a shroud of vindication. Tony Blair thanked each family member for coming along, gave each a signed copy of the apology and shook their hands. He gave an extra one to Gerry for his mother, who had remained back in Belfast.

Before leaving, Gerry Conlon reminded the prime minister that the families needed immediate psychological treatment to deal with the trauma he had referred to in his statement of apology. Blair turned to his parliamentary private secretary, David Hanson MP, and told him to make sure the appropriate remedies were put in place.

Gerry Conlon, a scarf wrapped around his neck and his arms around Ann and Bridie, with his nieces Sarah-Kate McKernan and Mary Brennan beside him, walked out of the Houses of Parliament. Reporters thronged around. Annie, Vincent and Patrick Maguire, Gerry's sisters Bridie and Ann, and Margaret Walsh joined him to face the press. Gerry's first reaction to Blair's apology was: 'He went beyond what we thought he would: he took time to listen to everyone. His sincerity shone through – you could see he was physically taken aback when he saw the trauma and knew of the suffering. Tony Blair has healed rifts; he is helping to heal wounds.'[24]

One of the rifts that was healed was the Conlon-Maguire rift and, although there were many photographs taken that day, probably the most powerful one was of Gerry with his arm around Annie, with Vincent smiling in the background. A beaming Annie Maguire said: 'This is a great day for us. It will help our children and their children. The people who were still doubting us should now believe that we are totally innocent.'[25]

On the issue of receiving medical help for the trauma the families had been put through, Conlon said: 'This hasn't ended for us. But today is the start and if you can repair them, it is your duty to do so. The good thing is that he [Tony Blair] has acknowledged it, and he accepts that we are in pain, that we are suffering terribly; terrible nightmares and terrible post-traumatic stress disorder. It has been harder to clear our names than to get out of prison.'[26]

Back in Belfast, Mark Durkan had called in to be with Sarah Conlon when the apology came through. But she wanted to greet it on her own, in her little bungalow. Mark Durkan explained: 'Sarah wanted this space for herself. The apology was hers. It was entirely private. So I left until after Prime Minister's Questions: it wasn't about me, and it was entirely private.' There was a lump in his throat as Mark Durkan said: 'And afterwards I went back to Sarah and we watched the TV and there was crying and hugs and tears, and then she whispered in my ear: "I'm not afraid to die now." She was a lovely woman. Joe Hendron [Sarah's doctor and a former SDLP MP] later said: "We shouldn't be praying for Sarah Conlon; we should be praying to her."'[27]

Fifteen

Peel Street in Belfast, where Gerry Conlon was born and reared, had the luxury of having its own Lord Mayor, a dapper-dressed man called 'Dougie' Toner, whose favourite adage was: 'It's nice to be nice'. It was a credo that Giuseppe Conlon would have wholeheartedly embraced and which he would have passed on to his son. Had he been alive, Giuseppe might well have whispered in Gerry's ear: 'The SDLP were good to you, son. It's nice to be nice.'

On 12 February 2005, three days after receiving the apology, MPs Seamus Mallon and Eddie McGrady escorted Conlon into the annual SDLP conference in Derry. This was drama and Conlon was the leading actor. The audience played their part, giving the three men a standing ovation. In his address to the conference, Conlon said: 'I am standing here feeling like I have never felt since I was a child. I thought I would never come here. What happened to the Conlons and the Maguires and to Johnny Walker, who is from Derry … it has happened to a load of other people from Ireland. These miscarriages of justice happen all over the world. It does not necessarily mean a court decision – it can mean poverty.'

Conlon then went on to commend the pivotal role that Seamus Mallon had played in securing the release of the Guildford Four. After praising the former SDLP leader John Hume, Mark Durkan, Eddie McGrady, Margaret Walsh, and West Belfast MLA Alex Attwood, Conlon said: 'I know if my father were alive, my father would be telling people: "Go out and do the right thing."'

Doing the right thing was what Tony Blair had done and yet the apology was never going to provide a cure for Conlon's psychological problems. How could it? Blair had only confirmed what Gerry had already known: his extended family had been innocents. And, when the euphoria of the apology died down, when Gerry's latest *raison d'être* had been realised, who was waiting for him like the Colossus of Rhodes? Giuseppe Conlon. In his son's mind, Giuseppe was as fixed as the definite article. And it was not as if Gerry was inoculated against the logic of Blair's apology; he knew that in the prime minister's act of contrition, there was implicit recognition that, if anyone had killed Giuseppe Conlon, it was the British government. It did not matter.

Miseries collided. The old Chinese maxim, 'Be careful what you wish for' came true for Conlon when he got his wish 'to get emphysema and suffer as Giuseppe had suffered'. Then, as if he hadn't enough to contend with, he woke up one morning coughing blood – he had contracted tuberculosis. By March 2005, he was finishing a six-month course of treatment for tuberculosis, which included taking antibiotics.

Conlon remained in his emotional time capsule for a considerable period after the government's apology, while he continued to live in Plymouth. He was still plagued by flashbacks and nightmares. He was still angry. A year passed and yet nothing had happened. In a newspaper interview in Joe and Ann McKernan's house in Belfast, in March 2006, Conlon told reporter Helen Murray: 'Tony Blair turned to his PA [David Hanson] and said to him to see that we get the help we need and it's been nearly a year and we haven't heard a word. I telephoned 10 Downing Street myself and spoke to a woman called Eve Adams and she said: "Put in the request in writing."'[1]

Had Tony Blair forgotten all about his promise to Gerry the minute the Conlon and Maguire families left his office? Had he forgotten how Gerry and Annie Maguire had praised him outside the Commons? Had it slipped his mind how Gerry had said the prime minister's 'sincerity shone through'? Where was that sincerity now that the camera and the smile had been turned off? In a press interview in 2010, Conlon pulled no punches: 'We followed up on Tony Blair's promise and were basically told to get lost. He lied to us – the apology means nothing.'[2]

Few people would fault Conlon for believing that Blair had reneged on his promise, but things were not as black and white as Gerry thought. Commenting on Blair's attitude, Barry Walle said: '"The apology means nothing" isn't entirely true, but it [the treatment Blair had promised] was minimal and a struggle to get.' Walle went on to say: 'Capio Nightingale [a psychiatric hospital in Marylebone, London, where Conlon received treatment from 19 November to 14 December 2006] was an outcome from the apology, but it wasn't automatic, still had to fight to get it. Arguments about where the funding would come from, etc. Ridiculous amount of meetings. I think in the end the health authority here [Plymouth] funded it. Some monies may have come from central sources but if they did, I didn't hear about them.'[3]

The bond between Paddy Hill and Conlon had been severed over the latter's drug-taking in 1991. However, this did not mean that Hill held any animosity towards Conlon. Far from it – Paddy had been around long enough to know that Emperor Coke had ruled Gerry back then and that he had had little control over his life. For his part, Gerry had no beef with Paddy or anybody else – with the exception of Tony Blair. Still, it took tears to water this withered friendship.

Seventy-three-year-old Richard 'Dicky' McIlkenny had been the first of the newly released Birmingham Six to speak to the press outside the Old Bailey, on 14 March 1991. Since then he had lived quietly with his wife, Kathleen, and six children, in Celbridge, Co. Kildare, in the Irish Republic. Like the vast majority of miscarriage of justice victims, Dicky had found it an almost impossible task to adjust to life outside of prison and, while some turned to drugs, his poison of choice was alcohol: 'I was a different person,' he said. 'I was drinking bottle after bottle of vodka. I'd wake up and I'd drink. It just crippled me. You think you're in charge, but you're not.'[4]

Dicky had been suffering from cancer and died on 21 May 2006. Over 400 people attended Dicky McIlkenny's funeral, a measure of the esteem in which the man was held. Amongst the congregation were those with whom he had been charged: Paddy Hill, Gerry Hunter, Hugh Callaghan, Johnny Walker and Billy Power. Also there were Gerry Conlon, Paul Hill and Paddy Armstrong of the Guildford Four. Gareth Peirce attended. At the funeral Mass, his daughter Ann described her father as 'a gentle soul who had the heart of a lion'.

After the funeral, Paddy Hill introduced Gerry Conlon to John McManus, the co-founder, along with Hill, of the Miscarriage of Justice Organisation (MOJO), which is based in Glasgow. Hill was in a bridge-building mood:

And I said to him: 'What are you on now?' and he said: 'I'm on nothing' and he started telling me what happened 'cause I'd been reading about him and hearing about him. Me and him sat down and I said: 'Right, if you're clean, it's time to go back into the fuckin' fold and start working. You should be doing what you were doing when you first came out, before you went on the drug trail.' And I brought him back in, with MOJO ... and I used to drive down to Plymouth and visit him, every two or three weeks from Scotland 'cause my daughter lives down there, in Cornwall. And that was it; he was clean then, but by that time the damage had been done to his health.[5]

John McManus had accompanied Hill on his visits to Conlon in Plymouth. More than anyone else, these two men – Paddy Hill in particular – were responsible for helping Gerry climb out of the bottomless pit in which he had found himself because, crucially, they provided him with a reason to live. Conlon was only too willing to climb the rope ladder that Hill and McManus had thrown him.

Glaswegian John McManus had been a political and trade union activist all his adult life:

> I was very active in the Electricians, Electronic, Telecommunications and Plumbing Union in London in the mid-eighties, and took part in the Wapping dispute [where 6,000 print workers were sacked by Rupert Murdoch for going on strike]. I was an electrician, and I was working on building sites at the time. I met these guys who were in the Socialist Workers Party. They weren't just political but trade unionists as well. They were coming on the building sites and talking about the issues of the day and socialism; so we were getting educated by these guys. Soon after that I joined the SWP. Then I read Chris Mullins's *Error of Judgement* in 1987, and for me that was like a clarion call to fight to free the Birmingham Six.[6]

Soon after the Birmingham Six were released on 14 March 1991, McManus met Paddy Hill at a talk Hill was giving in Glasgow Town Hall. On 9 October 1994, they accidentally met again in the London underground when they were separately going to a demonstration in Hyde Park against the Criminal Justice and Public Order Act 1994. A comradely friendship formed and whenever Hill was speaking in Glasgow, he would stay in McManus's house.

After his release, Paddy Hill was burning up with a desire to help other miscarriage of justice victims. At his own expense, he was visiting prisoners up and down the length of Britain, as well as fighting human rights cases abroad. McManus was worried about the pace of Hill's life: 'I told him he was killing himself, running all over the place. We needed to get this more organised and he and I sat down and came up with MOJO.'

MOJO was officially launched in the House of Commons on 14 March 2001, the tenth anniversary of the release of the Birmingham Six. A central aim of the new organisation was to campaign for a dedicated retreat, where released miscarriage of justice victims from around the UK would receive professional and medical help, in order to reintegrate them into society. It was an ambitious and potentially expensive project that would be unlikely to draw government funding since, at its core, lay a presumption that the criminal justice system was dysfunctional. The second basis for the body's existence was to be an effective pressure group for innocent people who found themselves wrongfully incarcerated. McManus elaborated:

> MOJO don't get people out of jail; the only people who get innocent people out of prison are three appeal judges. All MOJO can do is create as much pressure as possible by working with the media. People have asked me, 'How do you know they're innocent?' and it's a good question. My reply is that it's not down to me; MOJO contacts forensic experts and shows them the evidence and waits for their reply. We then give the reply to investigative journalists. All we can do is to try to hold the authorities to account and look at the evidence, and weigh up the possibility and probability of innocence. But the main thing for me was the retreat.

Hill and McManus realised that if the retreat was to become a reality, it would need the support of the professional classes and, in particular, politicians and psychiatrists. They also realised that Gerry Conlon was well acquainted with both. Paddy Hill had been trying to arrange a meeting with Professor Gordon Turnbull for years without success. So, when Conlon met Turnbull in Plymouth, in 2006, Hill and McManus went along with him, and also met the consultant psychiatrist. McManus explained the importance of having Turnbull involved with MOJO: 'You see, we were trying to get the retreat set up for almost six years and it wasn't happening. And we needed somebody like Turnbull to support the rationale behind the retreat, and not just that, we thought he could open doors.' McManus and Hill did meet Turnbull but nothing of substance came of the meeting.

On 19 November 2006, Professor Turnbull arranged for Conlon to be admitted to Capio Nightingale Hospital. Trauma therapist and independent counsellor Stewart Johnson was designated to counsel and treat Conlon. On the first day, Gerry had to complete four questionnaires designed to assess his PTSD and his mental health. On each of the score-based questionnaires, Conlon scored very high, prompting Johnson to write in his 'Opinion': 'It is evident that Gerard Conlon has experienced very traumatic event(s). The circumstances and nature of his imprisonment was compounded by a plethora of traumatic events thereafter. He believed he was about to die on many occasions. His continuing fear concerning prospects of being attacked or moved without notice and the welfare of his father fuelled a sense of vulnerability, isolation and complete helplessness.'[7]

In a diary, which he kept of his time in Capio Nightingale, Conlon recorded his first day with Johnson: 'I found today 20/11/06 hard going, particularly the morning. Some of the questions went right over my head. It was hard to stay focused but I think that I got the gist of it. The afternoon seemed to go better for me. I think the tranquillizers affected me more in the morning. Have no problems working with Stu [*sic*] Johnson.'[8] It did not get much better for Conlon the next day: 'Today was tough, much tougher than I thought it would be. Bloody painful, still painful even now at 10.00 p.m. Images and thoughts racing around my head. Voices from the past speaking to me. Feels like I've been cut with a surgeon's scalpel, feel wounded. Everything is so vivid, so real, so in focus. Feel like I can reach out and touch it all. Time had not diminished or faded the memories, it's like a cloak wrapped around me. Worried as how I'll sleep tonight.'[9]

Stewart Johnson was impressed with Conlon: 'Having engaged with the programme he demonstrated from the outset that he was obviously very motivated, fully committed to his recovery, and keen to maximise his time in Capio Nightingale'.[10]

Conlon's lucidity and turn-of-phrase sometimes made its way on to the pages of his diary: 'Emotionally and physically drained at this moment in time. Feels like I'm climbing Mount Everest in a deep diver's suit. Have to believe I'll reach the summit. Found it a relief to talk about my dad; he's been bottled up inside me for too long; it's almost as if up until now I have been denying his existence. I miss him so very much.'[11]

On 24 November, Conlon wrote: 'Spoke about the move from Wandsworth to "Monster Mansion" Wakefield. Even after all this time that place still has the capacity to make me shudder and feel like throwing up. No one can imagine the horror that exists there. A cesspit, for sure.'[12]

As ever, Gareth Peirce was supportive of Gerry and while in Capio Nightingale he frequently made his way around to her house in Kentish Town and usually stayed with her and her husband Bill at the weekends. Conlon found Bill a soothing influence: 'I enjoy Bill's company a lot. He's a nice person, nice to be around. He's also very interesting and we communicate well. Listened to some of his folk records. He has records stretching back to the thirties and forties, great singers who I'd never heard. One singer called Petra Weiss has the most amazing voice that comes from the land, haunting.'[13]

The fiercely loyal Angie called in to visit Conlon almost every night. Usually they went for a walk and occasionally had dinner together. Conlon said: 'Angie came to see me. She has been a tower of strength. We walked for ages. I cried a little. She knows me well, so she didn't push the conversation. We shared two bottles of wine with our food. I feel good with her, she knows and understands me. She's coming again on Wednesday. I think her mum may come as well.'[14]

Anniversaries had always been a problem with Conlon and the 32nd anniversary of his arrest from his Cyprus Street home in Belfast proved to be no different:

> Thirty-two years ago today this nightmare began. Please God it's going to end soon. My head is swimming with images, of people and places. Doors opening then slamming shut behind me, the jangling of keys and the heavy tread of steel-tipped boots. Screaming police car sirens and flashing blue lights; the bite of handcuffs on wrists. The smell of stinking cells, and disgusting, inedible prison food. The fear on prisoners' faces, the rage, the anger in their eyes. The uncertainty every morning at unlock of what the coming day will bring.[15]

Barry Walle came up from Plymouth to visit his former patient and friend: 'Went to meet Barry at Kentish Town tube station. So good to see him. We went to a café for a coffee. He thinks I'm looking well.'[16] The next day, Conlon wrote: 'Went to Camden market early this morning with Barry. Not many people about as it was early and it was raining. Found a quiet café to have breakfast and talk. He has been such a good friend to me.'[17] On 12 December, Paddy Hill called in to see Conlon: 'So good to see Paddy again, he came all the way from Scotland to spend a few hours with me. He has been a good friend indeed to me.'[18] There can be little doubt that Conlon appreciated the effort his friends were making.

Conlon was apprehensive as his time in Capio Nightingale drew to a close: 'My last full day at Capio Nightingale, and my feelings are mixed. I'm glad to be leaving having completed the first stage, hopefully, of my recovery. But it's tinged with a little fear, going back out is a bit daunting. But with luck and keeping up what I've learned here, I should be alright.'[19]

Would he be all right? He had faced up to the gruelling sessions with remarkable tenacity and in a progress report to Professor Turnbull, Stewart Johnson would write:

> Gerard Conlon reported that although he had spoken about many relevant matters in previous settings, this was the first time he had been able to fully ventilate some issues that had been the cause of intense distress and it is evident this was a cathartic experience for him.

In addition, Gerard Conlon has thereafter been able to benefit from cognitive restructuring to gain alternative perspectives to the completely negative responses that his co-morbid depression and fear had fuelled. He has also begun to regain some sense of control from being able to make relevant connections between his personal reactions to the trauma and the symptoms of PTSD.

Gerard Conlon reported feeling that he has made good progress during the intense treatment regime and has demonstrated that by commencing the difficult task of setting himself some short-term goals that are both realistic and achievable. He is more relaxed and has noted he has actually begun to laugh a great deal more.[20]

Before being discharged, Conlon was made aware that he would receive additional local support and that he had the option of returning to Capio Nightingale if he felt it necessary. While in hospital, Gerry had learned that his 81-year-old mother was poorly. He resolved to return permanently to Belfast to look after her.

Northern Ireland in 2007 was not the same place it had been in 1974 when Gerry Conlon had first taken flight to England. There were no bombs exploding, no gun battles, no British soldiers on the streets and few sectarian murders. On 28 July 2005, the IRA had announced that its war with Britain was over. This declaration was followed shortly afterwards by the UDA, the biggest loyalist paramilitary organisation, also confirming that its 'war was over'. In a lexicon of clichés, nobody wanted to 'go back to the bad old days', nobody wanted their children to 'go through what they had gone through' and everybody 'was working for the peace process'. And now that peace was at hand, no one wanted to shoot dead someone who had never cocked a gun in anger.

Conlon's decision to leave Plymouth had been a momentous one because it represented release from his self-imposed quarantine. But it should be remembered that Plymouth had been an escape from his self-imposed, drug-gorging life in London. In the end, the Plymouth experiment had partially worked; the Gerry Conlon who was leaving the picturesque Devon town in December 2006 was far removed from the last-chance drug addict who had arrived there in 1998.

At Christmas 2006, Conlon reached back into his youth and refreshed lifelong friendships. In the salubrious setting of Belfast's Europa Hotel, he joined some of 'The Comanche Creeks', his old childhood gang from Peel Street. No one sitting there that night would have guessed the torment that this man had endured, and he was not inclined to tell them. Instead, the Chief of the Comanche Creeks let rip, regaling his pals with amusing tales of his life behind bars. So rich were his spellbinding stories that his audience would have been forgiven for thinking they had missed something, that he had found it a delight to be locked up at Her Majesty's pleasure. Then, when asked, he named every man, woman and child in every house in Peel Street, a main thoroughfare which had over fifty houses in total. The pre-prison memory which Barry Walle had tried so desperately to retrieve had returned with laser-like precision. Of Conlon's performance that night, 'Celtic Pat' McDonnell said: '"Fadley" [Gerry's childhood nickname] was on top of his game, really. His eyes were sparkling and they were everywhere. He missed nothing. Nobody walked into that lounge that he didn't clock. And it was the old Gerry, y'know: the live-wire, the Jack-the-Lad Gerry. He was some craic, I'll tell ya.'[21]

Conlon stayed with his mother in her small bungalow in Lisfadden Way, in the Lower Falls. Sarah, as she had done all her life, pampered her son. A metamorphosis was underway. Conlon was assiduously cultivating an alternative lifestyle from that which he had experienced in Plymouth. He started going for games of snooker and the odd drink with friends. He was looking after his appearance. He sometimes went to the bookies and the barber's on his own. People were getting used to seeing him about the area. There was no hostility towards him. Almost every week he went for breakfast with this author. Both of us were ex-prisoners and had done hard time while in prison, and each could relate to the other's experiences. The conversation would be lively, often political, and always free from the politeness of censorship – each of us knew that we could tell the other to 'wise up', if we thought it necessary. We often went to the theatre and rock concerts. Conlon made friends like hillbillies made moonshine. CEOs, playwrights, doctors, journalists, postmen and store assistants – once they tasted Gerry's wit and charm, they were hooked. As a result, his rock concert entourage began to grow. He knew most of the big rock stars personally and was able not only to get his friends into the shows for nothing, but also into the VIP lounges. Despite his oft-expressed abhorrence of celebrity, he liked the trappings of VIP life: the idea of being feted held a certain appeal. On that point, there was still a little seam of rebellion within him: he could not quite purge himself of the notion that the party had to run its course, and this regularly prompted him to go back with the musicians to their hotel for drinks after the concerts. And sometimes these parties lasted until the next day. But, where previously he might have jumped on a plane and travelled with the band to their next venue, he went home instead: the Renaissance man now had the emotional wherewithal to pull himself back from the brink. Whatever life tools the psychiatrist Stewart Johnson had given him in Caprio Nightingale Hospital, they were working.

Besides sowing relationships in Belfast in 2007, Conlon, along with John McManus and Paddy Hill, toured universities and trade union halls in Britain and Ireland, lecturing on current and historical miscarriages of justice. Travelling in a camper van, the three arrived in Galway, where Conlon and Hill were lined up with Sunny Jacobs to speak on the subject 'Is there a life after life?' at the Galway Film Fleadh on 11 July 2007. Sunny Jacobs was a miscarriage of justice victim who had served seventeen years, five on death row, in a Florida prison for the murder of two policemen, before being exonerated. Supporting the MOJO party at the Fleadh were members of the Alabama 3, the band that composed and recorded 'Woke Up This Morning', the theme song of the television series, *The Sopranos*. A call was put in to Joey Cashman in Dublin, and he took a taxi across Ireland to Galway. John McManus recalled: 'So Joey turns up and somebody gives him a fiver to get a pint. Now, he's just come from Dublin and he's clean. He's trying to get away from the dope and, on top of that, he's knackered. He goes into the pub and he's no sooner in than he's back out again, and he says the barman won't serve him because he's "drunk". Joey couldn't believe it: "I'm drunk? Me? Fucking drunk? I haven't been this sober in forty years!" We were rolling with laughter. I swear, not one of us could talk for half an hour.'[22]

In December 2007, Conlon, Hill and McManus were accompanied by an all-party delegation that was lobbying the parliamentary under-secretary at the Ministry of Justice, Maria Eagle, for funding for a centre where miscarriage of justice victims could receive specialist treatment. Included in the delegation were Mark Durkan, Jeremy Corbyn and John McDonnell of the Labour Party, and Willie Rennie and John Hemming of the Liberal Democrat Party. Looking back, Conlon said: 'She [Maria Eagle] came out and seen me and Paddy Hill, and she came over and started crying. And she said: "I've been in the back room and I've been reading your files and youse weren't a miscarriage of justice – youse were something else."'[23] In response to these comments, Conlon had a view on what else they could be: 'We always knew we were something else! This wasn't a mistake; this was deliberate policy by the British government to stop a murderous campaign in England by the IRA!'[24]

Paddy Hill's memory of the meeting with the government minister accords with Conlon's:

> Maria Eagle came through the door and she walked up to me and Gerry Conlon. She put her arms around us and she hugged me and Gerry. She had tears in her eyes and she turned around and said to me and Gerry Conlon: 'I want to apologise to you two personally for what happened to you. I have just finished reading your files in the backroom and I want to tell you now: you were not a miscarriage of justice; you were something else.'[25]

Maria Eagle declined to meet this author to discuss Conlon's and Hill's claims. Mark Durkan MP, who had tried to set up the meeting with her, relayed her views on the matter:

> She told me that she has no recollection of saying such a thing and says she would not have been in a position to imply or divulge more about the cases. Maria said that she would not have had access to historic case papers. Her recollection is of being sympathetic with their lobbying objective of a bespoke treatment and recovery centre for victims of miscarriages of justice and appreciating that the personal impact is not allayed by the correction of verdicts and release.[26]

Gerry Conlon and Paddy Hill both had excellent memories. They could recall in minute detail their abuse at the hands of the authorities, and each fed off the other. Of the two, Conlon was the more eloquent speaker. However, if Hill lacked anything in articulation, he more than compensated for it in his dynamism and passion. Additionally, each had the ability to hold an audience; to open a heavy prison door and coax the listeners into their tiny cells; to invite them to experience the isolation, the brutality, the terror and the unyielding pessimism that comes from long years in prison without as much as a glimmer of hope. Some people believe that this constant time-travelling back to terrible times only irrigates the pain and prevents the victim, or victims, from moving on. Indeed, the German philosopher Friedrich Nietzsche said: 'If you gaze into the abyss, the abyss gazes also at you.'[27]

It had been a long, sometimes cruel journey from the day he had gone cold turkey, but miraculously, Gerry Conlon, the consummate survivalist, had pulled through. Perhaps he had pulled through because his mother believed in miracles: she prayed for them every day of her life. She did the Stations of the Cross three times a week, year after year, in St Peter's Cathedral, in the hope that God would hear her prayers and bring her husband and son back to her. Only her son returned alive.

Born in Mary Street, at its junction with Peel Street, on 20 November 1926, Sarah Maguire, as she was then, had had a hard but typical upbringing. Like most young girls of her generation, she left school at fourteen and went to work in one of the local linen mills, getting up at 5.30 a.m. to the sound of the factory horn. It was a horrific job, made unbearable by the swelteringly heat and the wholesome intake of flax dust. After leaving the mill, Sarah worked in Harry Kane's scrapyard and rag store in Cyprus Street, where she separated the more expensive woollen garments from other clothing. Here was another grimy, dusty job. In 1947, Sarah married Giuseppe Conlon, who worked for a time in the Harland and Wolff shipyard, where he painted the hulls of ships with red lead, an anti-corrosive paint. Requests to management for masks to protect the workers from the dangerous fumes given off by the red lead were ignored. Consequently,

Giuseppe contracted tuberculosis and he suffered from lung disease for the rest of his life.

Sarah's health had been failing ever since a shadow had been discovered on her lungs in 2003. Doctors who treated her at that time had recommended that she stop smoking, but she never got around to it. By the beginning of April 2008, Sarah's children could see that their mother's health was waning. Ann McKernan said: 'She was having trouble sleeping and she was sweating. I must have changed her bedclothes eight or nine times that night. And she was in excruciating pain. I sent for her GP, Dr Lenfesty.' The next morning Dr Lenfesty examined Sarah and told her that there was something on her lung. 'Mammy had pneumonia and Lenfesty prescribed her antibiotic tablets,' Ann said. 'But he was concerned, you know, and he said he'd be coming back the next morning.' When the GP returned the next day, he told Sarah that he was sending for an ambulance to bring her to hospital. 'The first thing my mammy said to me was: "I want a priest. I haven't been to confession." And I said to her: "Sure what sins have you committed?" And she said: "Never you mind. Get me a priest."' Ann fetched Father Brendan Mulhall out of Clonard Monastery. Sarah had gone on pilgrimage to the Knock Shrine with him. Ann said: 'Then we found out my mammy had lung cancer and it was only a matter of time.'[28]

Sarah Conlon died on 19 July 2008.

Speaking of his mother's strength, Gerry Conlon said: 'I couldn't have survived without her. The help Mum gave me was invaluable. Her background and beliefs and religion was what got her through, and that strength was transmitted to me and my father in letters and visits. We would look forward to Mum's letters. You got fortified from them. While others may have been daunted by the challenge ahead, she quietly met and convinced Church leaders and dignitaries, politicians and journalists, of our innocence.'[29]

At the Requiem Mass in a packed St Peter's Cathedral on 22 July, Father Mulhall said: 'In spite of the terrible, dreadful injustices that were done to Sarah and her family, there wasn't an ounce of bitterness in her. That's what everyone found so remarkable about Sarah when they met her and when they spent time in her company, that she was so peaceful, so serene, and so dignified.'[30]

Sarah's huge funeral was attended by leading members of the SDLP and Sinn Féin, as well as by Paddy Hill, John McManus and Gareth Peirce. Gerry and this author picked up Larry Love and Nick Reynolds at the airport, and the two Alabama 3 members sang and played the moving hymn 'Can the Circle Be Unbroken' by The Carter Family during the funeral Mass. As the song progressed, mourners clapped in unison and smiled. Smiles at Sarah Conlon's funeral? That seemed a fitting tribute.

Sixteen

Shortly after the death of his mother, Gerry told Ann that he was considering moving back to London, the very place from which he had fled in blind panic and terror in 1998. Maybe he thought that he was better equipped to handle London now that he had had psychiatric counselling. Or did he think he could handle a hit of crack cocaine, just one perhaps, for old time's sake? Did Gerry equate the old times with good times? Had he forgotten that night in Tufnell Park in 1994 when Joey Cashman pleaded with him not to take that first hit of crack? Had it escaped his mind how he had been reduced to eating discarded food from hotel bins and skips in Mayfair in 1995? And yet, at the very point at which the precocious Conlon was in grave danger of sipping a broth of hemlock, the happiest days of his life beckoned.

Approximately six weeks after their mother had passed away, Ann and Gerry were in the Lisfadden Way bungalow when a letter came through the postbox for him. He opened it and turned to Ann: 'Do you remember "Linda"? I used to go out with her.'

Ann shrugged: 'How can I remember the names of half the girls you went out with?'

Gerry reminded her that he had first met Linda at their cousin David Loughran's wedding in November 1989.

Ann McKernan had never been one for mincing her words: 'What does she want?'

Gerry replied that he did not know, but that Linda had left a telephone number on the letter and had written that she would meet him if he wanted – but it was entirely up to him.

They met a couple of days later, approximately six weeks after Sarah Conlon's death, with Linda picking him up in her car at the door of the bungalow. They went to lunch and repeated the experience a few days later. Conlon liked this girl; she owned a lavish bungalow in affluent south Belfast, was well-mannered, good-looking and unassuming. Twelve years his junior, Linda was a nurse by profession.

After meeting up with Linda a couple of times, Gerry approached Ann and said that he had something to tell her: 'Linda's got a daughter and she's mine.' He said his daughter was eighteen years old and was named Sara, after their mother, and that she was a law student at Queen's University Belfast. If Gerry wanted to grab Ann's attention, he certainly succeeded. When asked what she thought of this disclosure, Ann replied: 'It was such a shock. He wanted me to meet Sara, and we did meet, outside Belfast City Hall. Her mother was there. It was just a quick hello. She seemed a nice wee girl. Through time, I got to know Linda. She was a good girl – she was very good for Gerry – nobody can take that away from her. It was her who put the notion of going back to live in London out of his head. But I had questions.'[1]

Ann's questions revolved around Linda's timing. She wondered why it had taken eighteen years for Linda to let Gerry know that he had a daughter, and why she had waited until the Conlon matriarch had passed away before revealing her secret. Yet, despite their differences, Ann and Linda got along, even going on holidays together with Gerry.

The introvert and the extrovert began spending more and more time in each other's company, but each liked their own space; they would stop over in their respective homes but they preferred to return to their own bungalows the next day. Linda was considerate and attentive and, additionally, she had work experience in psychiatric therapy; she understood Gerry's psychological limitations. Accordingly, when he was stressed, she would drive him to the bookies to place his bets before going back to work. Sometimes she would call into his bungalow and make him breakfast. If he was meeting friends to go to a concert, or for a drink, she would drive them to their destination. In a newspaper article on 5 May 2009, Conlon said: 'I am now with a girl that I met when I first came out of prison and I owe her an enormous debt of gratitude.'[2]

Gerry Conlon may not quite have cast off the melancholy that had plagued him since his release from jail, but when he looked at himself in the mirror, he was a universe away from the wretched recluse who had smoked crack with the Yardies in the mid-nineties. This Gerry Conlon was full of joie de vivre. He was outgoing, committed to highlighting injustices wherever they occurred and determined to give his daughter every chance in life. As someone who had given up on ever experiencing the joy of having his own family unit, he was naturally euphoric at the way things had turned around. It was almost as if he could once again 'levitate to a higher level' – only this time it was a cocktail of love, rather than drugs, that provided the stimulus.

He had breakfast with this author in a café in Botanic Avenue, Belfast, soon after Linda had given him the good tidings. Even before the Ulster Fry hit the table, it was evident from his demeanour that a time bomb was ticking away inside him. 'I've got a daughter, Rich!' he said, his face alight. 'I've got a daughter! She's eighteen and, guess what? She's gonna be a solicitor! A solicitor … my daughter! What do you think of that?' Congratulations were offered and gratefully received. Gerry tended to bubble on when he was excited and, on that particular morning, it was hard to get a word in edgeways for, amongst other observations, he speculated that Sara had obviously inherited her brains from him.

Over the next four years, Conlon was the voice for those who had no voice. He campaigned for human rights in the United States, Australia, on the Continent and throughout Britain and Ireland. On 27 June 2008, Conlon, Hill, McManus and two other miscarriage of justice victims, Stevie Johnston and Paul Blackburn, went to Glastonbury Music Festival in Somerset, England. Amongst the many acts booked to perform were the trio's friends, the Alabama 3.

In his high-rise flat in Glasgow, in 2016, John McManus smiled. It was almost as if he was reliving the happy days of Glastonbury 2008: 'I always thought festivals were a good way to get your message through to people. We set up a stall, sold MOJO T-shirts and handed out leaflets.' Sharing the stall with the MOJO party were members of the National Union of Rail, Maritime, and Transport Workers (RMT), who were also selling T-shirts, one of which depicted a large, raised cobra and a warning: 'If provoked, will strike'. As a result of their chance meeting with the RMT members, MOJO was invited to go to London to meet the president of the union, Bob Crow, and other leading union personnel.

Gerry liked Glastonbury and, in 2008, Neil Diamond was one of the headliners. 'It doesn't matter how traumatised you are,' McManus said, 'if you're with good friends and Neil Diamond is singing "Sweet Caroline", and you're belting out "Good times never seemed so good" along with 100,000 people … it's dynamite.'[3]

On the Left Field stage, McManus introduced Conlon, Hill, Johnston and Blackburn to a receptive audience, and each spoke of their experiences and their determination to fight for others who were being unjustly held in prison. The inclusion of Johnston, from Fife in Scotland, and Blackwell, from Manchester, on stage was important because their presence reminded listeners that miscarriages of justice were not some Irish phenomenon from the 1970s, but rather an ongoing United Kingdom-wide occurrence.

Following the invitation from the RMT members, Conlon, Hill and Paul Blackburn addressed an assembly of union members. Such was their impact that they were invited to their union's annual conference the following year. John McManus described the moving atmosphere at that fringe meeting:

> You could cut the atmosphere with a knife. And this 60-year-old docker from Liverpool, a hard man, stood up, and said: 'My son's in prison. He's not like you guys; he was guilty. But what it did to my family—' And he just burst into tears, I mean real sobbing and everybody, these big builders, were hugging and comforting the man. It was almost spiritual. This … this was the power of Gerry and Paddy. I mean, Paddy had the fire. Gerry also had the fire but he connected more. Paddy's trauma took him really deep – not that it didn't take Gerry deep – but Gerry could pull himself back from it. Once Paddy is in that trauma, he goes all the way; he can take you into that cell; he can terrify you. At the same time, people loved Paddy. When you put the two of them together, my God, they were unbelievable.

Towards the end of the address, Christy Cain, the branch secretary of the Maritime Union of Australia (MUA) entered the room and listened to the discourse. When that meeting was over, Christy promised Conlon and Hill that he would arrange for them to come to Australia on a speaking tour. The trade unionist was as good as his word, and by December 2009 Conlon, Hill and McManus were Australia-bound.

They were in Australia for three weeks, during which time they gave talks in Perth, Melbourne, Brisbane and Sydney. McManus said:

> We thought there was an opportunity to get the retreat thing off the ground, but we didn't know what we were getting into. My opinion after Australia was that we were meeting the most switched-on people in the world 'cause we weren't meeting academics or business people, we were meeting workers, real thinkers, workers who had educated themselves, who fought for their communities. It was none of this 'Me, Me, Me'; it was all of us and how can we best help you. That's what really took Gerry by storm. Paddy had a trade union background but Gerry hadn't, and I don't think he realised the power of a real trade union until Australia. Christy Cain was phenomenal. He was secretary of the Dockers' union.

Conlon and Hill spoke out on a range of local issues, one of which was the case of 46-year-old Mr Ward from Warburton, Western Australia. Mr Ward was a multi-talented man who was an expert in native culture, arts and the land. An Aboriginal elder, he had taught Australian and British Special Forces the art of surviving in the remote bush. On 26 January 2008, he was arrested after an elders meeting in his desert home town of Laverton and placed in a metal 'pod' in the rear of a prison van. It was 40 degrees centigrade outside, and there was no air-conditioning inside the pod. Mr Ward was then transported 570 kilometres to a courthouse in Kalgoorlie, where he was remanded in custody, whereupon he was driven another 353 kilometres to jail in the same airless prison van. By the time the van stopped at the prison, Mr Ward was unconscious. It was noted that he had third-degree burns to his stomach. He died soon afterwards. Commenting on the treatment that Mr Ward received, Dennis Eggington of the Aboriginal Legal Service of Western Australia said: 'We don't treat animals like that. We don't treat our pets like that.'[4]

Conlon, Hill and McManus, now known by their sponsors in Australia as the 'MOJO 3', were briefed on the plight of Mr Ward by the 'Deaths in Custody Watch Committee'. Seamus Doherty, a Falls Road man, who was also a member of the committee said, 'It was clear that they were deeply interested in the plight of the Aboriginal people. They listened and asked questions about the over-jailing of Aboriginal people in the prison system. Gerry was particularly moved and still today the elders talk of Gerry's great understanding, and of how he related to the pain and anguish of Aboriginal suffering.'[5] Conlon and Hill highlighted the injustice that had been meted out to Mr Ward and to others of the Aboriginal community in subsequent public talks.

It was a punishing tour for Conlon and Hill. Besides a gruelling, inter-state speaking schedule, activists and victims were making their way to them in the hope that they would highlight their individual cases. 'Forget about priests and all that,' John McManus said, 'these people had heard Gerry and Paddy speak and they were relaying the most horrific stories about jail, and people who wouldn't talk to another sinner in the world about their trauma were queuing up to tell them about it. And the boys never complained once.'[6]

In June 2010, the MOJO 3 were invited back to Australia specifically to lend their support to a construction worker called Ark Tribe. Tribe was among a group of Adelaide workers who voted for a one-day strike on 30 May 2008 because of work-safety concerns. The building company, Hindmarsh Constructions, then contacted the police, who locked out the workers the next day.

The John Howard-led government had created the Australian Building and Construction Commission (ABCC), which was effectively an industry police force that had the power to summon workers before them and compel them to divulge information about their workmates and any breaches of industrial law in which they might have been involved. The penalty for ignoring an ABCC summons was six months' imprisonment. Ark Tribe was summoned to such an ABCC meeting, but he did not turn up and was subsequently charged with contempt. The Construction, Forestry, Mining and Energy Union (CFMEU) supported their member. Peter Ong, a union representative from the Electrical Trades Union, defined the issues: 'The legislation, along with the ABCC, was introduced to do one thing and that was to strike fear into the hearts of workers in the construction industry so they would not join a union, would not attend union meetings, would not be involved in any union activity and would not stand up against adverse and unsafe conditions. In other words, a compliant and controlled workforce.'[7]

The MOJO 3 arrived in Brisbane at midnight on Saturday, 12 June 2010 after a twenty-six-hour flight. Within three hours of arriving in Brisbane, Conlon and Hill were being interviewed by Graham Archer, the producer of the current affairs programme *Today Tonight*. The trio flew to Adelaide on the Monday. For John McManus it did not get any better:

> This was wonderful. This was one of the best experiences I've ever had in my life. We go to Adelaide on the Monday and we're taken straight from the airport to this big pub in the city, and it's full of these top trade unionists from all over the country. So, we're in the pub. We arrived at four o'clock in the afternoon and somebody said to me: 'Fucking hell. They're all here.' I told some people, 'We're gonna be on the news.' And it's all around the pub that Paddy and Gerry are there. So it comes six o'clock and everybody's talking and I just shouted, 'Shut up! Fucking shut up!' And they all looked at me 'cause they don't know me, and they didn't know what was going on: they don't know about the TV programme. And it came on and there was a silence. And see when it finished, fucking hell, not a sound. I was really worried. Then it went WHOOSH! They went fucking mad! Mental! Guys came up and said they had never, never seen a positive union message from the news broadcast like that one. They'd never seen anything like it.[8]

The message that Conlon had relayed on *Today Tonight* left no room for sentiment: 'Once you start going down this slippery path, where they start bringing in ... or taking bits of maybe Homeland Security in America, bits of the Prevention of Terrorism Act, taking them to a new country and employing them against the union, I mean, where do you stop with this Big Brother scenario?'[9]

The next day thousands of people, many holding trade union flags, gathered at the court to support Ark Tribe. As he made his way to the entrance of the court, he was escorted by the MOJO 3. McManus described the incredible scene:

> When we marched into the court the prosecution and defence teams were there, and the public and everyone just stopped what they were doing and looked at us. It was fucking incredible. And sure enough, six months later, all charges were dropped against Ark. He won it. I asked Ark how did he feel about Paddy and Gerry and he said – 'I'm totally honoured. These two guys – what they went through to come over here and support me. For me personally, as a trade unionist, to be taken into that circle and see the impact that we were having, it was just, just incredible.'[10]

Peter Ong, the hard-nosed union representative, summed up Conlon and Hill's effect on the Ark Tribe case:

> Obviously Gerry's and Paddy's notoriety played a huge part in bringing media attention, not just in Australia, but also internationally, to the injustice that was being dished out to Ark Tribe, and the fact that the normal judicial rights available to every other Australian are not available to construction workers. And the decision handed down in favour of Ark Tribe was momentous in that it ensured the ABCC's objective – the suppression of the trade unions – did not happen on our building sites. Now we have a strong and active union membership on our building sites, workers who are willing to stand up and take action if the employer is doing the wrong thing. And nearly six years after the Ark Tribe decision, not one worker has been charged with contempt even though most, if not all, refuse to even attend interviews when summoned.[11]

In January 2011, Hill, Conlon and McManus returned to Australia for the last time at the invitation of the Maritime Union of Australia. On this occasion they gave talks in Perth and Melbourne. When asked to give an assessment of Conlon's impact on MOJO, John McManus said: 'Nobody had heard of Gerry for a long time and people were very, very interested in why he was coming on board. More than anyone, I think Paddy had an idea of the impact he would have. Paddy knew him; I guess he knew that once Gerry was clean and had committed, he would be a major asset to us. His impact was profound. He was a charming man; a real charming individual.'

Conlon had always had enormous affection for 'The Home of the Brave'. He was enthralled with America and visited the country as often as possible. In April 2011, he was on a panel of miscarriage of justice victims from five different countries which discussed the topic 'An International Exploration of Wrongful Conviction' at the University of Connecticut's College of Law.

In April 2012, he made one of his numerous lecture tours to the United States to fundraise on behalf of Centurion Ministries, an American human rights organisation dedicated to fighting for those who have been unjustly sentenced by the courts. Since Centurion's birth in 1980, the organisation had secured the freedom of fifty-four innocent men and women who were serving life imprisonment, or had been on death row. Based in Princeton, New Jersey, this organisation has an impressive board of professionals: lawyers, award-winning journalists and analysts. In its mission statement it says: 'We take on the hard cases, the ones others leave behind. We are a small but mighty organization that goes boots to the ground, uncovering lost evidence, finding new evidence, convincing a coerced witness to come forward with the truth, overturning false confessions, and sometimes even finding the real criminal.' Centurion deals with approximately 1,500 requests for help every year and is developing 150 active cases. It costs in the region of $350,000 to get one innocent person out of prison and Centurion bears all the expenses. On this speaking tour, Conlon gave a talk on *In the Name of the Father* at Princeton Garden Theatre on 10 April, and five days later he repeated the exercise at the Arts Council of Princeton. He also gave lectures at schools and universities in Princeton and New York.

On 21 April, Conlon and Kate Germond, a director of Centurion Ministries, flew to Los Angeles to greet the newly released miscarriage of justice victim, Frank O'Connell, who had spent twenty-seven years in prison for a murder he did not commit. To Centurion's great credit, they uncovered new evidence which demonstrated that the sole witness against O'Connell had falsely picked his photo out of an assortment of other photos. Kate Germond had been working on O'Connell's case for fourteen years before his release.

Amongst the other interesting people whom Conlon met through Centurion Ministries on this trip were humanists, Bill and Judith Scheide, and, like most people, they warmed to the affable Irishman. William H. Scheide was an interesting man. He was a Johann Sebastian Bach scholar and has been described as a 'musician, musicologist, bibliophile and philanthropist'.[12] Bill was the grandson of wealthy oil executive William T. Scheide, who began collecting books in 1865, when only eighteen years old. By the time the library was passed on to Bill in 1954, it was already a formidable collection of rare books and manuscripts and he added greatly to it.

When the occasion of Bill's 96th birthday loomed, the Scheides decided to invite Gerry to the party and on 6 January 2010 he and Linda attended the birthday bash on the Princeton campus. But this was not the kind of party that Conlon was used to frequenting; this was a concert given by the Vienna Chamber Orchestra, under the baton of Mark Laycock, a favourite conductor of Bill's (the pair had worked out the programme between them beforehand). Although a rock 'n' roller at heart, Conlon was enthralled by the occasion and overawed by the music of Mozart and Schubert. Later, when he met Bill and Judith, Gerry presented them with a bodhrán on which was painted a Celtic cross and the American and Irish flags. Judith McCartin Scheide would later say: 'Bill and I believe in Centurion. We have loved meeting so many exonerees here in Princeton – during the concert for Bill's 96th birthday, when Gerry Conlon came to town for the screening of *In the Name of the Father*, and again in September.'[13] When Bill passed away in 2014, aged 100, he left his library to Princeton University and included in the texts were four first-edition copies of the Bible; a first printing of the United States Declaration of Independence; manuscripts by Abraham Lincoln, J.S. Bach and Ludwig van Beethoven and first editions of Shakespeare and Milton. The value of Bill Scheide's library was estimated at $300 million.

SIXTEEN

One of the most important trips that Conlon made to the United States occurred in November 2013, when he was invited by the National Irish Freedom Committee (NIFC) to New York to receive the Sister Sarah Clarke Human Rights Award. He was picked up at the airport by Mike Costello, a lifelong republican, who briefed him on the schedule. In Molly Wee Pub on Eighth Avenue and 30th Street, the two men met Sandy Boyer who, along with Conlon, had orchestrated the American campaign to free the Birmingham Six in 1990. After being approached by a drug dealer outside his accommodation, Conlon contacted his friend Kate Germond and arranged to stay with her and her family in New Jersey.

The NIFC had arranged a series of talks with Irish-American groups, whereby *In the Name of the Father* would be shown and Conlon would answer questions afterwards. Boyer recalled: 'People wondered why Gerry never watched the film. He just told them: "I lived it. I don't need to watch it." He said to me that if he saw it he might have to say something about how things really happened.'[14]

Boyer organised two meetings for Conlon with politicians over Martin Corey, a republican prisoner who had been released in 1992 after serving nineteen years for killing two police officers in an IRA attack in Aghalee, Co. Antrim. In April 2010, Corey's licence was revoked by the Secretary of State for Northern Ireland and he was returned to prison. At a closed hearing of the parole commission, evidence was withheld from Corey's defence team, and the commission ruled that he should stay in prison. Evidence withheld from defence teams? To Gerry Conlon, that had a ring to it. The two politicians whom Conlon met were Danny Dromm and New York State Comptroller, Tom DiNapoli, the sole custodian of the state's billion dollar pension funds. Boyer said: 'Gerry charmed each of them. He started with his own story and then connected that to Martin Corey. That enabled me to ask them to take action. Dromm wrote a letter supporting Martin Corey and DiNapoli raised the case with Theresa Villiers [the Northern Ireland Secretary of State] when she came looking for investment the day after our meeting.'

It was on this trip that a grand reconciliation had taken place. Boyer and Conlon had arranged to meet for lunch opposite Grand Central Station. Conlon was late. 'When Gerry arrived,' Boyer said, 'he was buzzing. I mean, he was really happy. He told me he had run into Jim Sheridan on the street and they wound up going for breakfast and reconciling completely after all those years.' Although they'd reconciled around the time of Blair's apology, Gerry still had a problem with Jim after that. However, Boyer continued: 'He was so happy he'd run into Jim. They were supposed to get together in Ireland later, but I don't think it ever happened. Gareth later told me that Gerry was reconciling with everybody because he was happy with himself for the first time since his release from the Old Bailey.'

Boyer set up a meeting for Conlon at the City University of New York Law School during this tour. It had stuck in Conlon's craw that he could not say whatever he wanted to without offending conservative Irish-Americans. 'And he let loose,' Boyer said. 'He talked about Martin Corey, the Craigavon Two and other Irish cases, and he linked them with the prisoners in Guantanamo Bay in a way I hadn't seen before.'[15]

After being presented with the Sister Sarah Clarke award, Conlon and some friends went to a local bar. Conlon was drinking shots. They went to another bar and again Conlon drank shots. By the time the drinking was over, all were drunk. Snow was on the ground. Conlon lagged behind. Ann McKernan recalled her brother telling her what happened next:

> He said he fell and they were drunk and walked on and left him. It was freezing cold, and somebody came along and phoned an ambulance. He was brought to hospital. He had a card on him identifying Centurion Ministries, and the hospital contacted them. Kate Germond went to the hospital, and they released him the next day – they didn't even do a brain scan. He said he told Kate he was all right, but I think this was where things took a wrong turn, health-wise. He came home and he had a flu and a cough ... so, I'm beginning to wonder.[16]

Sandy Boyer had one final memory of Gerry Conlon:

> I went shopping with Gerry at Abercrombie and Fitch on Fifth Avenue because he had a list of presents to bring home. When

we were leaving the store, Linda phoned on his mobile. I dropped back so as not to intrude on their conversation but I heard him say, 'You've got to come to New York.' It struck me that if Gerry was really enjoying something, he wanted to share it with Linda.[17]

Sandy Boyer, the indefatigable socialist and human rights advocate, passed away on 11 February 2016.

On 3 July 2010, Gareth Peirce introduced Conlon at the annual Marxist Festival in London. Alongside him on the platform was Moazzam Begg, a British Pakistani who claimed that he had been tortured in Bagram detention centre, after which he was held for three years by the Americans in Guantanamo Bay prison and then released on 25 January 2005. Conlon had campaigned to secure Begg's release and at that time he was still fighting for the release of another Guantanamo prisoner, Shaker Aamer. During an address to his 'Friends and Comrades', Conlon said:

> But three weeks after I got out, that auld bastard Lord Denning said – and I quote: 'If we'd have hung the Birmingham Six and the Guildford Four there'd have been no campaigns against British justice and it wouldn't have been dragged through the mud.' Now this is the Establishment's fear. I mean, it's an absolute pleasure to be here, but I think charity starts at home. I'm wearing a T-shirt from a friend of mine, Gary Crichley, who we took onto our wing in Long Larton in 1983. He's still in fucking prison! [Crichley, who always proclaimed his innocence, was eventually released in March 2012.] There's a young kid called Sam Hallam from down the road in Hoxton who was five miles away from a murder – he's still in prison [Hallam had his conviction quashed by the court of appeal on 16 May 2012]. We need to support the innocent people at home as well as the innocent people abroad. Thanks very much. It's been a pleasure.[18]

Besides Martin Corey's case, Conlon took up the case of Brian Shivers, a 41-year-old County Derry man who was charged with the Real IRA murders of British soldiers, Mark Quinsey and Cengiz 'Patrick'

Azimkar on 7 March 2009. Shivers suffered from cystic fibrosis and, at a High Court bail application, his consultant told the judge that if his patient did not get a lung replacement very soon, he might not be alive by the time the case came to trial. The judge, none other than the Lord Chief Justice for Northern Ireland, Sir Charles Declan Morgan, did not blink and dismissed the application. This refusal to grant bail to a dangerously ill man and to keep him in prison, where medical care was invariably inadequate, opened up a potentially appalling vista for human rights activists: Shivers had to be presumed innocent until proven guilty, but what if he died in prison by neglect before reaching trial? Conlon's memories of prison medical care always reverted back to his father, Giuseppe: 'My father took ill just before Christmas '79 and he had cancer and emphysema and they [prison doctors] were giving him Benylin [a cough mixture]. They were giving him Benylin for cancer!'[19] For Conlon there was no choice: he waded in.

In a press interview on 16 September 2009, Conlon roundly condemned the murders of sappers Quinsey and Azimkar. He then called for Shivers's release on 'humanitarian grounds,' before saying: 'Legal history shows that all too often the latest atrocity in the Northern Ireland conflict is followed by a miscarriage of justice.' In an obvious reference to Brian Shivers's ill-health, he said: 'I often wonder if my father would have lived if he'd been given proper medical treatment instead of being forced to die in prison. We can't afford a situation arising where potential victims of miscarriages of justice are allowed to die in custody prior to their trials.'[20] Solicitors for Shivers believe that Conlon's intervention directly influenced the High Court's decision to grant their client bail.

On 20 January 2012, Brian Shivers was found guilty of the two soldiers' murders, but this was overturned on appeal and, at a retrial in 2013, Shivers was exonerated, with Judge Donnell Deeny saying that the killers had been 'ferocious and ruthless' and that Shivers would have been 'an unlikely associate for this hardened gang to rely on'. Outside the court, Shivers's solicitor, Niall Murphy, told reporters: 'Brian Shivers has suffered the horror of having been wrongfully convicted in what now must be described as a miscarriage of justice.'

Another case that Conlon took up in Northern Ireland was that of the 'Craigavon Two'. On 9 March 2009, PSNI constable Stephen

Carroll was part of a police mobile unit that was sent to investigate an emergency 999 call in the Craigavon area of County Armagh. While in his police vehicle, a Continuity IRA gunman opened fire and shot Constable Carroll dead.

On 30 March 2012, a former Sinn Féin councillor, Brendan McConville, and John Paul Wootton were convicted of Constable Carroll's murder. Conlon came to the case with some reluctance:

> I'm not involved in politics. I don't support the IRA. I don't support republican violence. But I support the right for people to have a fair trial, for the right for justice to be done and to be seen to be done. It was something I didn't get involved lightly in, and it was something I didn't believe in for a couple of months after going to meetings, but when I did believe in it I saw a pattern, and it looked like MI5 had run an operation that had gone badly wrong. I think that Stephen Carroll was killed by accident, although people were out with guns that should never have been out with guns. I think that two innocent men have stood trial and been convicted on the most flimsy of evidence.[21]

Conlon elaborated further on his reasons for involving himself in the Craigavon Two case: 'If I'm working with the Aborigines in Australia and I'm working with the anti-death penalty groups in America – and I'm working with a great organisation called Centurion Ministries out of Princeton that had fifty-four people released from never-ending sentences, most from death row in the last twenty-five years – how could I not do this on my own doorstep? It's imperative I do! I have to do it because I can't sit back and not give help to others that I expected myself.'[22]

Conlon prudently warned the McConville and Wootton families that appeal court judges were loath to find fault with their colleagues' verdicts (McConville and Wootton were convicted in a no-jury Diplock court) and that they should not expect success. His cautious approach was vindicated when, on 29 May 2014, the appeal court in Belfast upheld the convictions, despite fresh witness evidence that Conlon and others believed had demolished the prosecution case. Reflecting on Conlon's input to the Craigavon Two campaign, the international human rights lawyer Kevin R. Winters said:

> I first met Gerry in 2013 in relation to the cases of the Craigavon Two, who were convicted for a murder of a policeman that they didn't commit, and for which they are currently serving life sentences. Gerry was a dynamo and he was actually very important in galvanising support, especially from sections and areas from which you may not have necessarily expected it. Also, he would have attended court cases, he would have made phone calls, door-stepped people, and he would have attended numerous meetings. So he did all the footwork and graft that was needed to make things happen. It was not his fault that justice for the Craigavon Two was denied.
>
> Not only had Gerry a long reach but his counsel was much sought after, for example, the case of Colin Fulton, who is a loyalist and makes no apologies for it. Colin was being targeted by the press as a leading loyalist and as someone who was agitating and causing problems in the communities, etc. He approached Gerry and asked his advice ... that was the thing about Gerry ... he was completely non-sectarian and non-political: he just saw the human rights issue no matter what sector of society an individual hailed from. In Colin's case he directed him to our law firm and we are acting for Colin at present.[23]

In 2012, Conlon asked Winters if his law firm would employ his daughter Sara, who had graduated from university. Winters recalled their conversation:

> He contacted me and it was one of my strongest memories of him. This was when his daughter, Sara, came to work for our firm as an apprentice. We felt humbled and privileged to be asked, you know, and we had no hesitation in taking her in – and not just because she was Gerry Conlon's daughter – the girl had qualities and she brought so much positivity to the place. She qualified with us and is now a proficient criminal defence lawyer who has an interest in human rights, and that's exactly what Gerry would have wanted.[24]

Another case that Conlon supported was the 'Stop the Extradition of Seán Garland' campaign. Garland was a lifelong republican who had been in a leadership position within the republican movement from the late 1950s. By the time 'The Troubles' started in 1969, he was firmly of the view that armed struggle against the British government was a tactic that was doomed to failure. The Provisional IRA, which split from Garland and his Official IRA comrades, thought otherwise.

The Officials liked money; they liked it so much, they stood accused of printing it themselves. The counterfeit notes, virtually flawless $100 bills, were supposedly printed in the early 1990s with the co-operation of the North Korean government. The accusation against Garland was that he was the bagman, the person who distributed millions of 'super dollars' through international crime syndicates in Dublin and in Birmingham, England. Pete Seeger, Christy Moore, the Alabama 3, John Spillane and Gerry Conlon backed the campaign against Garland's extradition to the United States, and on 20 December 2011 the High Court in Dublin rejected the application.

There were rumours that some of those who supported Garland had a celebratory drink in a top Dublin hotel and lit Cuban cigars with $100 bills. Gerry Conlon would never have done such a thing. He did not smoke cigars.

Seventeen

In all respects, Gerry Conlon was enjoying life. He had secured his daughter a placement in a very reputable Belfast law firm; there was talk that Linda and he would get married in Las Vegas, but no date was specified; and amid his frenetic, globe-spanning campaigning, there were holidays abroad, mostly cruises in the Caribbean. On a holiday to Las Vegas, Conlon won $2,000 at the poker table. His luck had turned, or so it seemed. He began cultivating a penchant for the theatre and West End musicals and was particularly taken with the plight of Jean Valjean, the tortured ex-prisoner in *Les Misérables*. He regularly went to Manchester United and Glasgow Celtic football matches, usually as a VIP. To those who were close to him, Conlon seemed intent on squeezing the pips out of life; it was as if unconsciously, he knew the clock was ticking.

At a talk in University College Dublin in November 2013, Gerry shared a platform with Chelsea (formerly 'Bradley') Manning's mother, Susan. Bradley Manning was a former United States soldier who was sentenced to thirty-five years after he revealed classified documents to WikiLeaks, a news organisation committed to revealing state secrets. During his speech, Conlon said:

> I'll tell you what: I wish there'd been a Julian Assange, Edward Snowden or a Bradley Manning around when we were in jail to get the papers the government are holding and refusing to let the public see. What Bradley Manning did was to expose the horror of what governments expect children, their sons and daughters, to do on their behalf, the pretext of going to war to liberate people ... we all need to be aware of what is being done in our name, because it's not my name they're doing it in.

Along with Paddy Hill, Conlon gave a lecture to law students at Limerick University on 18 March 2014. The message had not altered and, really, the only significance in mentioning the event at all is that outwardly, while Conlon looked well-fed and healthy, he was within weeks of his death. The end, when it came, was mercifully swift.

In a powerful and lucid testimony on her brother's last days, Ann McKernan recalled: 'Gerry had a cough. This was at the end of May. You see, he'd had a bad experience with one of his GPs, around November or December of 2013, when he thought he had pleurisy. I rang the GP to come out and visit him because Gerry couldn't go into a surgery because of his panic attacks, and the surgery was always packed.

'Then, in 2014, he met Dr Walsh. She was only a wee local, but he was over the moon with her. She gave him a third-degree check-up, and she was sending him to the Royal Victoria Hospital for a chest X-ray. This was three weeks before he died. Linda went with him for an outpatient appointment. Then I got a phone call from Linda to ring our Gerry.'

When asked what Linda had said to her, Ann replied: 'She said that Dr McGarvey, his chest consultant, was keeping him in because he was a bit short of breath and had pneumonia, and his oxygen levels had dropped. McGarvey said he'd prefer to give him antibiotics intravenously so they would get into his system quickly. They were going to give him an MRI scan on the Monday. So I rang Gerry and said: "Where are you, wee boy?" He said he was still in the outpatients, sitting there on his own. So me and my Sarah went to the outpatients. He was taken up to Ward 7A and put in a side-ward.

'He was taken down the next day for a CAT scan. It showed a massive clot on his lung, and the doctors were more interested in getting that clot down, so they were pumping antibiotics through the drip and he was on oxygen.

'He was alert. I was up with him on the Saturday and Sunday, and Gerry being Gerry, he was giving his orders. He wanted the papers and all up, and a portable TV. So I brought him up a TV, but there was no signal. I went out and bought him a booster and an aerial, and it still didn't work! Cost me seventy quid, it did. And all the Gerry fella was interested in was: "How am I going to see the horseracing and the football?" Anyway, we got TV working and he got his bet done; Linda put it on for him. He was in the best of form that Saturday.

'On the Sunday, Linda brought him over his dinner and he ate it, and he also ate the hospital dinner. Our Gerry was a great grubber,' Ann said. 'It was roasting in the side-ward; there were no windows that you could open, and he was sweating and he said: "Do you know what I'd love? I'd love custard and cake." So I got him the custard and cake from the hospital canteen, and he said, "I enjoyed that." When I told him I was going for a smoke, he asked me to bring him back a lollipop. When I brought him the lollipop back, he was licking it like a big child, his legs dangling out of the bed. After he dozed off, Linda dropped me home. I got a phone call from her at a quarter past six that night. She said Gerry had taken a turn. I was confused; I didn't understand. And when I got up to the hospital and saw the colour of him. ... He'd sorta come around by this time and I said, "What happened to you?" Linda said he'd got up to go to the toilet, and what he thought was a panic attack was a heart attack. He was afraid 'cause he'd had a heart attack before, brought on by crack. So I sat in the chair with him all night 'cause Linda had to go to work the next morning. He kept wakening up and saying to me: "I've got you up all night." And I said: "So what? You'd do it for me." And so he would have.

'Anyway, the next morning, Gerry was taken for another CAT scan and this was where it showed up he had cancer. They were doing tests and that, to see how bad it was. And every time they did a test I used to think: "Oh, my mammy. No, not again. It's [cancer] here; it's there." But on saying that, they did offer him chemotherapy, and he did say to McGarvey: "I don't want a long time; I only want a short period of time." The chemo would have prolonged his life for a couple of months. He was happy with that.

'They didn't tell him he had two weeks to live. But they told me. He thought he'd be getting chemo. I'll tell you one thing: Gerry Conlon wasn't afraid to die; that's one thing I can say about him. He wasn't a cry-baby. He asked me if I'd go to the bungalow with him when he got out of hospital 'cause he would've wanted to get up and he couldn't get up. We got the care package put in the bungalow. He didn't want anyone else there except Linda and me. The only ones he sent for when he was in hospital was you (this author) and Gareth.

'We were able to take him home on the following Monday. And, you know, he couldn't get his head around how he had walked into the hospital complaining of a sore chest and now he could barely stand up. And do you know something? He was at the X-ray clinic in February 2014. They put him on a treadmill and took an X-ray. He came into me that day, and he was laughing and, I swear on my mammy's grave, he said: "I was at the chest clinic and you'll never believe this. I've the lungs of a 47-year-old." And he started laughing. And I said: "Good for you."'

When this writer went up to the hospital to see Gerry, he brought with him two Ulster Frys from the hospital kitchens. Gerry was sitting up, alert and smiling. There was no suggestion of self-pity, no hint from him that he was approaching the end of his life. A young nurse entered the room, and Gerry lavished thanks and praise on her. She smiled and passed a comment that he was 'a charmer'. How very perceptive, I thought. He enthusiastically ate his Ulster Fry.

When asked about his lack of self, Ann said: 'Gerry didn't feel sorry for himself. He just didn't. When they told him the cancer was all through him and that he could get chemo, he just said: "That'll do. I'm not looking for a long time." And neither was he. And believe me, he wasn't weepy. But I'll tell you what, it broke my heart.'

'Why did Gerry not receive chemotherapy treatment?' I ask.

'Well,' Ann said, 'when we got him home, there were nurses. He had to get injections every day because they couldn't get the clot down. His stomach was black with the injections. You see, they couldn't understand why the clot wasn't breaking down. It was covering most of his lung; it was a massive, massive clot.'

'Was Gerry in much pain?'

'No, no, no … He was up every morning getting his papers and eating his Belfast bap, and doing his bet –'

'To the end?'

'Aye! Sure you couldn't stop him. He did his bet every morning, right up to the morning before he died, he did. I never left the bungalow the whole time. He didn't go off his food either. No tears. He wasn't looking for pity. He took it like a man.

'He pulled out the tubes the night before he died. Around about half-nine that night, he was a real bad colour, and his eyes were rolling. I saw the deterioration in him. My Sarah and Mary-Kate were there. This was the first night we sent for the Marie Curie nurse and she hadn't arrived. So I decided to send for the Bel Doc [the emergency after-hours doctor].

'The doctor came out about 10.30 p.m. He spoke to Gerry and asked him if he wanted the syringe-drive in [a syringe-drive is the last resort if you're in pain] and Gerry said, "No. I'm going to get a few hours' sleep." He was on the oxygen and morphine. I sent for the Bel Doc again at 1.30 in the morning. It was a different doctor this time. Gerry again refused the syringe-drive, so she gave him another morphine shot and he fell asleep.

'The Marie Curie nurse came and she was very nervous. Linda heard a bit of a kerfuffle. She was lying on the settee and I was in the chair, and there was Gerry trying to pull the oxygen mask off and the wee Marie Curie nurse was letting him. He said he needed to go to the toilet. Linda then told him to use the bottle and she put his oxygen mask back on him. I had to go in and I said: "Mister Gerry, get into bed! You'd better do what you're told! Get into bed now!" Linda and me got him back into bed. It was the morphine; he didn't know where he was or what he was doing. We had to get the Bel Doc out at six that morning and the Marie Curie nurse at seven again.

'Then Gerry fell asleep and Linda took his pulse and said to me: "Ann, I think Gerry's ready for going." And just then, my Sarah and her husband Mark came in. And at that, the front door rapped and his daughter, Sara, came in. And Gerry just passed away. He had a peaceful death, I have to say. And not once did he shed a tear. I'm so proud of him.'[1]

A press statement from the Conlon family said:

> He helped us to survive when we were not meant to survive. We recognise that what he achieved by fighting for justice for us had

a far, far greater importance – it forced the world's closed eyes to be opened to injustice. It forced unimaginable wickedness to be acknowledged. We believe it changed the course of history. We thank him for his life and we thank all his many friends for their love. He brought life, love, intelligence, wit and strength to our family through its darkest hours.

The President of Ireland, Michael D. Higgins, issued a statement saying that he was 'greatly saddened' by the news, and that Gerry Conlon's death was a loss 'not only in Ireland, but also among all those who struggle against injustice. The integrity and determination Mr Conlon brought to the fight for truth, and the tireless work of those who supported the Guildford Four, Birmingham Six and Maguire Seven campaigns, stands as an inspiration to all who stand up for justice.'

Paddy Hill said he was 'gutted' to hear of Gerry's death and he blamed prison conditions in Britain's old Victorian gaols for his friend's demise: 'The cells were like ice boxes in winter and ovens during the summer. In the old prisons, the damp ran down the walls. I've no doubt that affected his health. I was speaking to him only last week when he was in hospital. He said to me, "Give me a week until I get out of hospital and you can come over and visit," so I said, "Okay."' Hill referred to their recent talk at the law faculty of the University of Limerick in March and said that Conlon had been in 'great form'.[2]

Annie Maguire of the Maguire Seven said that Conlon's death was 'very sad news. I am sorry to hear he has died, so young, and am so sorry for his sisters.'[3]

Paul Hill, Conlon's co-accused, was reflective: 'I think he suffered a great deal more than the other individuals involved, myself included, because Gerard could never have release from his father. I always said that Gerard's father was continuously imprisoned in Gerard's mind.'[4]

Jim Sheridan paid tribute to Gerry: 'We fought, we were pals; we had a mad relationship, like brothers. I met him in New York six months ago, and we had a great day. He was in great form, and all he talked about were people who were locked up, who he could help. He got rid of his demons by helping other people, and he had enormous respect for campaigning lawyer Gareth Peirce who worked on their case.'[5]

Terry George, the man who, along with Sheridan, wrote the screenplay of *In the Name of the Father*, said that Conlon was 'a unique character – funny, outrageous and full of dogged determination'.[6]

Siobhan MacGowan, his close friend and confidante, paid Gerry a moving tribute: 'This is a guy I was proud to call my friend, even though he called me "Goat Face". He had a heart like a bonfire, a soul that soared like a lightning bolt, and a mind as broad as the sky. His being no longer on this earth makes it a poorer place. God bless you, Gerry, mo chara, a stór. My love goes with you. Goat Face.'[7]

Conlon's co-conspirator in the United States campaign to free the Birmingham Six in 1990, Sandy Boyer, said: 'I think Gerry always really enjoyed talking to people. His childhood friend Richard O'Rawe reminded me that he was great craic. He was one of the great storytellers. It was always great to sit and listen as Gerry unfolded one fascinating tale after another over a pint or a cup of coffee.'[8]

Gerry Conlon's death was reported in the broadcasting and print media, with the BBC, ITV and RTÉ all covering the story, as well as all the major national papers.

In the *New York Times*, Douglas Dalby wrote: 'Freedom did not bring Mr Conlon peace. He contemplated suicide. He became addicted to drugs and alcohol. But in a recent interview, he said counselling had helped him to come to terms with the suffering he had experienced.'[9]

Kevin Cullen, a friend of Conlon's, wrote in the *Boston Globe*: 'Gerry seemed to have turned a corner. He was doing better than ever. He had devoted his life to helping others wrongfully accused and imprisoned. He was 60, far too young, far too tortured, a man dead and reborn.'[10]

The Pogues issued a statement saying: 'All The Pogues send sincere condolences to the family of Gerry Conlon. How lucky we were to have known him. RIP.' Two weeks later, in front of a crowd of 75,000 fans in Hyde Park, The Pogues and The Libertines dedicated 'Time for Heroes' to Gerry Conlon.

The funeral of Gerry Conlon took place on 28 June 2014. Many hundreds of people followed his coffin from Ann's house to St Peter's

Pro-Cathedral, and over one thousand people filed in behind it when it came back out of the church. Besides Gerry's sisters and family circle, some of those paying their last respects were: a representative of the President of Ireland, An Tánaiste Eamon Gilmore (deputy prime minister of Ireland), Paddy Armstrong of the Guildford Four, Paddy Hill, Gareth Peirce, Siobhan MacGowan, Joey Cashman, Angie, John McManus, Martin Loughran, Barry Walle, Jim Sheridan, Terry George, Peter Ong (who flew in from Australia), Mark Durkan MP, Margaret Walsh, 'Celtic Pat' McDonnell, Kate Germond from Centurion Ministries, Kevin Winters, and representatives of Sinn Féin and the SDLP.

During the funeral Mass, members of the Alabama 3 played 'Can the Circle Be Unbroken', the song they had performed at Sarah Conlon's funeral. The packed church clapped in tune and, at the end, gave the band a standing ovation.

In her funeral homily, which drew another standing ovation, Gareth Peirce said:

> When he angrily, angrily stated the truth, it had an enormous effect and made the world understand that innocent men and women had been buried alive in English prisons year after year, and it had been allowed. Indeed, it had been organised to happen. It was no accident. So when he shouted out: 'I am an innocent man, my father was innocent, the Maguires are innocent and the Birmingham Six', he set something in motion that forced the rest of us, the rest of the world, Britain, to hold a mirror up to itself and see precisely who we were and what we had done.
>
> Life dealt Gerry a pretty poor hand. He was a gambler, and gambling was in his DNA, but with a poor hand he made a magnificent fist of it. If anyone thinks that this is someone who was beaten or terrified and pushed down forever, that wasn't so. With all the adversities: in the end Gerry Conlon won – the victory was his.

During the Mass, Father Ciaran Dallat recalled how Gerry had said to him, as he gave Gerry the Last Rites: "I'm ready to meet my father."

Father Ciaran took this to mean he was ready to meet his God. Ann McKernan, however, knew differently. She believed that, 'He was ready to meet *our* father, Giuseppe Conlon, not God. Our Gerry was saying that he could look his father in the face: he had finally forgiven himself.'[11]

Endnotes

One

1. Dáithí Ó Conaill interviewed by Mary Holland: *Weekend World*, London Weekend Television: 17 November 1974.
2. Grant McKee and Ros Franey, *Time Bomb: Irish Bombers, English Justice, and the Guildford Four* (London: Bloomsbury, 1988), p. 28.
3. Ibid. p. 64.
4. Gerry Conlon and David Pallister, *Éagóir: The Guildford Four Case of Injustice*, Michelle Nic Phaidín, TG4, 2013.
5. McKee and Franey, p. 140.
6. Gerry Conlon, *Proved Innocent* (London: Hamish Hamilton, 1990), p. 88.
7. McKee and Franey, p. 232.
8. Ibid.
9. Ibid. p. 325.
10. *Peoples News Service*, 24 November 1993.
11. Lord Denning, *The Spectator*, 17 August 1990.
12. Gerry Conlon, WBAI radio, New York, 5 January 2013.
13. McKee and Franey, p. 382.
14. Shakespeare, *Macbeth*, I. 3. 8.
15. Lord Denning, *The Spectator*, 17 August 1990.
16. Ibid.
17. Ann McKernan, interview with author, Belfast, 25 June 2015.
18. Gerry Conlon, *Proved Innocent*, pp. 193–4.
19. Paddy Hill, interview with author, Belfast, 25 June 2015.
20. Gerry Conlon, *Proved Innocent*, pp. 208–9.
21. Ibid.
22. Paddy Hill, *Forever Lost, Forever Gone* (London: Bloomsbury, 1995), p. 226.
23. Paddy Hill, interview with author, Belfast, 25 June 2015.
24. Ann McKernan, interview with author, Belfast, 25 June 2015.

Two

1. Paddy Hill, interview with author, Belfast, 25 June 2015.
2. Gerry Conlon, interview with Mary-Rachel McCabe, *The Justice Gap*, 1 October 2013.
3. Gerry Conlon, *Irish News*, 23 October 1989.
4. Seán Smyth, *Irish News*, 6 July 1991.
5. Gerry Conlon, *Irish News*, 6 November 1989.
6. Gerry Conlon, *The Guildford Four: Freedom to Speak*, ITN, 7 November 1989.
7. Michael Fisher, *Irish News*, 10 November 1989.
8. Martin Loughran, interview with author, Belfast, 28 August 2015.
9. *Irish News*, 20 November 1989.
10. Sandy Boyer, interview with author, Belfast/New York, 10 August 2015.
11. (Paul Dwyer was a leading US civil activist, and Brian Donnelly, Joe Kennedy, Charlie Rangel and Tom Lantos were US Congressmen. Jack O'Dell was a legendary civil rights activist). Gerry Conlon, WBAI radio, New York City, 5 January 2013.
12. Gerry Conlon, Shane MacGowan Forum.
13. Frank Murray, interview with author, Dublin, 20 April 2016.
14. Gerry Conlon, interview with ITN, 19 October 1989.
15. Ibid.
16. Gareth Peirce, *Guardian Unlimited*, 19 October 1999.
17. Gerry Conlon, *Éagóir: The Guildford Four Case of Injustice*, Michelle Nic Phaidín, TG4, 2013.
18. Martin Loughran, interview with author, Belfast, 28 August 2015.
19. David Pallister, interview with author, Belfast/London, 7 October 2015.
20. Ibid.

Three

1. Sandy Boyer, interview with author, Belfast/New York, 10 August 2015.
2. An extract from a briefing document prepared by staffers for the Congressional Human Rights Caucus, Washington DC, 1990.

3. Sandy Boyer, interview with author, Belfast/New York, 10 August 2015.
4. Ibid.
5. Congressman Joe Kennedy, *Irish Voice*, 3 April 1990.
6. Colman McCarthy, for 'The Bulletin', *Washington Post*, 13 April 1990.
7. Gerry Conlon, WBAI radio, New York, 2 November 2013.
8. *Irish News*, 14 June 1990.
9. Ibid.
10. Ibid.
11. Ibid.
12. Ibid.
13. Paul May, Inside Justice (an investigative body for alleged miscarriages of justice), 25 June 2014.
14. Siobhan MacGowan, interview with author, County Tipperary, 24 October 2015.
15. Barry Walle, Gerry Conlon papers (courtesy of Ann McKernan).
16. Gerry Conlon, *Independent*, 13 May 1995.
17. David Andrews, *Irish News*, 28 July 1990.
18. Gerry Conon, *Irish News*, 28 July 1990.
19. Edmund Burke: Third letter ... on the proposals for peace with the Regicide Directory (1797), p. 30.
20. Fiona Looney, interview with author, Dublin/Belfast, 25 November 2015.
21. Frank Murray, interview with author, Dublin, 20 April 2016.
22. Gerry Conlon, *Observer*, 6 April 1997.
23. Joey Cashman, interview with author, Dublin, 26 September 2015.
24. Siobhan MacGowan, interview with author, County Tipperary, 24 October 2015.

Four

1. Interview with Shane MacGowan, Victoria Mary Clarke and Joey Cashman, Dublin, 15 October 2015.
2. Gavin Martin, Shane MacGowan Official Website, 22 October 1994.
3. Ann McKernan, Mary-Kate McKernan, interview with author, Belfast, 8 November 2015.
4. *Irish News*, 14 June 1991.

5. Court of Appeal, Criminal Division, Lloyd, Mustill, and Farquharson, 14–27 March 1991.
6. Paddy Hill, *Forever Lost, Forever Gone* (London: Bloomsbury, 1995), p. 261.
7. Marion McKeone, interview with author, Los Angeles/Belfast, 17 November 2015.
8. Siobhan MacGowan, interview with author, County Tipperary, 24 October 2015.
9. Marion McKeone, interview with author, Los Angeles/Belfast, 14 November 2015.
10. Siobhan MacGowan, interview with author, County Tipperary, 24 October 2015.
11. Finola Geraghty, interview with author, London/Belfast, 4 December 2015.
12. Paddy Hill, *Forever Lost, Forever Gone*, p. 266.
13. Paddy Hill, interview with author, Belfast, 25 June 2015.
14. *The Sun*, 3 May 1991.
15. Ibid.
16. Joey Cashman, interview with author, Dublin, 29 August 2015.
17. Paddy Hill, interview with author, Belfast, 25 June 2015.
18. Joey Cashman, interview with author, Dublin, 29 August 2015.
19. Paddy Hill, interview with author, Belfast, 25 June 2015.
20. Oscar Wilde, *Lady Windermere's Fan* (1892), Act 3.

Five

1. Gerry Conlon, *Irish News*, 27 June 1991.
2. Annie Maguire, *Irish News*, 27 June 1991.
3. Sarah Conlon, *Irish News*, 27 June 2015.
4. *Irish Press*, 27 June 1991.
5. Joey Cashman, interview with author, Dublin, 29 August 2015.
6. Ann McKernan, interview with author, Belfast, 8 November 2015.
7. Barry Walle, interview with author, 16 December 2015.
8. Gerry Conlon, WBAI radio, New York, 2 November 2013.
9. Joey Cashman, interview with author, Dublin, 8 December 2015.
10. Finola Geraghty, interview with author, London/Belfast, 4 December 2015.

11. Terry George, interview with Robert Brent Poplin, *Perspectives on History*, April 1999.
12. Jim Sheridan, *New York Times*, 26 December 1993.
13. Jim Sheridan, *Guardian*, 12 October 2003.
14. 'Minty', interview with author, 19 May 2016.
15. Ibid.
16. Minty's diary, 17 March 1992.
17. Minty interview with author, 19 May 2016.
18. Ibid.
19. Minty's diary, 28 April 1992.
20. Minty interview with author, 3 October 2016.
21. Minty's diary, 24 May 1992.
22. Minty interview with author, 3 October 2016.
23. Minty's dairy, 11 January 1992.
24. Minty interview with author, 3 October 2016.
25. Gerry Conlon, *How Far Home*, Hotshot Films, 1998.
26. Dr Adrian Grounds, Honorary Research Fellow, University of Cambridge, AIDWYC, Journal No. 3, 2003 (The Gerry Conlon papers, courtesy of Ann McKernan).
27. Siobhan MacGowan, interview with author, County Tipperary, 24 October 2015.
28. Marion McKeone, interview with author, Los Angeles/Belfast, 14 November 2015.

Six

1. *Irish News*, 5 December 1993.
2. Daniel Day-Lewis, *Irish Times*, 11 December 1993.
3. Daniel Day-Lewis, *Irish News*, 31 December 1993.
4. Joey Cashman, interview with author, Dublin, 8 December 2015.
5. Gerry Conlon, WBAI radio, New York, 2 November 2013.
6. Gerry Conlon, *Independent*, 13 May 1995.
7. Daniel Day-Lewis, *Irish News*, 31 December 1993.
8. Gabriel Byrne, *Irish Times*, 8 May 1993.
9. Jim Sheridan, *Irish Times*, 8 May 1993.
10. Joey Cashman, interview with author, Dublin, 8 December 2015.

11. Ibid.
12. Gerry Conlon, *Observer* 'Review', 6 April 1997.
13. *Daily Mirror*, 12 June 1991.
14. *Guardian*, 20 May 1993.
15. Ibid.
16. Ibid.
17. Emma Thompson, *Irish News*, 16 November 1993.
18. Jim Sheridan, *Irish Times*, 8 May 1993.
19. Tony Judge, *Irish Times*, 8 May 1993.
20. Jim Sheridan, *Irish Times*, 8 May 1993.

Seven

1. Gerry Conlon, *Proved Innocent*, p. 113.
2. Scene from *In the Name of the Father*, Universal Pictures, 1993.
3. Jim Sheridan, interview, VPRO Cinema Collection, 29 July 2015.
4. Gerry Conlon, *Proved Innocent*, p. 191.
5. Siobhan MacGowan, interview with author, County Tipperary, 24 October 2015.
6. Gerry Conlon, *Proved Innocent*, p. 217.
7. *Irish Times*, 18 December 1993.
8. Jim Sheridan, VPRO Cinema Collection, 29 July 2015.
9. Ann McKernan, interview with author, Belfast, 18 December 1993.
10. Yasser Afarat, *Irish Times*, 15 January 1994.
11. Michael Dwyer, *Irish Times*, 15 January 1994.
12. Emer Mullins, *Irish Times*, 15 January 1994.
13. Gerry Conlon, *Observer* 'Review', 6 April 1997.
14. Julie Birchill, *Sunday Times*, 13 February 1994.

Eight

1. Gerry Conlon, *Proved Innocent*, p. 57.
2. Gerry Conlon, *Observer* 'Review', 6 April 1997.
3. Joey Cashman, interview with author, Dublin, 10 January 2016.
4. Conlon, *How Far Home*.

5. Interview with Shane MacGowan, Victoria Mary Clarke and Joey Cashman, Dublin, 15 October 2015.
6. Joey Cashman, interview with author, Dublin, 10 January 2016.
7. Gerry Conlon, *Observer Review*, 6 April 1997.
8. Barry Walle, interview with author, 16 December 2015.
9. Gerry Conlon, *Observer* 'Review', 6 April 1997.
10. Barry Walle, interview with author, Plymouth, 16 December 2015.
11. Dorothy Parker, *Writers at Work*, 1st Series (1958), p. 81.
12. Joey Cashman, Dublin, 8 December 2015.
13. Ibid.
14. Marion McKeone, interview with author, 17 November 2015.
15. Gerry Conlon, *Observer* 'Review', 6 April 1997.

Nine

1. Alastair Logan, *BBC News*, 3 October 2014.
2. Gerry Conlon, *Daily Telegraph*, 4 June 2010.
3. Chris Mullins, *Independent*, 31 July 1992.
4. Sir John May's 1994 interim report into the Guildford and Woolwich pub bombings, 30 June 1994, Vol 1/2, Chapter Eight, p. 86.
5. Ibid. p. 302.
6. A Sir John May Inquiry entry: *Chronicle to go in letters to Stitt/Mathew/Met/DPP/Miscon De Reya*, 17 June 1976, p. 115.
7. Sir John May Inquiry: File number – GPB742753.
8. Lord Denning, *The Spectator*, 18 August 1990.
9. Sir John May's interim report, 21. 24, p. 308.

Ten

1. Ann McKernan, interview with author, 18 December 2015.
2. Gerry Conlon, *Observer* 'Review', 6 April 1997.
3. Joey Cashman, interview with author, Dublin, 8 December 2015.
4. Conlon, *How Far Home*.
5. 'Angie', interview with author, 24 January 2016.
6. Gerry Conlon, *Observer* 'Review', 6 April 1997.

7. *Irish News*, 13 September 1994.
8. 'Angie', interview with author, 24 January 2016.
9. Luke 4.23.
10. Ann McKernan, interview with author, 18 December 2015.
11. 'Angie', interview with author, 24 January 2016.
12. Ibid.
13. Ibid.
14. Ibid.
15. Ann McKernan, interview with author, 18 December 2015.
16. 'Angie', interview with author, 24 January 2016.

Eleven

1. David Rose, *Observer* 'Review', 14 January 1996.
2. Ibid.
3. Ibid.
4. Barry Walle, interview with author, 11 March 2016.
5. 'Angie', interview with author, 24 January 2016.
6. Gerry Conlon, *Observer* 'Review', 6 April 1997.
7. 'Angie', interview with author, 24 January 2016.
8. Ibid.
9. Gerry Conlon, *Irish News*, 21 February 1997.
10. 'Angie', interview with author, 24 January 2016.
11. Gerry Conlon, *Observer* 'Review', 6 April 1997.

Twelve

1. 'Angie', interview with author, 24 January 2016.
2. Ibid.
3. Ann McKernan, interview with author, 18 December 2015.
4. 'Angie', interview with author, 24 January 2016.
5. Ibid.
6. *Sunday Times*, 15 November 2016.
7. Joey Cashman, interview with author, 17 March 2016.
8. 'Angie', interview with author, 24 January 2016.
9. Conlon, *How Far Home*.

10. David Pallister, *Guardian Unlimited*, 19 October 1999.
11. 'Angie', interview with author, 24 January 2016.

Thirteen

1. Barry Walle, interview with author, 23 January 2016.
2. Barry Walle, Cognitive Behavioural Psychotherapy Report, 24 June 2002 (the Gerry Conlon papers, courtesy of Ann McKernan).
3. Ibid.
4. Ibid.
5. Barry Walle, CBT Record Sheet, 12 May 2000 (the Gerry Conlon papers).
6. Barry Walle, Cognitive Behavioural Psychotherapy report, 24 June 2002.
7. Ibid.
8. Ibid.
9. *Guardian Unlimited*, 6 June 2000.
10. Ibid.
11. Barry Walle, CBT Record Sheet, 7 June 2000.
12. *Independent*, 7 July 2000.
13. Barry Walle, CBT Record Sheet, 30 August 2000.
14. Ibid. 12 September 2000.
15. Ibid. 2 November 2000.
16. Ibid.
17. Ibid. 1 December 2000.
18. Ibid. 2 February 2001.
19. Ibid. 16 February 2001.
20. Ibid. 21 February 2001.
21. Barry Walle, CBT Record Sheet, 6 March 2001.

Fourteen

1. Ann McKernan, interview with author, 18 April 2016.
2. The Gerry Conlon papers.
3. Ann McKernan, interview with author, 18 April 2016.
4. *Sunday Business Post*, 27 May 2001.
5. Ibid.

6. Barry Walle, CBT Record Sheet.
7. Dr Adrian Grounds, Psychiatric report, 10 June 2003 (the Gerry Conlon papers).
8. Ibid.
9. Ann McKernan, interview with author, 25 January 2016.
10. Barry Walle, CBT Record Sheet, 18 February 2002 (the Gerry Conlon papers).
11. Ann McKernan, interview with author, 18 April 2016.
12. 'Angie', interview with author, 24 January 2016.
13. Barry Walle, CBT Record Sheet, 3 June 2003.
14. Margaret Walsh, interview with author, 1 October 2015.
15. Mark Durkan MP, interview with author, 25 September 2015.
16. Marie-Louise McCrory, *Irish News*, 24 January 2005.
17. Ibid.
18. Margaret Walsh, interview with author, 1 October 2015.
19. Jim Sheridan, *Irish News*, 28 January 2005.
20. Mark Durkan MP, interview with author, 25 September 2015.
21. Mark Durkan MP, *Irish News*, 28 January 2005.
22. Bridie Brennan, *Irish News*, 10 February 2005.
23. Patrick Maguire and Carlo Gébler, *My Father's Watch: The Story of a Child Prisoner in 70s Britain* (London: Fourth Estate, 2008), pp. 417–18.
24. Gerry Conlon, *Independent*, 10 February 2005.
25. Annie Maguire, *Independent*, 10 February 2005.
26. Gerry Conlon, *Independent*, 10 February 2005.
27. Mark Durkan MP, interview with author, 25 September 2015.

Fifteen

1. Helen Murray, *Sunday Tribune*, 26 March 2006.
2. Richard Holt, *Daily Telegraph*, 4 June 2010.
3. Barry Walle, interview with author, 13 June 2016.
4. Neil Connor, *Birmingham Post*, 22 May 2006.
5. Paddy Hill, interview with author, Belfast, 25 June 2015.
6. John McManus, interview with author, Glasgow, 10 July 2016.
7. The Gerry Conlon papers.
8. Gerry Conlon's Capio Nightingale Hospital diary, 20 November 2006.

9. Ibid. 21 November 2006.
10. The Gerry Conlon Papers.
11. Gerry Conlon's Capio Nightingale Hospital diary, 24 November 2006.
12. Ibid. 24 November 2006.
13. Ibid. 10 December 2006.
14. Ibid. 30 November 2006.
15. Ibid.
16. Ibid. 2 December 2006.
17. Ibid. 3 December 2006.
18. Ibid. 12 December 2006.
19. Ibid. 14 December 2006.
20. The Gerry Conlon papers.
21. 'Celtic Pat' McDonnell, interview with author, Belfast, 16 March 2016.
22. John McManus, interview with author, Glasgow, 10 July 2016.
23. Gerry Conlon, WBAI Radio, New York, 5 January 2013.
24. Gerry Conlon, Trinity College Dublin, 29 November 2013.
25. Paddy Hill, Innocent Network (UK), March 2012.
26. Mark Durkan, email to author, 13 June 2016.
27. Friedrich Nietzsche, *Jensen von Gut und Böse* (1886) chapter 4, no. 157.
28. Ann McKernan, interview with author, 18 April 2016.
29. Gerry Conlon, *Irish News*, 21 July 2008.
30. Father Brendan Mulhall, *Irish News*, 22 July 2008.

Sixteen

1. Ann McKernan, interview with author, 18 April 2016.
2. Gerry Conlon, *Guardian*, 5 May 2009.
3. John McManus, interview with author, Glasgow, 10 July 2016.
4. 'Who killed Mr Ward?' *Four Corners*, ACC Network Australia, 15 June 2009.
5. Seamus Doherty, interview with author, Belfast/Western Australia, 27 September 2016.
6. John McManus, interview with author, Glasgow, 10 July 2016.
7. Peter Ong, interview with author, 1 August 2016.
8. John McManus, interview with author, Glasgow, 10 July 2016.
9. Gerry Conlon, *Today Tonight*, ABC Network Australia, 14 June 2010.

10. John McManus, interview with author, Glasgow, 10 July 2016.
11. Peter Ong, interview with author, 1 August 2016.
12. News at Princeton, 15 July 2016.
13. Judith McCartin Scheide, Centurion Ministries website, 20 November 2012.
14. Sandy Boyer, interview with author, Belfast/New York, 10 August 2010.
15. Sandy Boyer, interview with author, Belfast/New York, 17 August 2015.
16. Ann McKernan, interview with author, Belfast, 18 September 2015.
17. Sandy Boyer, interview with author, Belfast/New York, 10 August 2015.
18. Gerry Conlon, Marxist Festival, London, 3 July 2010.
19. Gerry Conlon, *Irish News*, 16 September 2009.
20. Ibid.
21. Gerry Conlon, *Irish Times*, 19 March 2014.
22. Sandy Boyer and John McDonagh, interview with Gerry Conlon, November 2013.
23. Kevin Winters, interview with author, Belfast, 5 July 2016.
24. Ibid.

Seventeen

1. Ann McKernan, interview with author, 5 October 2015.
2. Paddy Hill, *Irish Times*, 21 June 2014.
3. Annie Maguire, *BBC News*, 23 June 2014.
4. Paul Hill, *BBC News*, 23 June 2014.
5. Jim Sheridan, *Independent*, 23 June 2014.
6. Terry George, *Independent*, 23 June 2014.
7. Siobhan MacGowan, Shane MacGowan Forum.
8. Sandy Boyer, *The Pensive Quill*, 23 June 2014.
9. Douglas Dalby, *New York Times*, 22 June 2014.
10. Kevin Cullen, *Boston Globe*, 24 June 2014.
11. Ann McKernan, interview with author, 5 October 2014.

Bibliography

Armstrong, Paddy, *Life after Life: A Guildford Four Memoir* (Dublin: Gill Books, 2017).
Conlon, Gerry, and David Pallister, *Proved Innocent: The Story of Gerry Conlon of The Guildford Four* (London: Hamish Hamilton, 1990).
Hill, Paddy Joe, *Forever Lost, Forever Gone* (London: Bloomsbury Publishing Ltd, 1995).
Hill, Paul, and Ronan Bennett, *Stolen Years: Before and After Guildford* (London: Doubleday, 1990).
Kee, Robert, *Trial and Error: The Maguires, The Guildford Pub Bombings and British Justice* (London: Hamish Hamilton, 1986).
Maguire, Anne, and Jim Gallagher, *Why Me? One Woman's Fight for Justice and Dignity* (London: HarperCollins, 1994).
Maguire, Patrick, and Carlo Gébler, *My Father's Watch: The Story of a Child Prisoner in 70s Britain* (London: Fourth Estate, 2008).
Mansfield, Michael, *Memoirs of a Radical Lawyer* (London: Bloomsbury, 2009).
Moloney, Ed, *Voices from the Grave* (London: Faber and Faber, 2010).
—, *A Secret History of the IRA* (London: Penguin UK, 2002).
Mullin, Chris, *Error of Judgement: The Truth about the Birmingham Bombings* (Dublin: Poolbeg Press, 1997).
McGladdery, Gary, *The Provisional IRA in England, The Bombing Campaign*, 1973–1977 (Dublin: Irish Academic Press, 2006).
McKee, Grant, and Ros Franey, *Time Bomb: Irish Bombers, English Justice and the Guildford Four* (London: Bloomsbury Publishing Ltd, 1988).
O'Donnell, Ruán, *Special Category: The IRA IN English Prisons, Vol. 1: 1968–1978* (Dublin: Irish Academic Press, 2012).

Index

Aamer, Shaker, 197
Aasleagh Falls, Co. Mayo, 79
Aboriginal people, 189–90
Academy Awards, 107–10
Adams, Eve, 171
Adelaide, 191–2
Aghalee, Co. Antrim, 195
Ahern, Bertie, 165–6
Alabama 3, 180, 184, 187, 201, 209
Alan (friend), 128, 132, 134, 138, 140, 141, 142
alibi evidence, 23, 113–15, 116–17
American Protestants for Truth about Ireland, 24
Amnesty International, 36
Andrews, David, 41
Angie (girlfriend), 121, 123–9, 132–4, 136–45, 156, 161, 162, 166, 176, 209
appeal hearings: Birmingham Six, 15, 42–3, 54–5; Guildford Four, 11–12, 117; Maguire Seven, 63–4, 111
Arafat, Yasser, 97
Archer, Graham, 191
Armstrong, Paddy, 4, 6, 17, 28, 43, 56, 58–62, 87, 95–6, 115, 132, 172, 209; *see also* Guildford Four
Assange, Julian, 202
Attwell, Vernon, 86–8
Attwood, Alex, 170
Australia, 187, 189–92
Australian Building and Construction Commission (ABCC), 190–2
Azimkar, Cengiz 'Patrick', 197–8

Bacall, Lauren, 90
Baker, Don, 96
Baker, Kenneth, 42
Balcombe Street Active Service Unit (ASU), 2–4, 5, 7–12, 95, 112, 116, 117

Balcombe Street siege, 5
Balcombe Street trial, 7–10, 116
Ball, Jonathan, 78
Bamber, Helen, 147–8
Barrington, Brian, 164
Bartle, Ronald, 86–7
Basinger, Kim, 65
Begg, Moazzam, 197
Belfast, 16–17, 24, 29, 38, 45–6, 64, 72, 81, 119–22, 124–5, 133–4, 136–7, 149, 157–64, 170, 178–80, 182–3, 185–7, 208–9
Belfrage, Julian, 77
Bennett, Ronan, 32, 135
Bible, 124
Bird, Antonio, 135
Birmingham pub bombings, 14
Birmingham Six: appeal hearings, 15, 42–3, 54–5; charges against police officers dropped, 55; Conlon campaigns for, 21, 22, 23–8, 34–7, 38–9; forensic evidence, 35, 42–3, 54; interrogations and confessions, 35; release, 54–5; visited by Joe Kennedy, 24–5; *see also* Callaghan, Hugh; Hill, Paddy Joe; Hunter, Gerry; McIlkenny, Richard; Power, Billy; Walker, Johnny
Blackburn, Paul, 187–8
Blair, Tony, 14, 151, 154–5, 163–9, 170–2
Blake, Robin, 32
Boggan, Steve, 152
Bono, 95
Boreham, Leslie, 11
Boston Globe, 208
Bowen, Kerry, 24
Boyer, Sandy, 25–7, 34–6, 195–7, 208
Brady, Ian, 13
Brennan, Bridie (née Conlon), 17–18, 52, 95, 124, 159–60, 165, 166, 168

Brennan, Mary, 168
Brisbane, 189, 191
British army, 29
British Broadcasting Corporation (BBC), 23, 113, 116, 151–2, 208
Brixton Prison, 15, 17, 106
Bromley, Joanna, 40, 146
Burchill, Julie, 100–1, 122–3, 142
Burke, Charles Edward, 23, 113–15, 116–17
Butler, Eddie, 3, 5, 10, 11, 112, 117
Byrne, Gabriel, 36–7, 53–4, 65–6, 77, 81, 82–3, 86
Byrne, Gay, 27

Cain, Christy, 188–9
Callaghan, Hugh, 172; *see also* Birmingham Six
Callaghan, James, 10
Campbell, Naomi, 90
Cantley, Sir Joseph Donaldson, 7–9, 116
Capio Nightingale Hospital, London, 172, 175–8
Carey, Patrick, 23
Carl (friend from prison), 74
Carlyle, Robert, 135
Carroll, Stephen, 198–9
Cashman, Joey, 33, 44–51, 58–62, 64–6, 68, 78–80, 83–5, 90–1, 104–10, 120, 122, 128, 136, 142, 180, 185, 209
Caterham Arms bombing, 7
Celbridge, Co. Kildare, 172
Centurion Ministries, 193–4, 196, 209
Clarke, Kenneth, 87–8, 111
Clarke, Sr Sarah, 96
Clarke, Victoria Mary, 49–50, 55–6
Clarkson, Felicity, 113, 115
Clines, Francis X., 101–2
'Comanche Creeks', 179
compensation, 27, 30, 43, 126–8, 135–6, 144–5, 151, 155
Congressional Human Rights Caucus, 25, 34–6
Conlon, Ann *see* McKernan, Ann (née Conlon)
Conlon, Bridie *see* Brennan, Bridie (née Conlon)

Conlon, Gerry: adjustment to life outside prison, 22, 27–8, 39–40; apology from Tony Blair, 14, 163–9; appeal hearing, 11–12; arrested for drug possession, 61–2; attends the Academy Awards, 107–10; breaks into flat in London, 103; Burke's alibi for, 23, 113–15, 116–17; campaigns for the Birmingham Six, 21, 22, 23–8, 34–7, 38–9; charged with assaulting a police officer, 133–4, 136–7; comes off crack, 134–5, 138–44; compensation, 27, 30, 43, 126–8, 135–6, 144–5, 155; contracts tuberculosis, 171; daughter, 186–7, 200, 202, 206; dealing with death of father, 88, 119, 141, 149–50, 160–1, 171, 210; drug use, 20, 28, 30–1, 42, 43, 59, 61–2, 94, 103–7, 119–20, 122, 125–9, 134, 156; emotional and psychological impacts upon, 22, 27, 39–40, 57, 67–8, 75–6, 128–9, 144, 145–6, 147–56, 158–62, 171; flashbacks, 149, 151, 163, 171; and football, 27, 40, 43, 202; friendships, 14–16, 20–1, 43–7, 48–53, 55–62, 72–3, 172, 179–80; gambling, 30–1, 56, 120, 133, 141, 186, 202; girlfriends, 18, 19, 25–6, 28–9, 41–2, 70–6, 95, 121, 123–9, 136–45, 185–7; holidays, 43, 51–3, 58–61, 74, 95, 202; human rights campaigning, 187–201; illness, death and funeral, 203–10; imprisonment, 10–11, 13–15, 90–5, 120, 148–9, 175–6; and *In the Name of the Father*, 64–70, 73–4, 77–86, 88–102, 106–10, 120–1, 193, 194, 195; interrogation and confession, 4–5, 21–2, 36, 153; and Johnny Depp, 33, 51–3, 56–8, 81; *Late, Late Show* appearance, 27; lecture tours of the US, 193–7; libel action against *The Sun*, 61, 132; libel action against *Sunday Times*, 101, 122–3, 142; Maguire family's condemnation of, 21–2, 99, 166; memory, 34, 69, 106, 148–9, 179, 182; and MOJO, 172–5, 180–1, 187–93; moves back to Belfast, 120–2, 178–80; and music, 48, 122, 179–80, 187–8, 194; named in Paul Hill's confession, 4; need for an apology from British government, 144, 146, 150, 151, 155, 158, 163–6; nightmares, 27, 99, 123, 128–9, 144, 147, 153–4, 161, 162, 171; and Paddy Hill, 14–16, 20–1, 58–62, 172–5, 177, 180–2, 187–93; panic attacks, 19, 57, 73, 158, 161, 203; plans for film of life story, 36–7, 53–4; plays drug dealer in *Face*, 134–5; and the Pogues, 33, 42, 44–7, 48–51, 55–7, 71; post-release celebrations, 18–19; *Proved Innocent*, 14–15, 31–2, 38, 39, 65, 69, 90, 95; psychotherapy, 146, 147–56, 158–62, 171–2, 175–8; quashing of conviction, 16–18, 130–1; reading, 124; receives Sister Sarah Clarke Human Rights Award, 195, 196; reconciliation with Maguire family, 166–8; relationship with mother, 39, 119–20, 140–1, 158, 160–2; runs out of money, 128, 132, 138; sentencing, 7; settles in London, 29–31; suffers minor heart attacks, 122; suicidal thoughts, 144, 146, 152–3, 158; target for loyalist paramilitaries, 29, 120–1; trial, 6; *see also* Guildford Four

Conlon, Giuseppe, 4, 7, 13–14, 37–8, 63–4, 88, 90–3, 96, 119, 141, 149–50, 160–1, 163–5, 168, 170, 171, 182–3, 198, 210; *see also* Maguire Seven

Conlon, Sarah, 10, 13, 16–19, 23–4, 37, 39, 64, 81, 95, 119–20, 140–1, 157–65, 169, 179, 182–4

Construction, Forestry, Mining and Energy Union (CFMEU), 190–1

Continuity IRA, 199

Cool World (film), 65

Copenhagen, 38–9

Corbyn, Jeremy, 30, 181

Corey, Martin, 195–6

Corliss, Richard, 101

Craigavon Two, 196, 198–200

Crete, 58–61, 132

Crichley, Gary, 197

Crow, Bob, 187

Cullen, Kevin, 208

Dagenham, 132–3, 136, 137, 166

Daily Mirror, 62, 86–7

Dalby, Duglas, 208

Dallat, Fr Ciaran, 209–10

Davis, Philip, 135

Day-Lewis, Daniel, 58, 65–6, 77–82, 84, 85–6, 90, 107

Dear Sarah (RTÉ), 37–8, 98

Deaths in Custody Watch Committee, 190

Deeny, Donnell, 198

Denning, Alfred, Lord, 9, 12, 18, 117, 197

Depp, Johnny, 33, 49–53, 56–8, 77, 81

Devon and Cornwall Police, 54

Diamond, Neil, 188

DiNapoli, Tom, 195

Dingle, Co. Kerry, 53

'Direct Action Against Drugs' organisation, 125

Director of Public Prosecutions, Office of (DPP), 5, 23, 100

Doherty, Hugh, 3, 7

Doherty, Seamus, 190

Donaldson, John (detective sergeant), 86–8

Donaldson, Sir John (judge), 6–7, 111, 116–17

Donnelly, Brian, 24, 26

Dowd, Brendan, 2–3, 11

Downing, Stephen, 154–5

Doyle, Shane, 36

Dromm, Danny, 195

drugs, 6, 20, 28, 30–1, 42, 43, 59, 61–2, 94, 103–7, 119–29, 134–5, 138–44, 156

Dublin, 22, 28–9, 38, 41–2, 46, 48, 51, 52, 83–5, 95–7, 165, 201, 202

Dublin Castle, 97

Duggan, Harry, 3, 7, 11

Durham Prison, 95

Durkan, Mark, 163–6, 169, 170, 181, 209

Dwyer, Michael, 98

Dwyer, Paul, 26

Dylan, Bob, 109

Eagle, Maria, 181

Eggington, Dennis, 189

Ellen (Angie's mother), 132–3, 136, 140, 166
Error of Judgement (Mullins), 173
Evening Standard, 89
Eye Movement Desensitization and Reprocessing (EMDR) therapy, 149

Face (film), 134–5
Farquharson, Sir Donald, 54
Field, The (film), 66, 79, 91
Fisher, Michael, 23
Foley, Tom, 24
Foot, Michael, 6
football, 27, 40, 43, 202
forensic evidence: Birmingham Six, 35, 42–3, 54; Guildford Four, 8–9, 115–16; Maguire Seven, 4, 63, 111
Franey, Ros, 7
Fricker, Brenda, 66
Fulton, Colin, 200

Galway, 79, 180
gambling, 30–1, 56, 120, 133, 141, 186, 202
Garland, Seán, 201
Gartree Prison, 15–16, 20, 95
George, Terry, 65, 69, 78, 80, 83, 86, 90, 101, 107, 208, 209
Geraghty, Finola, 57–8, 68–9, 71
Germond, Kate, 193–4, 195, 196, 209
Gifford, Tony, 35, 36
Gilmore, Eamon, 209
Glasgow, 55–7, 173–4, 187
Glasgow Celtic, 40, 43, 202
Glastonbury Music Festival, 122, 187–8
Goa, 43
Gresham Hotel, Dublin, 95, 97
Grounds, Adrian, 76, 127–8, 145–6, 159–60
Guantanamo Bay prison, 196, 197
Guardian, 144–5, 151, 152
Guildford Four: alibi evidence, 23, 113–15, 116–17; apology from Tony Blair, 14, 163–9; appeal hearing, 11–12, 117; arrests, 4; compensation settlements, 144–5, 151; embargo on release of documents, 10, 112, 202; evidence withheld from defence counsel, 5, 9, 23, 113–17; forensic evidence, 8–9, 115–16; imprisonment, 10–11; interrogations and confessions, 4–5, 6, 21–2, 36, 112–13, 115; police acquitted of charges, 86–8, 111; police alterations to statements and interview notes, 8–9, 17, 87, 116; public inquiry into convictions, 111–18; quashing of convictions, 1, 16–18, 130–1; sentencing, 7; trial, 6–7, 113–17; *see also* Armstrong, Paddy; Conlon, Gerry; Hill, Paul; Richardson, Carole
Guildford Four: Free to Speak (ITV documentary), 22
Guildford pub bombings, 1, 2–3, 4, 5, 8, 10–12, 95, 112, 168

Hale, Don, 154
Hallam, Sam, 197
Hanson, David, 168, 171
Harris, Richard, 66
Haughey, Charles, 27
Havers, Sir Michael, 6, 11–12
Hemming, John, 181
Hendron, Joe, 169
Higgins, Michael D., 95, 207
Higgs, Douglas, 8–9, 115–16
Hill, Michael, 115
Hill, Paddy Joe, 14–16, 20–1, 54–5, 58–62, 172–5, 177, 180–2, 184, 187–93, 203, 207, 209; *see also* Birmingham Six
Hill, Paul, 4, 6, 7, 22, 27–8, 32, 95, 96, 99–100, 115, 117, 151–2, 172, 207; *see also* Guildford Four
Hill, Seán, 58–60, 61–2
Holland, Mary, 1–2
Hollywood, 53–4, 68, 94, 106–10
Horse and Groom, Guildford, 2–3
Houses of Parliament, 32, 38, 154, 166–9, 174
Howard, John, 190
Hucklesby, Bill, 10
Hulse, Michael, 4
Hume, John, 170
Hunter, Gerry, 172; *see also* Birmingham Six

Imbert, Sir Peter, 112
In the Name of the Father (film), 23, 64–70, 73–4, 77–86, 88–102, 106–10, 120–1, 142, 193, 194, 195
Independent, 152
Ingram, Scott, 87
interrogations: Birmingham Six, 35; Gerry Conlon, 4–5, 21–2, 36, 153; Guildford Four, 4–5, 6, 21–2, 36, 112–13, 115; Maguire Seven, 21–2
Into the West (film), 65, 83
Irish Echo, 27
Irish News, 21, 24, 37, 164–5
Irish Post, 49–50
Irish Republic Army (IRA): Army Council, 1, 2; assassination of Ross McWhirter, 5; attack at Aghalee, 195; Balcombe Street Active Service Unit (ASU), 2–4, 5, 7–12, 95, 112, 116, 117; bombing campaign, 1–4, 5, 7, 78, 95; campaign against drug dealers, 125; ceasefire (1975), 5; counterfeit money production, 201; declaration that war is over, 178; fighting in Belfast, 29; *see also* Continuity IRA; Real IRA
Irish Times, 98, 99
ITN News, 17, 18–19

Jacobs, Sunny, 180
Jamaica, 43, 95
Jenkins, Roy, 10
Johnson, Stewart, 175–6, 177–8
Johnston, Stevie, 187–8
Judge, Tony, 89
Juno (friend), 105–6, 121, 125, 128, 132, 134, 137, 138
Jurassic Park (film), 108

Katsouris, Monolis, 59
Keane, John B., 66
Kee, Robert, 100
Kelly, Oliver, 145
Kennedy, Joe, 24–5, 26, 34–5
Kennedy, Ludovic, 55
Kennedy, Robert, 58
Kennedy, Ted, 24
Kennedy-Hill, Courtney, 151, 164

Killary harbour, 79
Kings Arms, Woolwich, 3–4
Koch, Ed, 26

Lane, Geoffrey, Lord, 1, 130
Lantos, Tom, 25, 26, 34, 36
Las Vegas, 202
Last of the Mohicans (film), 82
Late, Late Show (RTÉ), 27
Lawrence, Sir Ivan, 131
Lawton, Frederick, 11
Laycock, Mark, 194
Lee, Spike, 90
Leenane, Co. Galway, 79
Libertines, The, 208
Limerick, 52–3, 203
Linda (girlfriend), 185–7, 194, 197, 202, 203–6
Liz (girlfriend), 95, 97
Lloyd, Anthony, Lord, 54
Logan, Alastair, 11, 87, 96, 111–12, 118
Long Lartin Prison, 14–15, 197
Looney, Fiona, 41–2
Los Angeles, 66, 107–10, 193–4
Los Angeles Times, 101
Loughran, David, 52–3, 97, 185
Loughran, Martin, 23–6, 30–1, 34, 209
Love, Larry, 184
loyalist paramilitaries, 29, 120–1, 178
Lyell, Sir Nicholas, 111

McAliskey, Bernadette, 28
McCarthy, Colman, 36
MacColl, Kirsty, 58
McConville, Brendan, 199–200
McDonnell, 'Celtic Pat', 179, 209
McDonnell, John, 145, 181
McGovern, Mario, 58–61
MacGowan, Shane, 33, 45, 48–51, 56, 88, 104
MacGowan, Siobhan, 39, 46–7, 49–50, 55–7, 71, 76, 93–4, 208, 209
McGrady, Eddie, 167, 170
McGurk, Tom, 37, 98–9
McIlkenny, Richard 'Dicky', 54, 172; *see also* Birmingham Six
McKee, Grant, 7

McKeone, Marion, 55–7, 71, 76, 109–10
McKernan, Ann (née Conlon), 13, 16–19, 37, 52–3, 67, 95, 97, 119, 124–5, 128, 140, 157–61, 165, 168, 183, 185–6, 196, 203–6, 210
McKernan, Joe, 13, 16–17, 121, 157, 159–60, 164, 165
McKernan, Mary-Kate, 52, 53, 206
McKernan, Sarah, 13, 121, 168, 206
McManus, John, 172–5, 180–1, 184, 187–93, 209
McNamara, Kevin, 64
McPhee, Ann, 36
Macpherson, William, 87–8
McWhirter, Ross, 5
Maguire, Annie, 4, 7, 63–4, 168–9, 171, 207; *see also* Maguire Seven
Maguire, Hughie, 17, 19
Maguire, Kate, 17
Maguire, Paddy, 7, 99; *see also* Maguire Seven
Maguire, Patrick, 7, 166–7, 168; *see also* Maguire Seven
Maguire, Vincent, 7, 167, 168–9; *see also* Maguire Seven
Maguire Seven: apology from Tony Blair, 14, 163–9; appeal hearing, 63–4, 111; arrests, 4; condemnation of Conlon, 21–2, 99, 166; forensic evidence, 4, 63, 111; interrogations, 21–2; public inquiry into convictions, 111–18; quashing of convictions, 63–4, 111; trial, 7; *see also* Conlon, Giuseppe; Maguire, Annie; Maguire, Paddy; Maguire, Patrick; Maguire, Vincent; O'Neill, Pat; Smyth, Seán
Mallon, Seamus, 35, 164, 170
Manchester United, 43, 202
Mann, Michael, 82
Manning, Chelsea, 202
Manning, Susan, 202
Maritime Union of Australia (MUA), 188–9, 192
Marxist Festival, London, 197
Mathew, John, 8, 116
May, Sir John, 111–18
May, Paul, 39

Melbourne, 189, 192
Metropolitan Police, 10, 112, 117
Mexico, 43
Mildon, Arthur, 6
Miller, Paul, 128
Milton, Frederick, 2
Minty (girlfriend), 70–6
Miscarriage of Justice Organisation (MOJO), 172–5, 180–1, 187–93
Misérables, Les (musical), 202
Miskin, Sir James, 40–1
Moore, Christy, 201
Morgan, Sir Charles Declan, 198
Morrison, Van, 93
Mulhall, Fr Brendan, 183
Mulholland, Joe, 38
Mullins, Chris, 64, 112, 118, 173
Mullins, Emer, 99
Murphy, Niall, 198
Murray, Frank, 28–9, 42, 45
Murray, Helen, 171
Museum of Modern Art, New York, 90
Mustill, Michael, 54
My Left Foot (film), 65–6

National Irish Freedom Committee (NIFC), 195
National Union of Rail, Maritime and Transport Workers (RMT), 187–8
Nevill, Jim, 9, 112
Neville, Louise, 55, 57
New York, 25–7, 36–7, 51, 90, 193, 195–7
New York Times, 101–2, 208
Newsnight (BBC), 23
noble cause corruption, 131–2

O'Brien, Owen, 3
Observer, 130–1, 137
Ó Conaill, Dáithí, 1–2
O'Connell, Frank, 193–4
O'Connell, Joe, 2–4, 5, 7–8, 10, 11, 95, 112, 117
O'Connor, John, 26–7
O'Connor, Sinead, 52, 100–1
O'Dell, Jack, 26
Ó Fiaich, Tomás, 35
O'Hagan, Mo, 46

O'Hagan, Seán, 104, 119–20, 134, 137
Old Bailey car bombing, 2
O'Neill, Pat, 7; *see also* Maguire Seven
O'Neill, Terry, 49
Ong, Peter, 190–1, 192, 209
O'Rawe, Richard, 179, 184, 187, 205, 208
Oscars, 107–10

Pallister, David, 31–3
'Parade of Innocence', 28
Parker, Dorothy, 106
Parry, Tim, 78
Pat Kenny Radio Show (RTÉ), 98–9
Patek, John, 68
Peirce, Bill, 29, 176
Peirce, Gareth, 16, 19, 23, 25, 29–32, 35, 135, 145, 155, 172, 176, 184, 197, 205, 209
Perth, 189, 192
Pinter, Harold, 83
Pitt, Brad, 65
Plymouth, 138–43, 147–8, 154–5, 171, 173, 175, 178
Pogues, The, 28, 33, 39, 42, 44–6, 48–51, 55–6, 71, 109, 208
police *see* Devon and Cornwall Police; Metropolitan Police; Surrey Police
Pollard, Charles, 131
post-traumatic stress disorder (PTSD), 147, 151, 159, 175, 178
Postlethwaite, Pete, 81, 90, 96, 99, 107
Power, Billy, 172; *see also* Birmingham Six
Power, Sr Michael, 23, 113, 114, 115, 116
Prince of Jutland (film), 83
Princeton, 193, 194
Proved Innocent (Conlon), 14–15, 31–3, 38, 39, 65, 69, 90, 95
Public Prosecution Service, 54, 87

Quinn, Liam, 2
Quinsey, Mark, 197–8

Ragged-Trousered Philanthropists, The (Tressell), 124
Rangel, Charlie, 26
Real IRA, 197–8
Rennie, Willie, 181

Reynolds, Nick, 184
Richardson, Carole, 4, 6, 87, 96, 113, 115; *see also* Guildford Four
Rose, David, 130–1
Roskill, Eustace, Lord, 11–12
Rowe, Christopher, 4
Russell, Candice, 101

St James, Diana, 18, 19, 25–6
St Peter's Cathedral, Belfast, 163, 164, 182, 183, 208–9
Sara (daughter), 186–7, 200, 202, 206
Savoy Cinema, Dublin, 95–6
Scheide, Bill, 194
Scheide, Judith, 194
Schindler's List (film), 108
Security and Co-operation in Europe conference, 39
Seeger, Pete, 201
Seven Stars, Guildford, 2–3
Sewell, Wendy, 154
Shapiro, Francine, 149
Shelbourne Hotel, Dublin, 165
Sheridan, Jim, 65–6, 69–70, 77–86, 88–91, 96, 99, 100, 107–8, 165, 196, 207–8, 209
Sheridan, Pete, 91, 96
Shivers, Brian, 197–8
Silverton, Pete, 37
Simmons, Wally, 4
Simon, Carly, 90
Sinn Féin, 184, 199, 209
Sister Sarah Clarke Human Rights Award, 195, 196
Skelhorn, Sir Norman, 9–10, 22–3
Skuse, Frank, 42–3, 54
Smyth, Seán, 7, 21–2; *see also* Maguire Seven
Snowden, Edward, 202
Social Democratic and Labour Party (SDLP), 35, 162–3, 167, 170, 184, 209
Socialist Workers Party, 173
South Florida Sun-Sentinel, 101
Spielberg, Steven, 108
Spillane, John, 201
Spotlight (BBC), 151–2
Springsteen, Bruce, 109

INDEX

Stacy, 'Spider', 57
Stanage, Niall, 158–9
Stolen Years: Before and After Guildford (Hill), 32
Strangeways Prison, 120
'Streets of Sorrow/Birmingham Six' (Pogues), 45–6
Style, Thomas, 86–8
Sun, 61, 132
Sunday Business Post, 158–9
Sunday Times, 100–1, 122–3, 142
Surrey Police, 4–5, 6, 86–8, 111–13, 130
Sydney, 189

Thompson, Emma, 88, 89, 101
Time Magazine, 101
Tipperary town, 53
Today Tonight (current affairs programme), 191
Tomlinson, Geoff, 40, 146
Toner, 'Dougie', 170
trade unions, 173, 187–92
Tressell, Robert, 124
Trial and Error (Kee), 100
Tribe, Ark, 190–2
Trouble and Strife theatre company, 58
Tunisia, 31–2
Turnbull, Gordon, 175

U2, 95
Ulster Defence Association (UDA), 178
United States, 23–7, 34–7, 66, 68–9, 90, 93, 97–8, 100–2, 107–10, 135, 187, 193–7, 202
Universal Pictures, 77, 80–1

University College Dublin, 202
University of Connecticut, 193
University of Limerick, 203

Vienna Chamber Orchestra, 194
Villiers, Theresa, 195
Vine, Peter Henry, 113–15, 116

Wakefield Prison, 10–11, 148–9, 176
Walker, Johnny, 170, 172; *see also* Birmingham Six
Walle, Barry, 39–40, 67–8, 105–6, 127, 138, 146–59, 161–2, 166, 171–2, 177, 179, 209
Walsh, Margaret, 162–6, 168, 170, 209
Walsh, Paddy Joe, 24
Walsh, Roy, 92, 95–6
Wandsworth Prison, 92, 176
Ward, Mr (aboriginal elder), 189–90
Warner Brothers Films, 68
Warrington bombing, 78
Washington, 24–5, 34–6
Washington Post, 36
WikiLeaks, 202
William Morris Agency, 68, 70
Winchester Prison, 90, 91
Winstone, Ray, 135
Winters, Kevin R., 200, 209
Woodcock, Sir John, 131
Woods, Terry, 45
Woolwich pub bombing, 1, 3–4, 5, 8–12, 95, 112, 116, 168
Wootton, John Paul, 199–200
World Cup football finals, 27
Wormwood Scrubs Prison, 13, 91, 95–6